Immersive Realm of Extended Reality

Navigating the future of virtual and augmented reality

Suman Dutta

www.bpbonline.com

FIRST EDITION 2024

ISBN: 978-93-55517-227

LIMITS OF LIABILITY AND DISCLAIMER OF WARRANTY

Distributors:

BPB PUBLICATIONS
20, Ansari Road, Darya Ganj
New Delhi-110002
Ph: 23254990/23254991

DECCAN AGENCIES
4-3-329, Bank Street,
Hyderabad-500195
Ph: 24756967/24756400

MICRO MEDIA
Shop No. 5, Mahendra Chambers,
150 DN Rd. Next to Capital Cinema,
V.T. (C.S.T.) Station, MUMBAI-400 001
Ph: 22078296/22078297

Published by Manish Jain for BPB Publications, 20 Ansari Road, Darya Ganj, New Delhi-110002 and Printed by him at Manipal Technologies, Manipal

www.bpbonline.com

Dedicated to

My parents:

Mrs. Kalpana Dutta** and **Mr. Rabindra Nath Dutta

My family and to my cute little son

Vivaan S. Dutta

About the Author

Suman Dutta is a seasoned technology enthusiast with a rich background in Software Engineering and IT, amassing 17 years of industry experience. He earned a Master's degree in Computer Application, laying a strong foundation for his career. Throughout his professional journey, Suman has collaborated with a diverse range of organizations, spanning from startups to major industry players such as Apple Inc, Oracle America, PagerDuty, etc. Notably, he has achieved success in delivering numerous multi-million-dollar projects, showcasing his expertise in the Software Industry.

Suman is recognized for specific skills and qualities, including meticulous attention to detail, innovative thinking, and excellent communication skills. He is deeply committed to particular goals and values, such as advancing the field of VR/AR, promoting diversity and inclusion, and enhancing user experiences.

Beyond his role as an established Software professional, Suman Dutta is also an entrepreneur. He co-founded SwipeTouch Edutech Private Ltd, an Ed-tech startup. The startup has achieved significant success, currently operating in multiple states of India and providing support to 40,000 or more students and over 50 schools.

Passionate about various interests, Suman enjoys travel, photography, and volunteering. His diverse activities include hiking, cooking, and playing musical instruments. Currently residing in Silicon Valley, California, USA, he values quality time with family and friends. During his leisure moments, Suman can be found playing with his toddler, indulging in his love for cooking, listening to good music, and delving into insightful books.

About the Reviewer

Indika Wijesooriya has over eight years of extensive experience working with Unity, coupled with profound involvement in crafting AR applications since 2014. In 2017, he successfully attained a degree in Engineering intertwined with Computer Science, further solidifying his expertise in the field.

Notably, Indika held the distinguished position of Chief of Innovation at Arimac, a prominent end-to-end digital solutions provider renowned for its active engagement in the development of AR and VR applications on a global scale. His instrumental contributions to advancing immersive and emergent technologies have garnered local and international accolades.

Indika's passion is towards 3D real-time development, AR VR, and research, sharing his knowledge with enthusiasts around the world.

Acknowledgement

I want to express my deepest gratitude to my family and friends, especially my parents, wife, and close friends, for their unwavering support and encouragement throughout this book's writing.

I am also grateful to BPB Publications for their guidance and expertise in bringing this book to fruition. It was a long journey of revising this book, with valuable participation and collaboration of reviewers, technical experts, and editors.

I would also like to acknowledge the valuable contributions of my colleagues and co-workers during many years working in the tech industry, who have taught me so much and provided valuable feedback on my work.

Finally, I would like to thank all the readers who have taken an interest in my book and for their support in making it a reality. Your encouragement has been invaluable.

Preface

Virtual and extended reality technologies have come a long way since their inception, and today, they are poised to change how we work, learn, and interact with the world. From gaming and entertainment to education, healthcare, and beyond, these technologies have the potential to revolutionize many aspects of our lives. However, with great power comes great responsibility, and it is important to understand the potential benefits and risks associated with these technologies. Immersive Realm: Navigating the Future of Virtual and Extended Reality comes here.

The book provides a comprehensive guide to understanding and navigating the rapidly evolving virtual and extended reality world. It is designed for a wide range of readers, including developers, designers, entrepreneurs, and anyone interested in these technologies' potential applications and impact across various industries. The book is divided into six chapters, each focusing on a different aspect of VR and AR. Overall, this book provides a comprehensive, practical, and forward-thinking approach to understanding and utilizing the power of VR and AR in the digital age. By the end of the book, readers will have a deep understanding of the potential benefits and risks of these technologies, as well as the knowledge and tools needed to build successful VR and AR applications that are both innovative and ethical.

Chapter 1: Immersive Technology Promise and Potential - In recent years, the world has witnessed a surge in the development of immersive technologies, such as augmented reality (AR), virtual reality (VR), and mixed reality (MR) or extended reality (XR). These technologies have the potential to transform how we perceive and interact with the world around us, from entertainment and gaming to education, healthcare, and even work. This chapter will overview AR, VR, and XR technologies and discuss their promise and potential. It will explore the history and evolution of these technologies, their current state of development, and their future applications. It will also examine the challenges and limitations that must be addressed for these technologies to reach their full potential.

Chapter 2: The Psychology of Presence in Immersive Technologies - When we experience immersive technologies such as virtual reality and augmented reality, we often feel like we have been transported to a different world or reality. This sense of being present in another environment, also known as presence is a key aspect of immersion and is crucial to the effectiveness and the success of these technologies. This chapter will explore the psychology of presence and how it relates to immersion in VR, AR, and other immersive technologies. It will examine the factors contributing to presence, such as sensory inputs, cognitive processes, and emotional responses. It will also discuss the importance of understanding presence for designing and developing immersive experiences.

Chapter 3: Designing Immersive Experience - In this chapter, we will explore the principles and best practices for designing immersive experiences that captivate and engage users. Immersive experiences are becoming increasingly popular in fields like gaming, virtual reality, and augmented reality, and the principles we discuss here can be applied to a wide range of industries. We will look at how to design for sensory immersion, emotional immersion, and narrative immersion, as well as best practices for user interface and experience design.

Chapter 4: Evolution of VR Hardware - This chapter will dive deeply into the history and development of virtual reality hardware, from the early days of clunky head-mounted displays to the latest advancements in haptic feedback. We will explore how VR hardware has evolved over the years, the challenges developers and designers have faced, and the new opportunities emerging technologies create. This chapter will interest anyone interested in VR, including designers, developers, and enthusiasts.

Chapter 5: The Role of AI in AR, VR, and XR - Artificial intelligence (AI) is playing an increasingly important role in virtual reality and extended reality applications, enabling more realistic and responsive experiences for users. In this chapter, we will explore the intersection of AI and VR/XR, looking at how AI is being used to improve everything from graphics rendering to user interaction. We will discuss the current state of the technology, emerging trends, and the future possibilities for AI in VR and XR.

Chapter 6: Business Landscape of AR, VR, and XR - Virtual reality and extended reality technologies are rapidly evolving, and their potential applications extend far beyond gaming and entertainment. In this chapter, we will examine the business landscape of VR/XR, exploring the trends, challenges, and opportunities facing companies working in these fields. From funding and monetization to user adoption and regulation, we will discuss the key factors driving the growth of VR/XR and the strategies companies are using to succeed in this space.

Chapter 7: Applications of AR, VR, and XR in Healthcare - Virtual reality and extended reality technologies have enormous potential in the healthcare industry, enabling more effective training, diagnosis, treatment, and rehabilitation. In this chapter, we will explore the applications of VR/XR in healthcare, discussing the latest research, the challenges, and the opportunities for healthcare professionals, patients, and caregivers.

Chapter 8: Applications of AR, VR, and XR in Education - Virtual reality and extended reality technologies have the potential to revolutionize the education industry by creating immersive, interactive learning experiences that engage and motivate students. In this chapter, we will explore the latest research on the applications of VR/XR in education, discussing the challenges and opportunities they present for students, teachers, and educational institutions.

Chapter 9: Ethics in Immersive Technologies - Virtual reality and augmented reality can potentially transform our lives in many positive ways, but they also raise various ethical concerns that must be addressed. In this chapter, we will examine the ethical considerations surrounding VR and AR, including issues related to privacy, safety, and social impact. We will explore the challenges and opportunities presented by these technologies and consider how they can be developed and deployed to benefit society.

Chapter 10: 3D Modeling and User Interface Design - Virtual reality and augmented reality technologies rely on sophisticated hardware and software systems to create immersive user experiences. In this chapter, we will delve into the technical aspects of VR and AR, exploring the hardware and software considerations that underpin these technologies. We will also examine the design principles that guide the creation of immersive experiences, from 3D modeling to user interface design.

Chapter 11: Building VR Applications with Unity - Unity is one of the most popular game engines for creating VR applications. This chapter will introduce Unity, including its basic features, architecture, and workflow. We will then explore how Unity can be used to build VR applications, discussing the various components that make up a typical VR project and the key considerations that need to be taken into account when developing for VR.

Chapter 12: Building and Monetizing Successful VR and AR Applications - This chapter will provide practical advice for building successful VR and AR applications, including tips for marketing and monetizing these products. We will discuss the key factors contributing to the success of VR and AR applications, including user experience, design, and performance. We will also explore the various strategies that can be used to market and monetize VR and AR applications, such as advertising, sponsorships, and in-app purchases.

Coloured Images

Please follow the link to download the
Coloured Images of the book:

https://rebrand.ly/5na7ant

We have code bundles from our rich catalogue of books and videos available at **https://github.com/bpbpublications**. Check them out!

Errata

We take immense pride in our work at BPB Publications and follow best practices to ensure the accuracy of our content to provide with an indulging reading experience to our subscribers. Our readers are our mirrors, and we use their inputs to reflect and improve upon human errors, if any, that may have occurred during the publishing processes involved. To let us maintain the quality and help us reach out to any readers who might be having difficulties due to any unforeseen errors, please write to us at :

errata@bpbonline.com

Your support, suggestions and feedbacks are highly appreciated by the BPB Publications' Family.

Piracy

If you come across any illegal copies of our works in any form on the internet, we would be grateful if you would provide us with the location address or website name. Please contact us at **business@bpbonline.com** with a link to the material.

If you are interested in becoming an author

If there is a topic that you have expertise in, and you are interested in either writing or contributing to a book, please visit **www.bpbonline.com**. We have worked with thousands of developers and tech professionals, just like you, to help them share their insights with the global tech community. You can make a general application, apply for a specific hot topic that we are recruiting an author for, or submit your own idea.

Reviews

Please leave a review. Once you have read and used this book, why not leave a review on the site that you purchased it from? Potential readers can then see and use your unbiased opinion to make purchase decisions. We at BPB can understand what you think about our products, and our authors can see your feedback on their book. Thank you!

For more information about BPB, please visit **www.bpbonline.com**.

Join our book's Discord space

Join the book's Discord Workspace for Latest updates, Offers, Tech happenings around the world, New Release and Sessions with the Authors:

https://discord.bpbonline.com

Table of Contents

1. Immersive Technology Promise and Potential 1
Introduction 1
Structure 1
Objectives 2
Knowing immersive technologies 2
Augmented reality 2
Virtual reality 3
Extended reality 3
Overview of immersive technologies 4
Milestones and breakthroughs 5
AR milestones 5
VR milestones 6
Current state of immersive technologies 6
Statistical data for immersive technologies 7
Potential of immersive technologies 8
Limitations of immersive technologies 9
Conclusion 9
Points to remember 9

2. The Psychology of Presence in Immersive Technologies 11
Introduction 11
Structure 11
Objectives 12
Knowing presence 12
Definition and explanation of presence 12
Importance of presence for immersion and user experience 13
Theories of presence 14
Overview of different theories of presence 14
Overview of different models of presence 15
Theories explaining the experience of presence 16

Factors contributing to presence 17
Measuring presence 19
The different methods to measure presence 19
Self-report measures 19
Physiological measures 19
Behavioral measures 20
Experience sampling 20
Hybrid approaches 20
Advantages and limitations of measuring presence 21
Advantages 21
Limitations 21
Application of presence 22
Importance of presence for different applications 23
Training 23
Therapy 23
Examples of successful applications of presence 24
Conclusion 25
Points to remember 25

3. Designing Immersive Experience 27
Introduction 27
Structure 27
Objectives 28
Introduction to immersive design 28
Importance of immersion 28
Understanding immersion 28
The importance of immersion 28
Immersive experience psychology and impact 29
Designing for sensory immersion 30
Immersive experience with engaging user senses 31
Immersive experience principles 32
Spatial design 32
Sound design 32

Haptic feedback.......... 33

Designing for emotional immersion.......... 34

Powerful emotions with immersive experience.......... 34

Role of design in an impactful user experience.......... 35

Designing for narrative immersion.......... 37

Importance of storytelling in the narrative immersion.......... 37

Compelling narrative and user engagement.......... 38

Best practices for user interface and experience design.......... 40

Importance of a well-designed user interface.......... 40

Conclusion.......... 41

Points to remember.......... 42

4. Evolution of VR Hardware.......... 43

Introduction.......... 43

Structure.......... 43

Objectives.......... 44

Introduction to virtual reality hardware.......... 44

Evolution of virtual reality hardware.......... 44

Early systems (1960s-1990s).......... 44

Modern era (2010s onward).......... 45

Recent advances.......... 46

First head-mounted displays.......... 47

The rise of consumer virtual reality.......... 48

Role of technology advancement in virtual reality industry.......... 48

Virtual reality hardware design challenges.......... 50

The future of virtual reality hardware.......... 51

Emerging technologies.......... 51

Impact of emerging virtual reality technologies on industries.......... 52

Role of haptic feedback on virtual reality hardware.......... 54

Evolution of haptic feedback.......... 54

Types of haptic feedback.......... 55

Benefits and limitations of haptic technology.......... 56

Benefits of haptic technology.......... 56

Limitations of haptic technology 57
Case studies 57
Conclusion 59
Points to remember 60

5. The Role of AI in AR, VR, and XR 61
Introduction 61
Structure 61
Objectives 62
Introduction to AI in AR/VR/XR 62
AI and its usage in VR/AR 62
Graphic rendering 63
AI for improving realism and details 63
Rendering complex scenes and environments 65
Natural language processing 66
Popularity of other natural language processing 66
NLPs contribution in natural and intuitive interaction 66
User interaction 67
Improved UI with gesture recognition and eye tracking 67
Predictive analytics 68
Role of predictive analytics for better user experience 68
Conclusion 69
Points to remember 69

6. Business Landscape of AR, VR, and XR 71
Introduction 71
Structure 71
Objectives 72
Introduction to business of VR/XR 72
Current state and evolution of VR/AR industry 72
Business landscape and key trends 73
Funding and investment 75
Funding and its challenges for VR/XR industry 75

Funding options and investment-securing strategies ... 76
Monetization strategies ... 78
Monetization challenges in VR/XR industry ... 78
Pros and cons of various monetization models ... 79
User adoption and marketing ... 82
VR/XR's adoption challenges among users ... 82
Marketing strategies of the companies for VR/XR ... 83
Technology challenges ... 84
Case studies ... 85
Oculus case study ... 85
Magic Leap case study ... 86
Conclusion ... 87
Points to remember ... 87

7. Applications of AR, VR, and XR in Healthcare ... 89
Introduction ... 89
Structure ... 89
Objectives ... 90
Introduction to AR, VR, and XR in healthcare ... 90
Current state of AR, VR, and XR in healthcare and its evolution ... 91
Major players and some of the key trends ... 92
Diagnosis and treatment ... 93
Doctors and nurses practice and refine skills using AR, VR, or XR ... 94
Use of AR/VR in various healthcare areas ... 95
Rehabilitation and physical therapy ... 97
AR, VR, and XR for rehabilitation and physical therapy ... 97
Use of VR/XR for stroke and other injuries ... 98
In stroke rehabilitation ... 98
In traumatic brain injury ... 99
VR/XR in spinal cord injuries ... 99
Medical education and training ... 99
Use of AR, VR, and XR for medical education ... 100
Immersive technologies for some other areas of medical education ... 101

Patient education and engagement 102
Use of immersive technology in patient education *102*
Case studies 103
Osso VR *104*
Design principles *104*
Medical realities *104*
Design principles *104*
Conclusion 105
Points to remember 105

8. Applications of AR, VR, and XR in Education 107
Introduction 107
Structure 107
Objectives 108
Introduction to AR, VR, and XR in education 108
Current state of AR, VR, and XR in education and its evolution *108*
VR/XR impact on education's efficacy *110*
Immersive learning environment 111
Simulations and training 112
Personalized learning 113
Customized and personalized learning experience *113*
VR/XR for adaptive learning, gamification, and assessment *114*
Collaborative learning 115
Benefits of collaborative learning using VR/XR *116*
Utilizing VR/XR for team building and project learning *117*
Case studies 118
Conclusion 120
Points to remember 121

9. Ethics in Immersive Technologies 123
Introduction 123
Structure 123
Objectives 124

Introduction to ethics in immersive technologies 124

Overview of the ethical challenges posed by VR and AR 124

Importance of ethical consideration in VR and AR 126

Privacy and data protection 126

Privacy of personal data and safeguard 127

Legal and ethical framework that governs data collection 127

Safety and physical health 129

Physical effect on users due to VR and AR technologies 129

Measures are taken to ensure user safety 130

Psychological and emotional impact 131

Psychological and emotional impact due to immersive technology 132

Potential risks of AR, VR, and XR technologies 132

VR, AR, or XR and their impact to promote well-being and mental health 133

Case studies 134

Conclusion 135

Points to remember 136

10. 3D Modeling and User Interface Design **137**

Introduction 137

Structure 137

Objectives 138

Introduction to 3D modeling 138

Key concepts 139

Modeling technique 140

Artistic and technical balance 144

Animating 3D models 144

Importance of animation and techniques 144

Challenges in animating for immersive environments 145

Real-time 3D and game engines 146

Understanding real-time 3D graphics 146

Game engines: The heart of immersive environments 146

Applications of game engines 147

The democratization of immersive content creation 147

User interface design principles 148
User interface design software and workflow 149
Understanding the workflow *149*
Tools of the trade *150*
Challenges and considerations *150*
Implementing UIs in 3D environment 151
Design principles and considerations *151*
Implementation workflow *151*
Tools and technologies *152*
Conclusion 153
Points to remember 153

11. Building VR Applications with Unity 155
Introduction 155
Structure 155
Objectives 156
Introduction to Unity 156
Unity architecture 157
Integration of Unity with 3D modeling and animation *157*
Unity workflow 160
Tools and features to edit game objects *161*
VR development in Unity 163
Creating scenes and environments 164
Best practices for scene optimization *166*
Occlusion culling *166*
Level of detail system *167*
Batching *168*
Shader optimization *168*
Texture atlasing *169*
Physics optimization *169*
Audio optimization *169*
Scripting in Unity 170
Programming languages in Unity *171*

C# 171

JavaScript (UnityScript) 172

UI Design in VR 172

Conclusion 174

Points to remember 175

12. Building and Monetizing Successful VR and AR Applications 177

Introduction 177

Structure 177

Objectives 178

Understanding your audience 178

Engaging user experience for retention 179

Optimal application performance boosts retention 180

Monetizing your app 181

Paid apps 181

In-app purchases and virtual goods 182

Freemium models 182

Subscriptions 182

Ads and sponsorships 183

Location-based services and partnerships 183

Data monetization 183

Marketing your app 184

Importance of effective marketing 185

Exploring various channels and tactics 185

App store optimization 186

Leveraging analytics 187

Tips for using analytics tools effectively 188

Engaging with your community 189

Conclusion 190

Points to remember 190

Index 193-202

CHAPTER 1
Immersive Technology Promise and Potential

Introduction

In recent years, the world has witnessed a surge in the development of immersive technologies, such as **Augmented Reality** (**AR**), **Virtual Reality** (**VR**), and **Extended Reality** (**XR**). These technologies have the potential to transform how we perceive and interact with the world around us, from entertainment and gaming to education, healthcare, and even work. This chapter will overview AR, VR, and XR technologies and discuss their promise and potential. It will explore the history and evolution of these technologies, their current state of development, and their future applications. It will also examine the challenges and limitations that must be addressed for these technologies to reach their full potential.

Structure

In this chapter, we will discuss the following topics:

- Knowing immersive technologies
- Overview of immersive technologies
- Current state of immersive technologies
- Statistical data for immersive technologies

- Potentials of immersive technologies
- Limitations of immersive technologies

Objectives

This chapter will provide an overview of AR, VR, and XR technologies, and discuss their promise and potential. It will explore the history and evolution of these technologies, their current state of development, and their future applications. It will also examine the challenges and limitations that must be addressed for these technologies to reach their full potential.

Knowing immersive technologies

AR, VR And XR are three pillars on which immersive experience rests. So, it is very imperative to know what are these technologies. In this unit we will be knowing what are AR, VR and XR.

Augmented reality

Augmented reality, commonly known as AR, is a cutting-edge technology that overlays digital content, such as images, sounds, and text, onto the real-world environment in real time. Unlike virtual reality, which creates a fully immersive and simulated environment, AR enhances real-world experience.

To operate, AR technology requires a device, such as a smartphone or a tablet, equipped with a camera, sensors, and software that can recognize and track specific objects or markers in the physical world and then superimpose digital content onto them. This technology has entered various industries, such as gaming, education, advertising, architecture, and so on.

The technology behind AR involves computer vision, sensor fusion, and advanced algorithms to track and understand the user's surroundings accurately. It also requires robust software development and content creation to create compelling and seamless AR experiences.

AR continues to evolve rapidly, with ongoing advancements in hardware capabilities, software development frameworks, and user experience design. It holds great potential for transforming various industries, enabling new forms of interaction, enhancing productivity, and shaping the way we perceive and interact with the world around us.

The applications of AR are diverse and span multiple industries. In the entertainment and gaming industry, AR enhances experiences by overlaying virtual characters or objects into the real world, creating immersive and interactive gameplay. AR also finds applications in education, where it can be used to provide interactive and engaging learning experiences, such as overlaying informative content onto textbooks or creating virtual experiments.

In the retail and e-commerce sector, AR enables customers to virtually try on products or visualize how furniture or home decor items would look in their space before making a purchase. AR is also utilized in fields like architecture and engineering, where it can aid in visualizing and simulating construction projects or assisting with design and planning processes.

Furthermore, AR has implications in healthcare, where it can assist surgeons during complex procedures by overlaying real-time medical information onto the patient's body or by providing guidance during training. It can also help improve accessibility by providing real-time captions or translations for individuals with hearing or language impairments.

Virtual reality

Virtual reality refers to three-dimensional computer interfaces or experiences that one can get by using some specialized devices, like headsets with screens or wristbands with sensors. This technology is pathbreaking as this helps in creating fully immersive and desirable interactive experience which can be used in gaming, training, education, and other fields.

Some of the areas where VR can be a game-changer:

- **Education**: VR can be used to create interactive and engaging educational experiences. Students can explore historical sites, learn scientific concepts, and experience multiculturalism immersively.
- **Tourism**: VR can live-stream various travel destinations, allowing people to see places without leaving their homes.
- **Therapy**: VR can be used therapeutically to treat panic attacks and PTSD. Patients can be placed in simulated situations in a controlled environment to help manage their fears.

Extended reality

Extended reality is a term that refers to a variety of technologies, including VR, AR, MR, and other related technologies. XR develops to describe the visual and digital experiences it provides them. This further allows users to create virtual environment which possibly interacts with objects and enhanced environments.

XR technology makes its way into many devices, such as embedded displays, smart glasses, mobile devices, etc., to enable users to experience digital content naturally and easily. As XR technology continues to evolve, it has the potential to change the way we interact with our digital products and the world around us.

There are many examples of XR applications across various industries. Here are a few:

- **Training**: XR technologies are often used in training applications to simulate real-world scenarios for individuals to practice and learn new skills. For example, aviation pilots can practice flying in a virtual environment, medical professionals can learn surgical procedures using augmented reality simulations, and military personnel can train for combat scenarios in a mixed reality environment.
- **Gaming and entertainment**: The gaming and entertainment industry is the original area where XR is used predominantly. In these industries, XR provides an immersive and interactive experience to users.

  Games like Pokemon Go and Minecraft Earth use augmented reality to overlay digital objects onto the real world, while VR gaming platforms, such as PlayStation VR provide fully immersive experiences.
- **Retail and marketing**: XR can be used in retail and marketing to create interactive and engaging customer experiences. For example, AR applications can allow customers to try on clothing or see how furniture would look in their homes before purchasing.
- **Architecture and design**: XR technologies can be used in virtual tours of buildings and in visualizing more immersive and interactive designs.

The following is an illustration of an AR experience to find the usability of a furniture:

***Figure 1.1**: Illustration of usage of augmented reality in furniture selection*

Overview of immersive technologies

AR overlays digital information in the real world. AR applications typically use a camera and a mobile device or smart glasses to enable users to see and interact with digital content, such as images, videos, or 3D objects, overlaid in the physical environment. Examples of AR applications include Snapchat filters and Pokémon Go.

VR is a technology that immerses users in a wholly digital environment. It typically uses a headset with a screen and sometimes handheld controllers to let users see and interact with a virtual environment. VR applications can be used for gaming, training, education, and other applications where a fully immersive and interactive experience is desired. Examples of VR applications include Oculus Quest and HTC Vive.

XR is a term that encompasses both AR and VR, as well as other related technologies, such as mixed reality, which combines elements of both AR and VR. XR technologies are designed to provide immersive, interactive experiences that allow users to interact with digital content in new and innovative ways.

Overall, AR, VR, and XR technologies are becoming increasingly popular across various industries and are being used to provide users with unique and engaging experiences.

Milestones and breakthroughs

Here we will learn about the various milestones and breakthroughs that AR, VR And XR technologies went through before it reaches where it is currently in. There is a first a pictorial representation and then we would go through the timeline with a brief set of information:

AR milestones

Figure 1.2 showcases the various milestones that AR passes to reach the current state:

***Figure 1.2:** Important milestones of AR*

The following section shows how year over year AR made progress:

- **1992**: The first AR system, virtual fixtures, was developed by researchers at the U.S. Air Force.
- **2008**: Nokia Point and Find AR application was an early AR-based application developed on Symbian platform. Wikitude is a popular AR platform and mobile application that allows users to create, share, and discover AR content.
- **2010**: Layar, a mobile AR app, allowed users to view digital information overlaid on the physical world .
- **2013**: Microsoft released the first version of its AR headset, HoloLens.
- **2016**: Pokémon Go, an AR-based mobile game, became a worldwide phenomenon.
- **2018**: Apple released ARKit 2, supporting multi-user AR experiences.

- **2019**: Apple released ARKit 3, a platform that enables developers to create AR applications for iOS devices.
- **2020**: Facebook announced Project Aria, a research project on developing AR glasses.

VR milestones

Figure 1.3 graphically depicts various stages which present VR technology successfully passed to reach what we see the current format of VR:

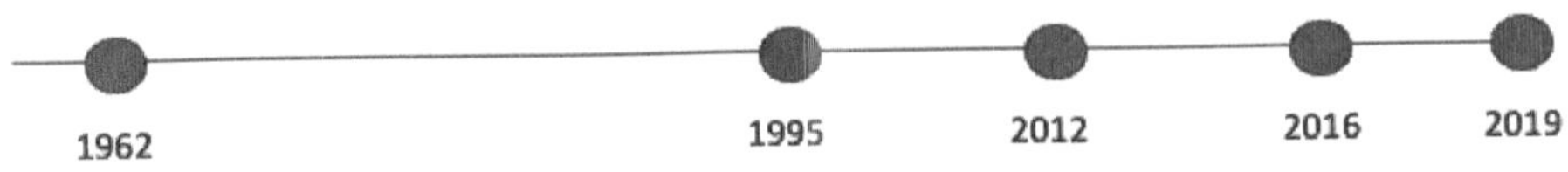

***Figure 1.3:** Important milestones of VR*

The following section shows how year over year VR made progress:

- **1962**: Sword of Damocles was one of the earliest HMD based VR product.
- **1995**: One of the first 32-bit tabletop portable video game console developed by Nintendo was released. It was called Virtual Boy. It was capable of producing stereoscopic 3D.
- **2012**: Oculus VR, a company specializing in VR hardware and software, was founded.
- **2014**: Google released its first VR platform, Cardboard.
- **2016**: The first consumer VR headset, the Oculus Rift, was released.
- **2019**: The release of Oculus Quest, a standalone VR headset that does not require a PC or smartphone.

  *(**Sources**: Forbes, Wikipedia, forbes.com)*

Current state of immersive technologies

Immersive technologies are rapidly advancing and have grown significantly in recent years. Here is an overview of the current state of development and adoption:

- **XR technology**: It encompasses both AR and VR, has the potential to provide even more immersive and interactive experiences, and is being adopted across various industries and is making path-breaking progress. The development of mixed reality headsets, such as Microsoft's HoloLens 2 and the Magic Leap One, have enabled more seamless transitions between real and virtual environments. However, the technology is still in its early stages, and challenges include the need for more advanced sensors and software to enable more natural interactions.

- **AR**: It has seen significant growth and adoption in recent years, with applications in industries such as retail, entertainment, automobile, and healthcare. The release of *ARKit* by Apple and *ARCore* by Google has made it easier for developers to create AR applications for mobile devices, and the adoption of smart glasses such as Microsoft's HoloLens and Magic Leap has enabled more immersive AR experiences.
- **VR:** This technology has also seen significant growth in recent years, with applications in gaming, education, and training. The release of standalone VR headsets such as the Oculus Quest has made it easier for consumers to access VR experiences, and the development of VR arcades and theme parks has helped to drive adoption.

Overall, Immersive technologies are advancing and being adopted across various industries. However, limitations and challenges still need to be addressed to enable even more widespread adoption and development of these technologies. For example, AR has a limited field of view and battery life, which can hinder adoption. There are issues such as motion sickness and the need for powerful hardware to run high-end VR experiences in VR.

Statistical data for immersive technologies

The global market size for each of these techs based on the data available in 2020 are \$2.39 billion, \$ 7.3 billion and \$ 11.4 billion (in USDs) for AR, VR, and XR, consecutively. The *future growth projection of AR* will be at a CAGR of 40% from 2021 to 2028. By 2025, AR business in retail and e-commerce will reach 11.14 billion.

The top industries for AR adoption are retail, gaming, and healthcare. Regarding demographics, most AR users are millennials and the younger generation (Gen-Z), with 62% of AR users under 35.

The *global VR market* was valued at USD 7.3 billion in 2020 and is expected to grow at a CAGR of 21.6% from 2021 to 2028. The VR gaming market is expected to reach USD 42.50 billion by 2027. The top industries for VR adoption are gaming, healthcare, and education. Demographics of the VR tech's user base; 57% of VR users are male, and 43% are female.

The *global XR market size* was valued at USD 11.4 billion in 2020 and is expected to grow at a CAGR of 43.8% from 2021 to 2028. The market for this is going to be USD 1.6 trillion by 2030. The top industries for XR adoption are retail, education, gaming, healthcare, Space tech, etc.

Demographics of the user base are millennials and the younger generation (Gen-Z), with 70% of XR users under 35.

*(**Sources:** Deloitte, Grand View Research, Statista, eMarketer, and Markets)*

Potential of immersive technologies

Under this topic, we will try to understand the potential of each of these technologies. How much this immersive and virtual reality related technology is going to affect various industries and what the immense potential that we have already started tapping.

The following illustration is a futuristic representation of VR:

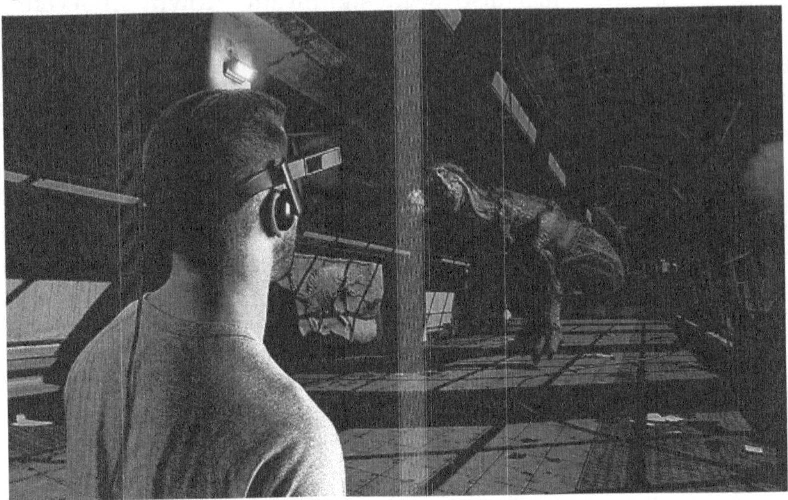

***Figure 1.4**: Illustration of virtual reality in VR gaming*

These technologies can potentially transform how we interact with the world around us. Here are some examples of the promise and potential of these technologies:

- **AR** has the potential to revolutionize educational experiences, with immersive and interactive AR content helping students learn and engage with subjects in a more engaging way. It can improve healthcare, with AR applications helping doctors and nurses visualize and diagnose medical conditions and aid in surgical procedures.

  It can change the shopping experience, with virtual try-on technologies enabling consumers to see how products look on them before purchasing.

- **VR** can provide immersive training experiences for professionals in various industries, from aviation to healthcare to law enforcement.

  It can enable virtual tourism, allowing people to experience destinations they may not be able to visit in person. It can offer new forms of entertainment, from immersive gaming experiences to virtual concerts and events.

Overall, the promise and potential of Immersive technologies are vast. As these technologies continue to develop and mature, we can expect to see even more transformative and innovative use cases emerge.

Limitations of immersive technologies

Despite the significant promise and potential of AR and VR technologies, several challenges and limitations must be addressed.

The following are the points which tells us about the reasoning behind limitations in AR and VR technologies:

- **Limited hardware**: This requires specialized hardware, such as smartphones with depth-sensing cameras or AR headsets, which can be costly and limit the reach of AR applications.
- **Expensive hardware**: VR headsets can be costly and require high-performance PCs or gaming consoles, limiting the reach of VR applications.
- **Motion sickness**: Some users experience motion sickness or discomfort when using VR applications, which can limit the adoption and use of VR technologies.
- **Limited content**: There is currently a limited amount of high-quality AR content available, which can hinder the adoption and use of AR applications.
- **Integration challenges**: XR technologies require integrating various hardware and software components, which can be complex and challenging to implement.
- **User experience**: AR applications must provide a seamless and intuitive user experience to be successful, which can be challenging given the complexity of AR technologies.

Conclusion

In this chapter we tried to take a closer look into the immersive technologies. We tried to take a holistic overview of these technologies. We tried to get to know how they reached their current state and what are the milestones achieved to get into the current state. We also came to know about their current state and the potential they are having. We understood that even though it is immensely powerful, it has a few limitations.

In the next chapter, we are going to learn about the psychology of presence and how it relates to immersion.

Points to remember

- AR is a technology that superimposes digital content, such as virtual objects or information, onto the real-world environment, blending the physical and digital realms. AR enhances the user's perception of reality by adding contextually relevant digital elements to their view, usually through a device like a smartphone or AR glasses.

- AR has the potential to revolutionize various industries, such as retail, where it can enhance the shopping experience by enabling virtual try-ons and product visualization and in healthcare AR can assist surgeons with real-time information during procedures.
- One of the main challenges for AR adoption is the need for sophisticated and expensive hardware. Secondly, this technology also faces issues related to user privacy, as AR applications may collect and process personal data.
- VR is an immersive technology that transports users to a computer-generated 3D environment, simulating presence in a virtual world. XR is an umbrella term that encompasses VR, AR, blurring the lines between the physical and digital worlds.
- VR relies on head-mounted displays and motion-tracking controllers to immerse users in a fully artificial environment.
- VR has the potential to revolutionize various industries, such as education, where it can create engaging and interactive learning experiences. XR holds promise for enhancing workplace productivity through hands-free access to information and guided instructions.
- High-quality VR experiences often require powerful and expensive hardware, limiting accessibility for some users. Both VR and XR face challenges related to motion sickness and discomfort during prolonged use.

CHAPTER 2
The Psychology of Presence in Immersive Technologies

Introduction

When we experience immersive technologies such as **Virtual Reality (VR)** and **Augmented Reality (AR)**, we often feel like we have been transported to a different world or reality. This sense of being present in another environment, also known as **presence**, is a key aspect of immersion and is crucial to the effectiveness and success of these technologies.

This chapter will explore the psychology of presence and how it relates to immersion in VR, AR, and other immersive technologies. It will examine the different factors that contribute to presence, such as sensory inputs, cognitive processes, and emotional responses. It will also discuss the importance of understanding presence for the design and development of immersive experiences.

Structure

In this chapter, we will discuss the following topics:

- Knowing presence
- Theories of presence
- Factors that contribute to presence
- Measuring presence
- Application of presence

Objectives

At the end of this chapter, you will be able to know in detail about presence. How presence plays an important and vital role in **Immersive Realm** and all the underlying technologies like AR, VR and XR. You will learn about the various factors that contribute to presence. Along with this, you will understand the way to measure this and finally how this can be applied in immersive technologies.

Knowing presence

First, we will learn what is presence and what are various factors that contribute to the presence in immersive technologies.

Definition and explanation of presence

Presence, in the context of immersive technologies such as VR and AR, refers to the subjective experience of being fully immersed and feeling as if you are physically present in a virtual or augmented environment. It is the feeling of being there in the virtual world or having virtual elements seamlessly integrated into the real world.

The *presence* of these devices is a crucial aspect of immersive technologies as they aim to create a *sense of realism* and *engagement* for users. When users experience a strong sense of presence, they tend to perceive the virtual or augmented environment as if it were real, and their responses and reactions can mirror those in the physical world.

There are various factors that contribute to the sense of presence in immersive technologies. These include:

- **Visual realism**: The visual fidelity and quality of the virtual or augmented environment play a significant role in creating a sense of presence. High-resolution graphics, accurate lighting, realistic textures, and detailed objects contribute to a more immersive experience.

- **Audio immersion**: Immersive audio, including spatial sound and realistic sound effects, helps to enhance presence. Spatial audio enables users to perceive sounds coming from different directions, creating a more convincing and realistic experience.

- **Interaction and input**: The ability to interact with and manipulate the virtual or augmented environment reinforces the feeling of presence. Natural and intuitive input methods, such as hand tracking or motion controllers, allow users to engage with the digital content, enhancing the sense of being present in the environment.

- **Body sensations**: Sensations that mimic real-world experiences, such as haptic feedback (vibrations or tactile sensations), can enhance presence. Feeling physical feedback when interacting with virtual objects or environments adds a layer of realism to the experience.

- **Social presence**: Interacting with other users in virtual or augmented environments can enhance the feeling of presence. The ability to see and communicate with others in real-time creates a sense of shared presence and social interaction, making the experience more immersive.
- **Narrative and context**: Engaging narratives, compelling storytelling, and meaningful context can contribute to a stronger sense of presence. When users have a clear purpose and context within the virtual or augmented world, it enhances their connection and involvement in the experience.

Developers and designers of immersive technologies aim to optimize these factors to create a sense of presence that transports users to a different reality, blurring the line between the virtual and physical worlds. Maximizing the sense of presence, immersive technologies can provide more engaging, realistic, and transformative experiences across a wide range of applications, from entertainment and gaming to training, education, and beyond.

Importance of presence for immersion and user experience

Presence plays a crucial role in creating immersive and engaging user experiences in VR, AR, and other immersive technologies. Here are some key reasons why presence is important for immersion and user experience:

- **Realism and believability**: Presence helps to create a sense of realism and believability in the virtual or augmented environment. When users feel present and connected to the digital content, they are more likely to suspend disbelief and perceive the experience as if it were real. This enhances the overall immersion and makes the experience more compelling.
- **Emotional engagement**: Presence has a significant impact on emotional engagement. When users feel present in the virtual or augmented environment, their emotional responses can mirror those in the physical world. This allows for a deeper emotional connection with the content and can evoke stronger feelings of excitement, empathy, or awe, enhancing the overall user experience.
- **Increased focus and attention**: Presence helps to captivate users' attention and focus. When users feel fully immersed and present in the experience, they are less likely to be distracted by external factors. This heightened focus allows users to engage more deeply with the content, leading to a more impactful and enjoyable experience.
- **Sense of agency and control**: Presence enhances users' sense of agency and control within the virtual or augmented environment. When users feel present, their actions and interactions have a direct impact on the digital world, reinforcing their sense of influence and empowerment. This sense of agency contributes to a more engaging and satisfying user experience.

- **Enhanced learning and skill development**: Presence can facilitate effective learning and skill development. Immersive experiences that generate a strong sense of presence can provide realistic training simulations, allowing users to practice and acquire new skills in a safe and controlled environment. This promotes active learning, muscle memory development, and better retention of information.
- **Social interaction and collaboration**: Presence enables social interaction and collaboration in virtual or augmented environments. When users feel present with others, they can communicate, interact, and collaborate in a more natural and meaningful way. This fosters a sense of shared presence and social presence, making the experience more enjoyable and fostering connections between users.

By prioritizing and optimizing presence, developers and designers can create immersive experiences that transport users to different worlds, provide meaningful interactions, and enhance the overall user experience. Presence is a key factor in enabling the transformative potential of immersive technologies across a wide range of applications, from entertainment and gaming to education, training, and beyond.

Theories of presence

Here we will learn about various theories and key concepts related to them.

Overview of different theories of presence

The concept of presence in the context of VR, AR, and other immersive technologies has been studied and theorized by researchers in various disciplines. Here is an overview of different theories of presence:

- **The spatial presence theory**: This theory, proposed by *Lombard* and *Ditton*, suggests that presence is primarily influenced by the perceptual illusion of being in a spatially located environment. According to this theory, the quality of sensory information, including visual and auditory cues, contributes to the feeling of presence. The more realistic and immersive the sensory input, the stronger the sense of presence.
- **The social presence theory**: This theory focuses on the role of social interactions and the feeling of being with others in virtual environments. It suggests that social cues, such as the presence of avatars or real-time communication with other users, can enhance the sense of presence. The theory posits that social presence is a critical component in creating a more immersive and engaging experience.
- **The transportation theory**: Proposed by *Green* and *Brock*, this theory suggests that presence arises from a state of transportation, where users become fully absorbed and mentally transported into a narrative or virtual environment. According to this theory, a compelling story, meaningful context, and engaging content can facilitate a state of transportation, leading to a stronger sense of presence.

- **The co-presence theory**: This theory emphasizes the importance of shared presence or co-presence in virtual environments. It suggests that the presence of others, either real or virtual, can enhance the feeling of being present. The theory argues that the presence of others can create a sense of social realism, interaction, and connectedness, contributing to a more immersive and engaging experience.
- **The psychological presence theory**: This theory focuses on the cognitive and psychological factors that influence presence. It suggests that the subjective mental state of being present is influenced by individual characteristics, such as attention, engagement, and involvement. Factors like user motivation, involvement in activities, and personal relevance can contribute to the sense of psychological presence.
- **The situated presence theory**: This theory considers presence as a situated experience that is influenced by the context and environment in which it occurs. It suggests that the physical environment, social context, cultural background, and personal experiences shape the sense of presence. According to this theory, the interaction between the virtual environment and the physical world impacts the overall sense of presence.

These theories provide different perspectives on the nature and determinants of presence in immersive technologies. They highlight the multidimensional nature of presence, considering factors such as sensory input, social interaction, cognitive processes, narrative engagement, and contextual factors. Understanding these theories can inform the design and development of immersive experiences, aiming to optimize presence and enhance the overall user experience.

Overview of different models of presence

Let us dive into perceptual and cognitive models of presence in immersive technology.

Perceptual models of presence focus on the *sensory aspects of immersion* and how they contribute to the feeling of being present in a virtual environment. These models emphasize the role of sensory inputs and their fidelity. Here are a few examples:

- **The Depth of Presence (DoP) model**: Developed by *Slater* and *Steed* in 2000, the DoP model proposes that presence is determined by the quality and amount of sensory information provided by the virtual environment. It suggests that higher levels of sensory immersion, such as realistic graphics, sound, and haptic feedback, lead to a stronger sense of presence.
- **The Perceptual Illusion of Non-Embodiment (PINE) model:** Introduced by *Kilteni, Normand,* and *Slater* in 2012, the PINE model focuses on the perception of one's own body within a virtual environment. It suggests that the sense of presence is influenced by the degree to which users perceive and identify with an avatar or virtual body. The model highlights the importance of body ownership and agency in enhancing presence.

Cognitive models of presence, on the other hand, emphasize the *cognitive and psychological* factors that contribute to the feeling of presence. These models consider the user's cognitive processing, attention, and engagement. Here are a couple of examples:

- **The Absorption-Realism-Attention (ARA) model**: Proposed by *Witmer* and *Singer* in 1998, the ARA model suggests that presence is influenced by three factors: absorption, realism, and attention. Absorption refers to the user's level of cognitive involvement and engagement in the virtual environment. Realism pertains to the perceived fidelity and authenticity of the virtual environment. Attention refers to the user's focus and cognitive resources dedicated to the virtual experience.
- **The attentional tunneling model**: Introduced by *Hoffman* and *Novak* in 1996, this model explains presence in terms of attentional processes. It suggests that presence arises when users become fully engrossed in the virtual environment, leading to a narrowing of attentional focus. As users direct their attention primarily towards the virtual environment, they become less aware of the physical world, resulting in a stronger sense of presence.

These perceptual and cognitive models provide valuable insights into the mechanisms underlying presence in immersive technology. Considering the sensory inputs, cognitive processing, and attentional factors, researchers and designers can create more immersive and engaging experiences that enhance the sense of presence for users.

Theories explaining the experience of presence

These theories and models of presence in immersive technology offer different perspectives on how individuals experience and perceive presence in virtual or augmented environments. Let us discuss how these theories and models contribute to the actual experience of presence:

- Perceptual model or DoP model and *PINE* model suggests that haptic feedbacks can enhance the sense of being present in virtual environment. This theory/model suggests that, how sensory experience contributes to the overall sense of presence.
- ARA models consider the user's cognitive processing, attention, and engagement with the virtual environment. They suggest that a high level of cognitive involvement, combined with perceived realism and focused attention, can enhance the feeling of presence. These models emphasize the importance of cognitive and attentional processes in shaping the experience of presence.
- On the other hand, *social model* suggests that the presence experienced by individuals is influenced by their perception and interaction with others in the virtual environment. Social cues, real-time communication, and the feeling of being together with others play a significant role in creating a sense of presence. These models highlight the social dimension of presence and how interactions with virtual entities or other participants can contribute to the overall experience.

- Some models take a multidimensional approach to explain presence. For example, the **Immersive Virtual Environment** (**IVE**) model combines sensory fidelity, interactivity, and the experience of control to explain presence. This model recognizes the multiple factors that contribute to the feeling of presence, including technological aspects, user agency, and the ability to navigate and manipulate the virtual environment.

Factors contributing to presence

In this topic you will learn how various factors contribute to the presence and how these factors are used to design and development of immersive experience. Different factors contributing to the presence.

Sensory inputs, cognitive processes, and emotional responses are critical factors that contribute to the experience of presence in immersive technology. Let us explore how each of these factors influences presence:

- **Sensory inputs:** Sensory inputs, including visual, auditory, and haptic cues, play a crucial role in creating a sense of presence. Realistic and high-fidelity sensory stimuli help to immerse users in the virtual environment, making it easier for them to suspend disbelief and feel present. For example, realistic visuals can enhance the perception of being in a different location, while accurate soundscapes can reinforce the sense of spatial presence. Additionally, haptic feedback, such as vibrations or force feedback, can provide a tactile sense of interaction, further enhancing the feeling of presence.

- **Cognitive processes:** Cognitive processes contribute significantly to the experience of presence. Attention, engagement, and cognitive involvement are central to the cognitive models of presence. When users direct their attention to the virtual environment, their cognitive resources become focused on processing the information and stimuli within that environment. This narrowing of attentional focus leads to a diminished awareness of the physical surroundings and strengthens the feeling of presence. Additionally, cognitive engagement and involvement in the virtual experience, such as active exploration, problem-solving, and decision-making, can enhance the sense of presence by increasing the user's investment in the virtual environment.

- **Emotional responses:** Emotional responses also play a significant role in the experience of presence. Emotions can be evoked through the content, narrative, or social interactions within the virtual environment. Positive emotions, such as excitement, joy, or awe, can enhance the feeling of presence by creating a sense of immersion and engagement. On the other hand, negative emotions, such as fear or anxiety, can intensify presence by triggering a strong emotional response and heightening the perceived reality of the virtual environment. Emotional engagement and resonance with the virtual content contribute to a more immersive and present experience.

It is important to note that these factors are interrelated and influence each other. For example, sensory inputs can evoke emotional responses, which, in turn, can affect cognitive processes and attention. Similarly, cognitive engagement and attention can shape the emotional experience within the virtual environment. Understanding how these factors interact and influence presence is essential for designing immersive technologies that effectively engage users and create compelling virtual experiences.

Let us now discuss how these factors are used in the designing and development of immersive experience:

- **Visual realism:** Designers focus on creating visually realistic virtual environments by using high-resolution graphics, realistic lighting, and detailed textures. This enhances the sense of presence by making the virtual world visually convincing.
- **Spatial audio:** By using binaural or spatial audio techniques, designers create a realistic soundscape that corresponds to the virtual environment, providing users with an immersive auditory experience. This contributes to a greater sense of presence.
- **Haptic feedback:** Incorporating haptic feedback devices, such as haptic gloves or controllers, allows users to feel tactile sensations, textures, or forces within the virtual environment. This enhances the sense of presence by adding a sense of touch and interaction.
- **Interactive elements:** Designers create interactive elements within the virtual environment that require cognitive engagement, decision-making, and problem-solving. This keeps users mentally engaged and invested in the virtual experience, enhancing their sense of presence.
- **Meaningful interactions:** Providing users with meaningful interactions with objects, characters, or the environment stimulates cognitive processes and fosters a stronger sense of presence. This can include realistic physics-based interactions or responsive feedback systems that mimic real-world behaviors.
- **Attentional guidance:** Designers direct users' attention through visual cues or narrative techniques to guide them towards important elements or events within the virtual environment. This helps focus users' attention and increases their sense of presence.
- **Compelling storytelling:** Designers create narratives, characters, and storylines that evoke emotional responses from users. Engaging storytelling techniques, such as strong character development, emotional arcs, or impactful plot twists, enhance the emotional connection to the virtual world, contributing to a heightened sense of presence.
- **Evoking emotion through visuals and audio:** Designers carefully craft the visual and auditory aspects of the virtual environment to elicit specific emotional responses

from users. For example, incorporating breathtaking vistas, atmospheric music, or dynamic sound effects can evoke awe, excitement, or suspense, deepening the sense of presence.

- **Emotional feedback:** Designers utilize emotional feedback mechanisms within the virtual environment to respond to user actions or decisions. This can include adaptive AI-driven characters that exhibit emotions, personalized reactions based on user choices, or emotional cues that provide a sense of empathy and connection.

Strategically employing these factors in the design and development process, designers and developers aim to create immersive experiences that captivate users, enhance their sense of presence, and create compelling virtual worlds that feel vivid and engaging.

Measuring presence

In this unit you will learn about the overview of different methods and tools used to measure presence. And then there will be discussion on the advantages and limitation of these methods.

The different methods to measure presence

When it comes to measuring presence in immersive technology, various methods and tools are utilized to capture different aspects of the user experience. Let us discuss some commonly used methods and measures.

Self-report measures

Self-report measures involve participants providing subjective feedback about their experience of presence through questionnaires, interviews, or rating scales. These measures rely on participants' self-perception and reflection. Examples include:

- **Presence Questionnaire (PQ)**: A widely used self-report measure that assesses the subjective sense of presence by asking participants to rate their experience based on specific items related to presence.
- **Slater-Usoh-Steed Presence Questionnaire (SUS-PQ)**: An extended version of the PQ that incorporates additional dimensions such as involvement and realism.
- **Subjective mental effort questionnaire**: Assesses the perceived mental effort required during the virtual experience, which can indirectly reflect the level of presence.

Physiological measures

Physiological measures aim to capture bodily responses that may be associated with presence. These measures assess physiological changes such as heart rate, skin conductance, brain activity, or eye movements. Some commonly used physiological measures include:

- **Electrocardiography (ECG/EKG)**: Measures the electrical activity of the heart to assess changes in heart rate and heart rate variability, which can indicate arousal and emotional response.
- **Galvanic Skin Response (GSR)**: Measures changes in skin conductance, which is associated with changes in emotional arousal and stress levels.
- **Electroencephalography (EEG)**: Records brainwave activity to identify patterns of attention, cognitive load, or emotional engagement during the virtual experience.

Behavioral measures

Behavioral measures focus on the observable actions and interactions of users within the virtual environment. These measures can provide insights into user engagement and presence. Examples include:

- **Task performance metrics**: Assessing the efficiency, accuracy, or completion time of specific tasks or activities performed within the virtual environment can indicate the level of engagement and presence.
- **Interaction logs**: Capturing user interactions, such as navigation patterns, object interactions, or communication behaviors, provides information about the extent of user engagement and presence.

Experience sampling

Experience sampling methods involve periodically interrupting the user's virtual experience to gather momentary self-reports about their sense of presence. This method allows for capturing in-the-moment experiences and fluctuations in presence throughout the session.

Hybrid approaches

In some cases, researchers employ a combination of different methods and measures to gain a more comprehensive understanding of presence. This may involve triangulating self-report measures, physiological measures, and behavioral data to capture multiple dimensions of presence simultaneously.

It is important to note that each method has its own strengths and limitations. Researchers must carefully select the measures based on their research goals, context, and resources. Additionally, advances in technology and research continue to expand the range of measurement tools available for assessing presence in immersive technology.

Advantages and limitations of measuring presence

Following is the holistic collection of advantages and limitations of various methods and models to measure presence. That is being said, we covered for: Self report, behavioral, physiological, experience sampling, and so on.

Advantages

The advantages of these methods are as follows:

- Provides direct insight into participants' subjective experiences of presence.
- Allows for capturing rich and detailed information about the nuances of presence.
- Relatively easy to administer and cost-effective.
- Provides objective and real-time data on physiological responses associated with presence.
- Less susceptible to conscious manipulation or biases.
- Can capture implicit or automatic responses that participants may not be aware of.
- Allows for assessing the physiological correlates of presence.
- Captures observable actions and interactions within the virtual environment.
- Allows for assessing presence in real-time during the interaction.
- Can offer insights into the user's behavioral patterns and preferences.
- Allows for studying the temporal aspects of presence.
- Can capture experiences that may be forgotten or distorted in retrospective reports.
- Combining multiple methods can offer a more comprehensive understanding of presence.
- Allows for triangulation of data, increasing the validity of the findings.
- Enables a multi-dimensional assessment of presence.

Limitations

The limitations of these methods are as follows:

- Relies on participants' self-perception and ability to accurately report their experiences.

- Subject to response biases, such as social desirability or acquiescence bias.
- May be influenced by memory recall and retrospective judgments.
- Variability in interpreting and understanding questionnaire items across individuals.
- Requires specialized equipment and expertise to collect and analyze physiological data.
- Individual differences in physiological responses may exist, making it challenging to establish universal markers of presence.
- Physiological measures may be influenced by factors other than presence (for example, general arousal or emotional states).
- Contextual factors and artifacts (for example, motion artifacts in EEG recordings) can impact the quality of data.
- Interpretation of behavioral data may be subjective and require careful analysis.
- Difficult to capture the full range of user experiences and emotions solely through behavioral observations.
- May not capture internal cognitive processes or emotional responses.
- Interrupting the virtual experience for sampling may disrupt immersion and potentially influence presence.
- Relies on participants' ability to recall and report their experiences accurately.
- Sampled moments may not be representative of the overall experience.
- Requires timely administration and coordination during the virtual session.
- Requires expertise in multiple measurement techniques.
- Challenges in integrating and interpreting data from different sources.
- Potential inconsistencies or discrepancies between different measures.
- Researchers should carefully consider the advantages and limitations of each method and select the most appropriate combination of measures based on their research goals, context, and available resources. Combining multiple methods and considering converging evidence can help enhance the reliability and validity of presence measurement in immersive technology.

Application of presence

In this unit you will know the discussion of the importance of presence for different applications of immersive technologies, such as training and therapy.

You will go through some successful applications of presence in different domain.

Importance of presence for different applications

The concept of presence plays a significant role in various applications of immersive technologies, including training and therapy. Presence refers to the subjective feeling of being there in a virtual environment, where the user's senses and cognitive processes perceive the virtual world as real. It is a crucial factor for the effectiveness and success of immersive experiences. Here is a discussion on the importance of presence in training and therapy applications.

Training

Immersive technologies, such as VR and AR, offer unique advantages for training scenarios. Presence enhances training effectiveness by creating realistic simulations and engaging the trainees' cognitive processes. Let us discuss them in detail:

- **Skill acquisition**: Immersive training allows individuals to practice and develop skills in a safe and controlled virtual environment. With a strong sense of presence, trainees can experience scenarios that closely resemble real-life situations, enabling them to acquire and refine skills more effectively.
- **Emotional engagement**: Presence can evoke emotional responses and facilitate emotional engagement during training. By creating a sense of being there, immersive technologies can elicit emotional reactions like those experienced in real-world situations, helping trainees develop emotional intelligence and decision-making skills.
- **Memory retention**: The immersive nature of virtual environments can improve memory retention. When trainees feel present in a training scenario, their cognitive processes are more likely to encode and retrieve information effectively, leading to enhanced learning and knowledge retention.

Therapy

Immersive technologies are increasingly being used in therapeutic applications, such as exposure therapy, pain management, and mental health treatments. Presence plays a vital role in therapeutic experiences, offering several benefits:

- **Enhanced immersion**: Presence enables a higher level of immersion in therapy sessions, allowing individuals to fully engage with the therapeutic environment. This heightened immersion can foster a sense of safety, relaxation, and openness, facilitating the therapeutic process.
- **Exposure and desensitization**: In exposure therapy, presence is crucial for creating realistic and immersive scenarios that expose individuals to their fears or anxieties.

By feeling present in the virtual environment, patients can gradually confront and overcome their fears, leading to desensitization and therapeutic progress.

- **Empathy and rapport**: Presence in therapy can foster a stronger sense of empathy and rapport between the patient and the therapist. Immersive technologies can create a shared virtual space where both parties can interact and communicate, enhancing the therapeutic alliance and facilitating effective therapy.
- **Distraction and pain management**: In the context of pain management, presence can help distract individuals from pain sensations by immersing them in engaging virtual environments. By redirecting attention and creating a sense of presence, immersive technologies have the potential to alleviate pain and discomfort during medical procedures or rehabilitation exercises.

In summary, presence is a vital aspect of immersive technologies for training and therapy applications. By creating realistic and engaging virtual environments, presence enhances skill acquisition, emotional engagement, memory retention, therapeutic outcomes, empathy, and pain management. The subjective feeling of being there contributes to the overall effectiveness and success of these immersive experiences.

Examples of successful applications of presence

Here are some examples of successful applications of presence in different domains:

- **Medical training**: Immersive technologies like virtual reality have been used to train medical professionals in various procedures. For example, surgical simulations with a high sense of presence allow surgeons to practice complex procedures in a realistic virtual environment, improving their skills and reducing the risk of errors during actual surgeries.
- **Military training**: Presence has been instrumental in military training, where realistic simulations are crucial for combat readiness. Virtual reality-based training programs provide soldiers with immersive combat scenarios, allowing them to practice tactical decision-making, teamwork, and situational awareness in a safe and controlled environment.
- **Occupational safety training**: Presence has proven valuable in training programs for high-risk professions, such as firefighters and construction workers. Virtual reality simulations can recreate hazardous situations, enabling trainees to develop critical skills, experience realistic emergencies, and make split-second decisions without real-world consequences.
- **Sports training**: Immersive technologies, including virtual reality and augmented reality, have found applications in sports training. Athletes can use VR to simulate game scenarios, improving their decision-making abilities and enhancing their performance. The sense of presence helps athletes immerse themselves mentally and emotionally in the training environment.

- **Mental health therapy**: Virtual reality is increasingly being used in mental health therapy. For instance, exposure therapy for phobias and **Post-Traumatic Stress Disorder (PTSD)** leverages presence to recreate triggering situations and help patients confront their fears in a controlled environment. By feeling present, patients can engage in gradual desensitization and emotional processing.
- **Architectural design**: Presence has been utilized in the field of architecture and design. Architects and clients can use virtual reality to experience and explore virtual building models, allowing them to assess the spatial layout, aesthetics, and functionality of the design before construction begins. This enhances the design process and enables more effective communication between stakeholders.
- **Tourism and cultural heritage**: Immersive technologies have transformed the way people experience tourism and cultural heritage. Virtual reality and augmented reality can create realistic virtual tours of historical sites, museums, and landmarks, providing users with a strong sense of presence and an interactive learning experience, even if they are physically distant from the location.

These are just a few examples that highlight the successful applications of presence in various domains. As technology continues to advance, the potential for creating immersive experiences with a high sense of presence will likely expand into new areas, benefiting a wide range of industries and fields.

Conclusion

In this chapter we tried to take a closer look into the concept of presence, various theories of presence, factors that contribute to presence and how we can measure presence also the various application of presence.

In the next chapter, we are going to learn the principles and best practices for designing immersive experiences that captivate and engage users.

Points to remember

- Presence is a crucial aspect of immersive technologies as it aims to create a *sense of realism* and *engagement* for users. Understanding these key points about knowing presence, theories related to presence, methods to measure it, and its applications will provide you with valuable insights into the importance of presence in immersive technologies and how it impacts user experiences.
- Presence refers to the subjective sense of being there or feeling immersed in a virtual or mediated environment. Understanding presence is crucial for designing immersive technologies that evoke realistic and engaging experiences.
- The Social Presence Theory suggests that the feeling of presence is influenced by the social cues and interactions experienced in a virtual environment.

- The Spatial Presence Theory emphasizes the importance of spatial characteristics and the extent to which a virtual environment feels spatially coherent.
- The Coherence Theory of Presence focuses on the consistency of the virtual environment with the user's expectations and prior experiences.
- Presence is a multi-dimensional construct and can be challenging to quantify objectively.
- Presence can be measured through self-report questionnaires, physiological measures, behavioral indicators, and qualitative assessments of user experiences.
- Presence plays a significant role in various fields, such as VR, AR, video gaming, teleconferencing, and simulation-based training.
- In VR, a high sense of presence can lead to more realistic and impactful experiences, benefiting areas like gaming, education, and training simulations.
- Design elements that enhance presence include realistic graphics, accurate spatial sound, intuitive user interfaces, and seamless interactions.
- Creating a sense of agency, embodiment, and emotional engagement in virtual environments can heighten the feeling of presence.

CHAPTER 3

Designing Immersive Experience

Introduction

In this chapter, we will explore the principles and best practices for designing immersive experiences that captivate and engage users. Immersive experiences are becoming increasingly popular in fields like gaming, virtual reality, and augmented reality, and the principles we discuss here can be applied to a wide range of industries. We will look at how to design sensory immersion, emotional immersion, and narrative immersion, as well as some of the best user interface and experience design practices.

Structure

In this chapter, we will discuss the following topics:

- Introduction to immersive design
- Designing for sensory immersion
- Designing for emotional immersion
- Designing for narrative immersion
- Best practices for user interface and experience design

Objectives

At the end of this chapter, you will be able to know in detail about *immersive designing*. How sensory, emotional, and narrative immersion plays an important role in the entire user interface and experience of an augmented or virtual real environment. You will also learn about some of the best practices for user interface and experience design.

Introduction to immersive design

First, we will learn what is presence and what various factors contribute to the presence in immersive technologies.

Importance of immersion

Have you ever been so engrossed in a book, movie, or video game that you lost track of time and felt completely transported to another world? That captivating feeling is none other than immersion. In this chapter, we will delve into immersion, its significance in various domains, and why it holds a crucial place in our modern digital landscape.

Understanding immersion

Immersion can be described as being fully absorbed and engaged in an experience to the point where one's awareness of the external world diminishes. It involves creating a sense of presence, where the boundaries between reality and the simulated or imagined world blur. Immersive experiences can captivate our senses, evoke emotions, and provide a heightened level of engagement.

The importance of immersion

Let us discuss the importance of immersion in detail:

- **Enhanced engagement**: Immersion holds the key to unlocking heightened levels of engagement. By immersing users in a rich and compelling experience, whether it is through **Virtual Reality** (**VR**), **Augmented Reality** (**AR**), or other mediums, we can capture their attention and create a deep connection between the user and the content.
- **Emotional impact**: Immersive experiences can evoke powerful emotions and leave a lasting impact on individuals. Whether experiencing the thrill of a rollercoaster ride in VR or feeling empathy for a character in a virtual storytelling experience, immersion enables us to tap into emotions in a way that traditional media often cannot replicate.
- **Learning and training**: Immersion has proven to be an effective tool for learning and training in various fields. Placing individuals in simulated environments, they can actively participate and learn through hands-on experiences. For example,

flight simulators provide pilots with realistic training scenarios without the risks associated with real flights.

- **Entertainment and media**: Immersive technologies have revolutionized the entertainment and media industries. From immersive video games that transport players to fantastical worlds to immersive theater experiences that blur the line between performer and audience, immersion offers a new dimension of storytelling and entertainment possibilities.
- **Architectural and design visualization**: Immersive technologies like VR and AR have transformed how architectural designs and prototypes are visualized. Architects and designers can provide realistic and interactive representations of their projects by immersing clients and stakeholders in virtual environments, enabling better decision-making and collaboration.

Figure 3.1 shows how an immersive experience of nature gives an experience of real nature to the user:

***Figure 3.1**: Illustration of the immersive experience of nature*

Immersive experience psychology and impact

Immersive experiences have a profound psychological impact on users, captivating their attention, evoking emotions, and influencing their perceptions. In this chapter, we will delve into the psychology behind immersive experiences and explore how they affect users on cognitive, emotional, and behavioral levels. By understanding the psychological mechanisms at play, we can gain insights into the power and potential of immersive technologies:

- **Presence and perceived realness**: Immersive experiences strive to create a sense of presence, where users perceive the virtual environment as real and their actions within it as meaningful. This feeling of presence is influenced by factors such as sensory fidelity, interactivity, and narrative coherence. When users feel a high level of presence, their cognitive and emotional responses align with those of real-world experiences, leading to a more authentic and engaging encounter.

- **Cognitive engagement and attention**: Immersive experiences demand focused attention from users, drawing them into the presented environment and reducing distractions from the external world. The heightened cognitive engagement facilitates deep information processing, enhancing learning, memory formation, and problem-solving abilities. Immersive technologies also leverage the power of spatial cognition, spatial presence, and embodied cognition to immerse users in realistic and contextually rich environments.

- **Emotional responses and empathy**: Immersive experiences can remarkably elicit emotional responses in users. Leveraging sensory inputs, storytelling techniques, and interactive elements can evoke a wide range of emotions, from excitement and joy to fear and empathy. Users often experience a heightened emotional intensity in immersive environments, leading to increased emotional immersion and a stronger connection to the content. This emotional engagement can enhance the user experience and leave a lasting impact.

- **Behavioral influence and empowerment**: Immersive experiences can shape users' behavior and influence their decision-making processes. Users can practice skills, explore possibilities, and experiment with different choices in a safe and controlled environment through interactive scenarios, simulations, and role-playing. This behavioral influence can extend to training, therapy, and behavior change interventions, where immersive experiences offer a unique platform for guided practice and behavioral modification.

- **Presence and social interaction**: Immersive experiences also have implications for social psychology. Virtual environments can facilitate social presence, enabling users to interact and collaborate with others, even when physically separated. This social interaction can enhance feelings of connectedness, foster empathy, and facilitate the formation of social bonds. Additionally, virtual representations of oneself, known as avatars, can impact self-perception, self-esteem, and social behaviors.

Designing for sensory immersion

This chapter will explore the fascinating world of sensory immersion and its role in creating truly captivating experiences. We will delve into the importance of designing for multiple senses, understanding sensory perception, and utilizing sensory cues to enhance immersion. From visual aesthetics to auditory landscapes, haptic feedback to olfactory stimuli, we will uncover the key considerations and best practices for designing immersive experiences that engage all the senses.

Immersive experience with engaging user senses

Creating immersive experiences that engage users' senses is a multidimensional task that requires careful consideration and intentional design. To craft truly captivating experiences, designers can follow these key principles and techniques:

- **Understand the power of each sense**: Begin by understanding the unique capabilities and characteristics of each sense. Explore how sight, hearing, touch, taste, and smell can contribute to the overall immersive experience. Consider how different senses can complement and reinforce each other to create a more holistic and engaging environment.

- **Set the scene with visual design**: Visual elements play a significant role in establishing the foundation of an immersive experience. Pay attention to the aesthetics, colors, lighting, and visual composition to create visually appealing and cohesive environments. Use visuals to guide users' attention, convey emotions, and establish the desired atmosphere.

- **Harness the power of sound**: Sound is a powerful tool for enhancing immersion. Utilize high-quality audio and sound effects to create realistic and immersive auditory landscapes. Consider spatial audio techniques to give users a sense of direction and depth within the virtual environment. Align sound design with the visual elements to create a more cohesive and immersive experience.

- **Incorporate tactile feedback**: Tactile feedback adds another layer of immersion by engaging the sense of touch. Explore haptic feedback technologies and incorporate them thoughtfully into the experience. Use vibrations, textures, and physical interactions to provide users a tangible connection to the virtual world, enhancing their sense of presence and interaction.

- **Design for cross-sensory integration**: Aim for a cohesive and harmonious integration of sensory cues. Ensure that the sensory elements work together seamlessly, supporting and enhancing each other rather than competing or conflicting. Align sensory stimuli to create a synchronized, immersive experience that feels natural to users.

- **Emphasize interaction and agency**: Immersive experiences are not passive; they thrive on interaction and user agency. Provide opportunities for users to actively engage with the environment, objects, or characters. Design meaningful interactions that respond to users' actions, giving them a sense of control and influence over the experience.

- **Storytelling and narrative**: Engaging storytelling and compelling narratives can significantly enhance immersion. Create a coherent and captivating storyline that draws users into the experience and provides a context for their interactions. Use narrative elements to guide users' emotional journey and establish a connection between them and the virtual world.

Following these principles and techniques, designers can create immersive experiences that engage users' senses and transport them into captivating and memorable worlds. The thoughtful integration of sight, sound, touch, taste, and smell can create a truly immersive and transformative experience, unlocking the full potential of immersive technologies.

Figure 3.2 shows how an immersive experience can be produced in real estate touring, and this helps the user to understand the actual layout of the living or office space:

***Figure 3.2**: Illustration of immersive experience in real estate tour*

Immersive experience principles

Let us understand the principles for creating immersive experiences, mainly spatial design, sound design, and haptic feedback.

Spatial design

Spatial design is fundamental to creating immersive experiences, particularly in VR and AR applications. It involves meticulously arranging and organizing physical and virtual elements within a space to evoke a sense of presence and realism. Carefully considering scale, proportion, depth, layout, and interactivity, designers can create virtual environments that captivate users and transport them into a world that feels authentic and engaging. Attention to detail, such as incorporating appropriate depth cues, thoughtfully designing navigation systems, and adding realistic environmental details, enhances the overall immersive quality of the experience. Spatial design fosters a sense of presence, enabling users to interact seamlessly with the virtual environment and facilitating a truly immersive and memorable experience.

Sound design

Sound design is crucial to creating immersive experiences in various media forms, including VR, AR, films, and video games. It involves the intentional and creative use of audio elements to enhance the overall immersion and emotional impact of the experience. Sound design encompasses background music, sound effects, dialogue, and spatial audio. By carefully crafting and integrating these elements, designers can transport users into rich and believable worlds, creating a sense of presence and engagement.

One key aspect of sound design is ambient sounds and background music. These elements set the mood, establish the environment, and evoke specific emotions. From soft and tranquil melodies to intense and suspenseful soundscapes, the right choice of music can greatly enhance immersion and draw users deeper into the experience. Sound effects are also crucial in providing auditory cues corresponding to visual events or actions within the experience. Whether it's the sound of footsteps, the swishing of a sword, or the roar of a spaceship engine, these effects add realism and help users make sense of the virtual environment. Additionally, spatial audio techniques can create a sense of depth and directionality, making the audio feel more three-dimensional and further enhancing the immersive quality of the experience.

In summary, sound design is essential for designers to create immersive experiences. Using ambient sounds, music, sound effects, and spatial audio, they can transport users to new worlds, elicit emotional responses, and provide a more engaging and believable experience. Sound design enriches the overall sensory experience, making it a vital component in creating truly immersive and memorable experiences.

Haptic feedback

Haptic feedback, also known as tactile feedback, is a technology that adds a sense of touch to virtual and AR experiences. It provides physical sensations and vibrations that mimic real-world tactile experiences, allowing users to feel and interact with virtual objects and environments. Haptic feedback plays a crucial role in enhancing immersion and realism, as touch is an essential aspect of how we perceive and understand the world around us.

One aspect of haptic feedback is the use of vibration or force feedback. Applying precise vibrations or forces to a user's hands or body, haptic feedback can simulate various sensations like impact, texture, or movement. For example, when a user interacts with a virtual object and presses a button, they can feel a subtle vibration or resistance that mimics the sensation of pressing a physical button. This feedback helps bridge the gap between the virtual and physical worlds, making the experience more engaging and believable.

Another aspect of haptic feedback is the use of wearable devices like haptic gloves or suits. These devices use actuators or motors to provide localized vibrations or pressure on specific parts of the body, such as the hands, fingers, or torso. This enables users to feel the shape, texture, or even the weight of virtual objects they interact with. For instance, wearing haptic gloves can create the sensation of touching different surfaces or feeling the impact of objects within a virtual environment. These gloves are a welcome step in the dimension of immersive experience. However, it needs more technological advancement before we can actually feel it as a part of our body. At this stage, the gloves seem a little bulky and heavy to carry.

Figure 3.3 shows how haptic feedback provides a haptic response to the user:

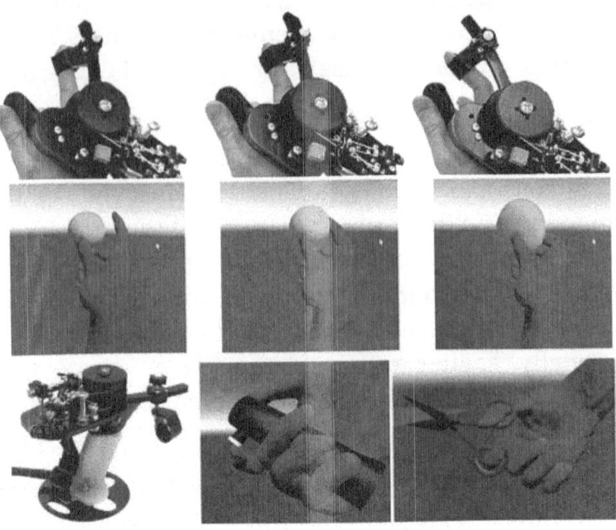

***Figure 3.3:** Illustration of haptic feedback*
*(**Source:** Microsoft Corporation)*

Applying these principles of spatial design, sound design, and haptic feedback, designers can create immersive experiences that engage multiple senses, enhance the sense of presence, and provide users with a more compelling and captivating interaction with the virtual or physical world.

Designing for emotional immersion

In this topic, we will explore the profound impact of emotional immersion in creating truly memorable and engaging experiences. We will delve into the importance of designing for emotional resonance, understanding the psychology of emotions, and employing effective techniques to elicit and shape users' emotional responses. From storytelling to aesthetics, audiovisual cues to interactive elements, we will uncover the key considerations and best practices for designing immersive experiences that deeply resonate with users on an emotional level.

Powerful emotions with immersive experience

We will begin by exploring the significance of emotional immersion in creating transformative experiences. We will discuss the ways in which emotions can heighten user engagement, influence decision-making, and foster a sense of connection and empathy with the virtual world.

Let us dive into the psychology of emotions, including the different types of emotions, their underlying mechanisms, and the role they play in human experiences. Gain insights into how emotions are triggered, influenced, and expressed and how they can be effectively harnessed in immersive design:

- **Storytelling and narrative**: Examine the art of storytelling and its pivotal role in evoking emotions. Learn how to craft compelling narratives that engage users' emotions, create meaningful character arcs, and establish a sense of purpose and emotional investment within the immersive experience.
- **Visual and aesthetic design**: Explore the impact of visual aesthetics on emotional immersion. Discuss the use of color palettes, lighting, visual composition, and art direction to evoke specific emotions and set the desired mood within the virtual environment.
- **Soundscapes and music**: Uncover the power of audio in eliciting emotions and enhancing immersion. Discover how sound effects, ambient sounds, and carefully selected music can evoke specific emotional responses and enhance the overall emotional impact of the experience.
- **Interactive elements and agency**: Investigate the role of interactivity in emotional immersion. Explore how meaningful interactions, choices, and consequences can empower users, deepen their emotional engagement, and create a sense of agency and ownership within the immersive environment.
- **Empathy and connection**: Examine the importance of fostering empathy and emotional connection between users and virtual characters or environments. Discuss techniques such as realistic character behavior, non-verbal communication cues, and engaging narratives that promote emotional resonance and empathy.

Role of design in an impactful user experience

Design has the power to evoke strong emotions and create experiences that leave a lasting impact on users. By implementing efficient design principles and strategies, designers can tap into users' emotions and create meaningful and memorable experiences. Here are keyways in which efficient design can achieve this:

- **User-centered approach**: An efficient design begins with a deep understanding of the target audience. Conducting user research, personas, and empathy mapping helps identify users' needs, preferences, and emotional triggers. Designing with users in mind, designers can create experiences that resonate on a personal level, connecting with users' emotions.
- **Emotional storytelling**: Storytelling is a powerful tool to engage users emotionally. Crafting compelling narratives that evoke empathy, suspense, joy, or nostalgia can create a deep emotional connection. Efficient design incorporates storytelling elements such as character development, plot progression, and conflict resolution to engage users and elicit emotional responses.

- **Visual communication**: Visual elements play a crucial role in creating emotional impact. Efficient design utilizes visual cues, aesthetics, and graphical elements to convey emotions effectively. The choice of colors, typography, imagery, and graphic design elements should align with the intended emotional tone and reinforce the narrative or message.
- **Seamless user experience**: An efficient design seamlessly guides users through an experience, enabling them to engage with content effortlessly. Smooth navigation, intuitive interactions, and responsive interfaces reduce friction and frustration, allowing users to focus on the emotional aspects of the experience. Eliminating distractions and providing clear paths for users enhances their emotional connection to the content.
- **Multi-sensory integration**: Incorporating multiple senses into the design enhances emotional immersion. Efficient design utilizes audio, visuals, haptics, and other sensory elements to create a holistic experience. Sound design, for instance, can evoke specific emotions, while haptic feedback can enhance user engagement and provide a tangible connection to the experience.
- **Emotional feedback and validation**: Design that acknowledges and validates users' emotions can have a profound impact. Efficient design incorporates feedback mechanisms that respond to users' actions and emotional cues. It acknowledges achievements, provides positive reinforcement, and offers support when needed. This validation strengthens the emotional bond between users and the experience.
- **Surprise and delight**: Efficient design includes elements of surprise and delight to create memorable moments. Unexpected surprises, Easter eggs, or hidden interactions can evoke positive emotions such as joy, excitement, or curiosity. These moments of delight leave a lasting impact on users and encourage them to share their experiences with others.
- **Authenticity and empathy**: An efficient design captures authenticity and empathy by understanding users' perspectives and emotions. Designers empathize with users' needs, challenges, and aspirations, creating experiences that reflect their values and resonate with their emotions. Authenticity fosters a genuine emotional connection, leading to a more meaningful and impactful experience.
- **Long-term engagement**: An efficient design aims to create an experience that users remember long after their initial interaction. It considers strategies for fostering long-term engagement and encourages users to revisit the experience. This can include personalized content, social features, rewards, or ongoing updates that maintain users' emotional connection and interest over time.

Implementing efficient design principles that prioritize user-centeredness, emotional storytelling, seamless user experience, multi-sensory integration, emotional feedback, surprise and delight, authenticity, empathy, and long-term engagement, designers can create experiences that tap into users' emotions and leave a lasting impact. Such experiences have the potential to evoke deep emotional connections, inspire action, and become memorable moments in users' lives.

Designing for narrative immersion

In this chapter, we will explore the art and science of designing for emotional immersion. We will delve into the importance of emotions in user experiences, the psychological impact of emotional immersion, and the strategies and techniques for creating experiences that deeply engage users on an emotional level. From empathy-driven design to emotional cues and triggers, we will uncover the key principles and best practices for designing immersive experiences that elicit powerful emotional responses and leave a lasting impact.

Importance of storytelling in the narrative immersion

In this topic, we will explore the profound impact of storytelling on creating narrative immersion in experiences. We will delve into the importance of narrative structure, character development, plot progression, and thematic elements in capturing users' attention and creating a deep sense of immersion. From traditional storytelling techniques to interactive narratives, we will uncover the key principles and best practices for leveraging storytelling to enhance narrative immersion and engage users on an emotional and cognitive level. Let us discuss them in detail:

- **Understanding narrative immersion**: Explore the concept of narrative immersion and its significance in creating compelling experiences. Discuss the role of storytelling in captivating users' attention, fostering emotional engagement, and creating a sense of presence within the narrative world. Understand the psychological aspects of narrative immersion and its effects on users' perceptions and empathy.

- **The elements of effective storytelling**: Examine the fundamental elements of storytelling and how they contribute to narrative immersion. Discuss the importance of a well-defined narrative structure, engaging characters, and a compelling plot. Explore techniques for crafting captivating beginnings, building tension and suspense, and delivering satisfying conclusions.

- **Character development**: Delve into the art of character development and its impact on narrative immersion. Learn how to create relatable and multi-dimensional characters that resonate with users' emotions. Explore techniques for designing character arcs, motivations, and conflicts that drive the narrative and create a sense of investment and empathy.

- **Plot progression and pacing**: Discuss the role of plot progression and pacing in maintaining users' interest and sustaining narrative immersion. Explore techniques for creating tension, surprises, and plot twists that keep users engaged and eager to uncover the next chapter of the story. Learn how to balance exposition, rising action, climax, and resolution for a satisfying narrative experience.

- **Thematic cohesion**: Explore the importance of thematic cohesion in creating narrative immersion. Discuss how a consistent and well-developed theme can enhance users' understanding, emotional connection, and overall engagement with the story. Learn how to align visual, audio, and interactive elements with the central themes to reinforce narrative immersion.

- **Interactive narratives**: Examine the role of interactivity in narrative immersion. Explore techniques for designing interactive elements and choices that empower users to shape the story and feel a sense of agency. Discuss the challenges and opportunities of branching narratives, multiple endings, and adaptive storytelling in creating personalized and immersive experiences.

- **Cross-media storytelling**: Explore the potential of cross-media storytelling to enhance narrative immersion. Discuss the integration of visuals, audio, music, animation, and other media elements to create a cohesive and immersive narrative experience. Learn how to leverage the strengths of different media platforms to expand the narrative world and engage users across multiple channels.

Storytelling is a powerful tool for enhancing narrative immersion in experiences. Understanding the elements of effective storytelling, developing compelling characters, crafting engaging plots, maintaining thematic cohesion, incorporating interactivity, evoking emotional resonance, and exploring cross-media possibilities, designers can create immersive experiences that captivate users' attention, evoke emotions, and leave a lasting impact. A well-crafted narrative can transport users to new worlds, spark their imagination, and provide meaningful and memorable experiences.

Compelling narrative and user engagement

In this topic, we will explore the art of creating compelling narratives that captivate users and keep them engaged and invested in the experience. We will examine the key elements of narrative design, storytelling techniques, and strategies for maintaining user interest throughout the journey. From establishing a strong hook to building tension and delivering satisfying resolutions, we will uncover the principles and best practices for crafting narratives that immerse users and leave a lasting impact:

- **Understanding the power of narrative**: Explore the significance of narratives in engaging users and creating immersive experiences. Discuss the psychological aspects of storytelling, including the impact of narratives on attention, emotions, and memory. Understand the role of narrative immersion in fostering user engagement and enhancing the overall experience.

- **Defining the narrative objective**: Define the narrative objective and identify the desired impact on users. Discuss how different experiences, such as games, interactive stories, or educational applications, require specific narrative goals. Explore techniques for aligning the narrative objective with the intended user experience.

- **Establishing a strong hook**: Learn the importance of a strong hook to capture users' attention and draw them into the narrative. Discuss techniques for creating compelling introductions, intriguing premises, or memorable opening moments that immediately pique users' curiosity and motivate them to continue exploring.

- **Character development and user empathy**: Examine the role of well-developed characters in fostering user empathy and investment in the narrative. Learn how to create relatable, multi-dimensional characters with distinct personalities, motivations, and conflicts. Explore techniques for engaging users through character-driven storytelling and their emotional connections to the characters.

- **Building tension and conflict**: Discover strategies for building tension and conflict within the narrative. Discuss the importance of obstacles, challenges, and rising action in keeping users engaged and invested. Explore techniques for pacing the narrative, introducing plot twists, and maintaining a sense of suspense throughout the experience.

- **Narrative structure and progression**: Understand the significance of narrative structure and progression in maintaining user interest. Explore different narrative structures, such as linear, non-linear, or branching, and their suitability for different experiences. Learn how to create well-paced narratives with compelling story arcs and turning points.

- **Satisfying resolutions and endings**: Examine the importance of satisfying resolutions and endings in creating a memorable narrative experience. Discuss techniques for delivering emotional payoffs, resolving conflicts, and providing closure to users. Explore the impact of different endings, such as open-ended, conclusive, or cliffhangers, on user satisfaction and anticipation for future experiences.

- **Iterative storytelling and user feedback**: Understand the iterative nature of storytelling and the importance of user feedback in refining the narrative. Explore methods for collecting user feedback, analyzing narrative flow, and making iterative improvements based on user insights. Learn how to adapt the narrative based on user preferences and engagement metrics.

Crafting compelling narratives is a key component of creating engaging and immersive experiences. By understanding the power of narrative, defining clear objectives, establishing strong hooks, developing relatable characters, building tension and conflict, structuring the narrative effectively, balancing exploration and direction, providing satisfying resolutions, and incorporating iterative storytelling processes, designers can create narratives that captivate users and keep them invested throughout the experience. Storytelling can potentially elevate the user experience, leaving a lasting impression and ensuring users' continued engagement with the narrative-driven product or application.

Best practices for user interface and experience design

In this part, we will explore the best practices for designing user interfaces and experiences that are intuitive, user-friendly, and engaging. We will delve into the principles and strategies that guide the creation of effective interfaces, focusing on usability, visual design, interaction design, and accessibility. From understanding user needs to implementing intuitive navigation and providing feedback, we will uncover the key considerations and techniques for designing exceptional user interfaces and experiences.

Importance of a well-designed user interface

In this chapter, we will explore the crucial role of user interface design in creating immersive experiences. We will delve into the principles and strategies that guide the design of user interfaces to enhance immersion, engagement, and interaction. From intuitive controls and seamless navigation to visual aesthetics and interactive feedback, we will uncover the key considerations and techniques for designing a well-crafted user interface that elevates the overall immersive experience:

- **User-centric interface design**: Learn the importance of a user-centric approach in interface design. Understand the target audience, their goals, and preferences. Explore techniques for gathering user feedback, conducting user research, and creating user personas to inform the design decisions and ensure a personalized and immersive experience.

- **Intuitive and responsive controls**: Discuss the significance of intuitive controls in facilitating user interaction and enhancing immersion. Explore techniques for designing control schemes that are easy to learn and use. Discuss the importance of responsiveness and feedback in creating a sense of agency and connection between user actions and the virtual environment.

- **Seamless navigation and information architecture**: Explore the role of seamless navigation and information architecture in maintaining immersion. Discuss techniques for designing clear and logical navigation systems that allow users to move through the experience effortlessly. Learn how to organize content effectively, provide contextual cues, and optimize information flow for a smooth, immersive journey.

- **Visual aesthetics and atmospheric design**: Discuss the impact of visual aesthetics on immersion. Explore techniques for visually appealing interfaces that align with the overall experience and narrative. Discuss the importance of consistent visual language, appropriate colors, typography, and visual elements to evoke desired emotions and enhance immersion.
- **Audio design for immersion**: Understand the significance of audio design in creating immersive experiences. Discuss techniques for designing spatial audio, sound effects, and background music that enhance the sense of presence and create an immersive atmosphere. Explore the importance of audio cues and feedback in guiding user actions and reinforcing the virtual environment.
- **Interactive feedback and responsiveness**: Explore the role of interactive feedback in enhancing immersion and user engagement. Discuss techniques for providing real-time feedback through animations, haptic feedback, and visual cues. Learn how to create a sense of responsiveness to user actions, ensuring a seamless and immersive interaction with the interface.
- **Contextual and dynamic user interfaces**: Discuss the benefits of contextual and dynamic user interfaces in creating immersive experiences. Explore techniques for adapting the interface based on user context, such as adjusting controls, layout, or content based on the environment or user preferences. Learn how to leverage real-time data and user behavior to create personalized and immersive interfaces.
- **Iterative design and user testing**: Understand the iterative nature of interface design and the importance of user testing in refining immersive experience. Discuss methods for collecting user feedback, conducting usability tests, and iterating the design based on user insights. Learn how to balance user feedback with creative vision to create an interface that enhances immersion and meets user expectations.

A well-designed user interface is essential for creating immersive experiences. Understanding the principles of immersion, adopting a user-centric approach, designing intuitive controls and navigation, considering visual aesthetics and atmospheric design, incorporating audio elements, providing interactive feedback, and embracing contextual and dynamic interfaces, designers can craft interfaces that enhance immersion and elevate the overall user experience. Careful consideration of user needs, seamless interaction, and attention to detail in interface design plays a crucial role in creating unforgettable and immersive experiences that impact users.

Conclusion

In this chapter, we tried to take a closer look at the concept of immersive experience. We learned about various ways to design immersion, like sensory, emotional, and narrative-based immersion. In the end, we learned about some of the best practices for user interface and experience design. We further explored how a well-designed user interface is essential for creating easy-to-use and navigate immersive experiences.

In the next chapter, we will learn about the history and development of VR hardware, the challenges developers and designers have faced, and the new opportunities emerging technologies create.

Points to remember

- Clearly define the purpose and objectives of the experience, understanding the target audience and their expectations.
- Adopt a user-centered design approach, researching to gain insights into their needs and preferences.
- Incorporate a compelling narrative or storyline to engage users throughout the experience.
- Utilize spatial design principles to create a realistic environment.
- Engage multiple senses to enhance immersion, such as visuals, audio, and haptic feedback.
- Design intuitive interactions and provide responsive feedback.
- Incorporate dynamic and adaptive elements that respond to user input.
- Optimize performance to ensure a seamless experience.
- Iterate on the design based on user feedback and testing.

CHAPTER 4
Evolution of VR Hardware

Introduction

This chapter will take a deep dive into the history and development of **Virtual Reality (VR)** hardware, from the early days of clunky head-mounted displays to the latest advancements in haptic feedback. We will explore how VR hardware has evolved over the years, the challenges that developers and designers have faced, and the new opportunities that emerging technologies are creating. This chapter will be of interest to anyone interested in VR, including designers, developers, and enthusiasts.

Structure

In this chapter, we will discuss the following topics:

- Introduction to virtual reality hardware
- The rise of consumer virtual reality
- Virtual reality hardware design challenges
- The future of virtual reality hardware
- Role of haptic feedback on virtual reality hardware
- Case studies

Objectives

At the end of this chapter, you will see the evolution of the VR hardware ecosystem over time. We will learn about the rise of consumer-centric VR, various challenges that the VR industry faced over design, and how they overcame them.

We will dive deep into the future of the VR hardware industry. Then, we will study haptic feedback in VR, the different types of haptic feedback, and the benefits and limitations of the technology. Finally, we will end up with some case studies to examine examples of successful VR hardware.

Introduction to virtual reality hardware

First, we will learn what VR hardware is and how it evolved. We will also investigate the early history of VR and the first mounted displays.

Evolution of virtual reality hardware

VR hardware refers to the physical devices and equipment used to experience virtual reality, a computer-generated simulation or recreation of a real or imagined environment that a user can interact with and explore. VR hardware has evolved significantly, progressing from rudimentary systems to more advanced and immersive technologies. Let us discuss the evolution of VR hardware in detail.

Early systems (1960s-1990s)

The following are some of the VR systems that existed between the 1960s and 1990s:

- **Sensorama (1962)**: Considered one of the earliest attempts at VR, Sensorama was a machine that displayed stereoscopic 3D visuals with accompanying sounds, vibrations, and even scents.
- **The Sword of Damocles (1968)**: Developed by Ivan Sutherland, it was a bulky **Head-Mounted Display (HMD)** system connected to a large computer. It featured basic 3D graphics but was limited to immersion and interactivity.

Figure 4.1 displays the Sensorama VR system:

***Figure 4.1**: Illustration of early VR device, Sensorama*
*(**Source**: Wikipedia.com)*

Commercialization and gaming (1990s-2000s)

The following are some of the early gaming and commercial VR devices that existed from the 1990s till the 2000s:

- **Virtuality (1991)**: This pioneering VR gaming system included headsets, wired gloves, and an arcade-style booth. It offered multiplayer experiences but had limited tracking and low-resolution visuals.
- **Nintendo Virtual Boy (1995)**: A consumer-grade VR console featuring a tabletop HMD and handheld controller. It suffered from a monochromatic red display, limited game library, and discomfort during prolonged use.
- **Vuzix iWear VR920 (2007)**: A milestone in consumer VR, it was a head-mounted display with head tracking and stereoscopic 3D visuals. It primarily targeted PC gaming.

Modern era (2010s onward)

Here are some of the modern era devices that came to market post-2010:

- **Oculus Rift (2016)**: Considered a turning point for VR, the Rift was a high-quality HMD with positional tracking, a wide field of view, and precise motion controllers. It popularized the concept of modern VR.
- **HTC Vive (2016)**: Developed in collaboration with Valve Corporation, the Vive offered room-scale VR with accurate tracking using base stations. It introduced motion-tracked handheld controllers for natural interaction.

- **PlayStation VR (2016)**: Sony's VR headset for the PlayStation 4 console provided a more accessible entry point to VR for gamers, leveraging the existing console ecosystem.
- **Oculus Quest (2019)**: A standalone VR headset, Quest eliminated the need for a PC or console, offering wireless freedom. It incorporated inside-out tracking and hand tracking, enabling greater mobility.
- **Valve Index (2019)**: A premium VR system with high-resolution displays, wider field of view, and advanced tracking using external base stations. It provided a premium experience for enthusiasts.
- **HP Reverb G2 (2020)**: Known for its high-resolution displays, the Reverb G2 targeted gaming and professional applications such as virtual training and simulation.

Recent advances

Most recent advancements happened in the commercial/gaming VR industry, and below are some of those devices:

- **Meta Quest 3 (2023)**: After several generations of headsets offering pure immersive VR, the Meta Quest 3 also leans into mixed reality with an upgraded suite of six outward-facing cameras that show your real-world surroundings in full color, track your hand movements far more accurately than on Quest 2, and allow the gizmo to place digital objects like ghostly keeps within reach.
- **Apple Vision Pro (2023)**: Apple Vision Pro is going for design excellence. The front of the headset is composed solely of one piece of glass, while the frame is made of lightweight aluminum. However, through a slightly more controversial design choice. The battery pack of the headset is external, and headsets are connected by a wire to a battery pack around their waist. This reduces weight and helps battery life but, sadly, does not give you truly wireless experience.
- **Customizable fit for Apple Vision Pro:** Apple has also confirmed that it will be possible to customize the fit of the Vision Pro, stating *Light Seal (the cushion around the front of the headset) is made of a soft textile, and comes in a range of shapes and sizes, flexing to conform to a user's face for a precise fit.*
- **Transparent design and eyesight technology in Apple Vision Pro:** The most striking element of the Vision Pro's design is the transparent front of the device, allowing you to see the user's eyes. Apple's Eyesight technology will blur VR and AR technology together, keeping experiences immersive while also helping *users stay connected with those around them.*
- **Varjo VR-3 (2021):** A professional-grade VR headset with exceptional visual fidelity and eye-tracking technology. It caters to industries like design, engineering, and research.

- **Oculus Quest 2 (2020)**: An upgraded version of its predecessor, it offered improved visuals, performance, and affordability. It further popularized standalone VR with a large user base.

These examples represent a fraction of the VR hardware available, and the technology continues to advance rapidly. With ongoing developments in resolution, field of view, tracking, ergonomics, and haptic feedback, VR hardware is becoming more immersive, comfortable, and accessible to a wider range of users.

First head-mounted displays

In terms of HMDs, one of the pioneering devices was the Sword of Damocles, developed by Ivan Sutherland in 1968. It was a bulky apparatus that hung from the ceiling and featured a head-mounted display connected to a computer system. Although it was rudimentary by today's standards, the Sword of Damocles introduced the concept of wearing a display on the head to create a simulated virtual environment. However, the device was cumbersome, limiting its practicality and user experience.

These early experiments laid the foundation for further exploration and development in VR. While the technology was still in its infancy during this period, these early attempts at creating immersive environments and head-mounted displays set the stage for the evolution and eventual commercialization of VR hardware in the following decades.

Refer to *Figure 4.2*:

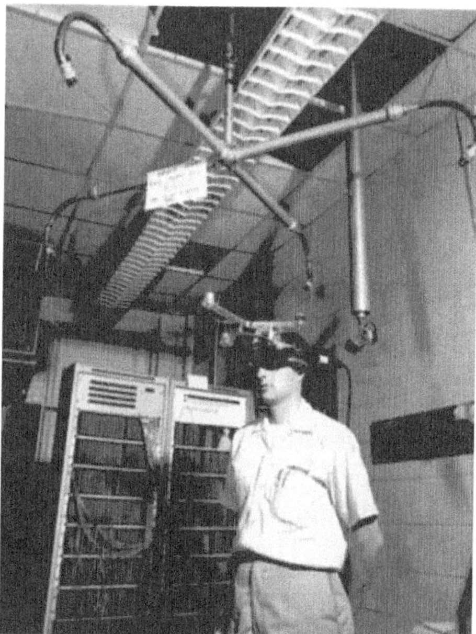

***Figure 4.2**: Illustration of early VR as head-mounted devices, also known as Sword of Damocles 1968*

*(**Source**: https://www.britannica.com/)*

The rise of consumer virtual reality

The rise of consumer VR began in the 2010s with significant advancements in technology and the introduction of several key devices. This period marked a turning point for VR as it transitioned from niche applications to a more accessible and mainstream consumer market.

One of the pivotal moments was the introduction of the Oculus Rift in 2016. Developed by *Oculus VR*, a company later acquired by Facebook, the Rift was a high-quality VR headset that offered immersive experiences to consumers. It featured a wide field of view, positional tracking, and precise motion controllers, revolutionizing how people interacted with virtual environments. The Rift, along with other early devices like the HTC Vive and PlayStation VR, played a crucial role in popularizing consumer VR and driving its adoption.

The availability of consumer VR hardware also expanded with the introduction of standalone headsets. The Oculus Quest, launched in 2019, was a notable breakthrough in this regard. It eliminated the need for a separate computer or console, providing wireless freedom and ease of use. Quest's inside-out tracking, and hand-tracking capabilities enhanced user mobility and interaction. The success of Quest demonstrated the demand for standalone VR. It encouraged other companies to develop standalone devices, making VR more accessible and appealing to a wider audience.

With the rise of consumer VR, various industries beyond gaming have also embraced the technology. VR applications now span education, healthcare, architecture, training, and entertainment. The continued advancement of consumer VR hardware, along with the growing ecosystem of software and experiences, is driving the expansion of virtual reality into new frontiers and shaping the way we interact with digital content.

Role of technology advancement in virtual reality industry

Several technological advancements played a crucial role in making consumer VR devices possible and shaping the industry. Here are some key advancements and their impact:

- **Display technology**: High-resolution and low-latency displays were essential for creating immersive VR experiences. Advances in display technology, including OLED and LCD panels with higher pixel densities, allowed for sharper and more realistic visuals in VR headsets. These displays, combined with optics and lenses, gave users a convincing sense of presence in virtual environments.

- **Tracking and positional sensors**: Accurate tracking of head movements and positional tracking were fundamental for creating a sense of immersion in VR. **Inertial Measurement Units (IMUs)**, accelerometers, gyroscopes, and magnetometers were integrated into VR headsets to track users' head movements and render corresponding virtual viewpoints in real-time. This tracking capability, combined with external sensors like cameras or base stations, enabled precise and responsive interaction within virtual environments.

- **Graphics processing power**: VR demands significant computational power to render complex 3D graphics at high frame rates. The advancement of **Graphics Processing Units (GPUs)** and their ability to handle real-time rendering of high-resolution content played a critical role in delivering smooth and visually appealing VR experiences. This allowed for more realistic environments, lighting effects, and textures in virtual worlds.

- **Input devices and controllers**: VR input devices and controllers have evolved to provide more natural and intuitive interaction within virtual environments. The introduction of motion-tracked handheld controllers allowed users to interact with objects, manipulate virtual elements, and enhance the feeling of presence and immersion. These devices, often equipped with buttons, triggers, and haptic feedback, provided tactile feedback and increased the sense of engagement.

- **Wireless and standalone VR**: The development of wireless and standalone VR headsets eliminated the need for wired connections and external computing devices. Standalone devices like the Oculus Quest, powered by onboard processors and memory, offered the convenience of all-in-one systems, enabling users to experience VR without being tethered to a PC or console. This advancement greatly expanded accessibility, making VR more portable and user-friendly.

The impact of these technological advancements on the VR industry has been significant. Consumer VR devices have become more affordable, user-friendly, and accessible, attracting a broader audience beyond early adopters. The improved hardware capabilities have facilitated the growth of VR applications in gaming, entertainment, education, training, healthcare, and other industries. Additionally, these advancements have spurred the development of a robust VR software ecosystem, including games, simulations, and productivity tools, further enriching the VR experience for users.

The following figure illustrates a head-mounted VR/AR device developed by NASA:

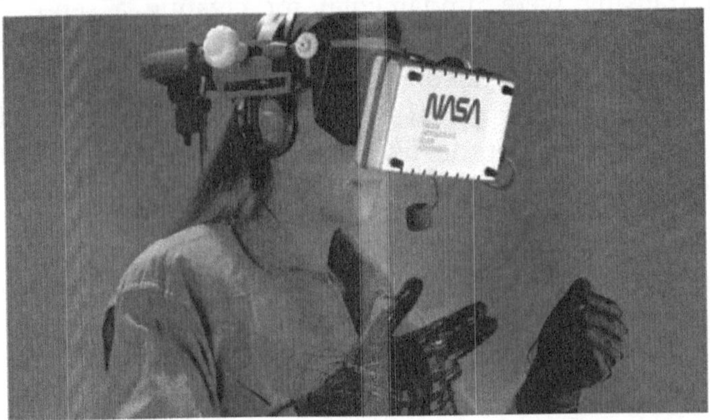

***Figure 4.3:** Illustration of advancement in mounted devices; one of the pioneers in this was NASA*

Virtual reality hardware design challenges

Designing VR hardware comes with several challenges that manufacturers and developers need to overcome:

- **Comfort and ergonomics**: VR hardware must be comfortable for extended periods to prevent fatigue and discomfort. Achieving a balance between weight, fit, and adjustability is crucial. Ensuring proper weight distribution, sufficient padding, and adjustable straps can enhance comfort and accommodate a wide range of head sizes and shapes.

- **Optics and display quality**: VR headsets rely on optics and displays to deliver immersive visuals. Designing high-quality lenses with a wide field of view and minimal distortion is essential to provide a natural viewing experience. Maintaining high-resolution displays with low persistence, high refresh rates, and reduced screen-door effects is crucial to minimize motion sickness and enhance immersion.

- **Tracking and input**: Accurate and responsive tracking of head movements and user input is vital for a seamless VR experience. Designing tracking systems that are robust, reliable, and can handle a variety of environments is challenging. Implementing intuitive and precise input methods, such as motion-tracked controllers or hand-tracking, adds complexity to the hardware design.

- **Heat dissipation and power efficiency**: VR hardware, particularly devices with high-performance components, can generate significant heat. Efficient heat dissipation mechanisms, such as passive or active cooling solutions, must be integrated to prevent discomfort and performance degradation. Additionally, optimizing power consumption to prolong battery life for standalone devices is crucial for uninterrupted VR experiences.

- **Cost and affordability**: While VR technology continues to evolve, cost remains a significant barrier to entry for many potential users. Designing hardware that balances performance, quality, and affordability is a challenge. Manufacturers must find ways to leverage economies of scale, optimize production processes, and use cost-effective components to make VR hardware more accessible.
- **User interface and accessibility**: The user interface design of VR hardware should be intuitive and easy to navigate, considering that users may be fully immersed in virtual environments. Incorporating user-friendly controls, clear indicators, and intuitive menu systems is essential. Additionally, ensuring compatibility with a range of devices, platforms, and software frameworks promotes accessibility and user adoption.

Addressing these challenges requires iterative design processes, user testing, and continuous refinement. As VR technology evolves, hardware designers must keep pace with user expectations, technological advancements, and emerging industry standards to create compelling and immersive experiences.

The future of virtual reality hardware

In the future, VR hardware is expected to undergo significant advancements, resulting in more immersive and realistic experiences. Display technology will continue to improve, with higher-resolution and pixel-dense screens, reducing the screen-door effect and enhancing visual fidelity. Lightweight and compact form factors will become standard, increasing comfort during extended usage. This will help in the extended use of the device in terms of time, and also, more comfort will help in longer hours of operation.

Tracking systems will become more accurate and seamless, enabling precise and natural movements within virtual environments. Additionally, haptic feedback systems will be refined, offering realistic touch sensations and further enhancing immersion. The integration of eye-tracking technology will allow for foveated rendering, optimizing performance by focusing rendering resources on the user's focal point. Furthermore, advancements in wireless communication and computing power will enable untethered VR experiences, freeing users from physical constraints and expanding the potential for large-scale virtual worlds. Overall, the future of VR hardware holds the promise of more lifelike and engaging experiences, making virtual reality an increasingly integral part of entertainment, communication, education, and various industries.

Emerging technologies

Emerging technologies such as haptic feedback and eye-tracking have indeed opened new possibilities for VR hardware. These advancements enhance the immersive experience and allow users to interact with virtual environments in more natural and intuitive ways.

The following is the list of emerging technologies that play a significant role in modern VR devices:

- Haptic feedback refers to the sense of touch or tactile sensations. In the context of VR, haptic feedback technology enables users to feel virtual objects and receive physical feedback when interacting with them. This can be achieved through various means, such as wearable gloves, suits, or controllers that provide vibrations, pressure, or even more intricate sensations like texture and temperature. Haptic feedback enhances the realism and immersion of VR experiences by adding a sense of touch, making it feel more lifelike and engaging.

- Eye-tracking technology, on the other hand, involves tracking the movement and position of a user's eyes. Incorporating eye-tracking sensors into VR headsets, the system can accurately determine where the user is looking within the virtual environment. This information can be utilized in several ways. For instance, it enables foveated rendering, a technique where only the area the user is directly looking at is rendered in high detail, while peripheral areas are rendered at lower quality. This optimization significantly reduces the computational requirements, allowing for more efficient rendering and better overall performance. Eye-tracking also enables gaze-based interaction, where users can control objects or navigate menus simply by looking at them, offering a more intuitive and hands-free way of interacting with virtual environments.

These technologies not only enhance the immersive qualities of VR but also have practical applications. For example, haptic feedback can be beneficial in training simulations, where users can feel the feedback of a virtual tool or instrument they are manipulating. Eye-tracking can be used in social VR experiences, where avatars can make eye contact with each other, leading to more realistic and engaging social interactions.

As these technologies continue to advance, we can expect further improvements in VR hardware, leading to even more realistic and immersive experiences. Their integration into VR systems opens exciting possibilities for gaming, education, training, healthcare, and various other fields.

Impact of emerging virtual reality technologies on industries

Emerging VR technologies have the potential to make a significant impact across various industries. Here are some examples of how these technologies can revolutionize different sectors:

- **Gaming and entertainment**: VR has already made a significant impact on the gaming industry by providing immersive and interactive experiences. With advancements in haptic feedback and eye-tracking, gaming experiences can become even more realistic, allowing players to feel the impact of in-game actions and interact with virtual environments in more natural ways. This technology opens new possibilities for game developers to create more engaging and compelling experiences.

- **Education and training**: VR has immense potential in the field of education and training. By simulating real-world scenarios, students and professionals can practice and gain practical skills in a safe and controlled environment. Emerging technologies like haptic feedback can enhance training simulations by providing users with tactile sensations, making the learning experience more immersive and effective. VR can be applied in fields such as medical training, engineering, aviation, and military simulations.
- **Healthcare**: VR technologies have already shown promise in healthcare applications, such as pain management, mental health therapy, and rehabilitation. The incorporation of haptic feedback can further enhance these applications by providing realistic tactile feedback to patients. Additionally, eye-tracking can be used to track patients' gaze and monitor their visual attention during diagnostic procedures or therapy sessions.
- **Architecture and real estate**: VR allows architects and real estate developers to create virtual walkthroughs and immersive experiences of buildings and properties that are yet to be constructed. With haptic feedback, users can also interact with virtual furniture or objects within these virtual spaces, providing a sense of scale and usability.
- **Manufacturing and design**: VR technologies can streamline product design and manufacturing processes. Engineers and designers can visualize and test their prototypes in virtual environments, allowing for rapid iterations and reducing the need for physical prototypes. Haptic feedback can aid in the design process by providing realistic touch sensations, allowing designers to assess the ergonomics and functionality of virtual products.
- **Tourism and hospitality**: VR can offer virtual tourism experiences, allowing users to explore destinations and landmarks from the comfort of their homes. With haptic feedback, users can also experience sensations related to the visited locations, such as feeling the wind or vibrations. This technology can also assist in hotel and venue selection, as users can virtually tour and experience the facilities before making a booking.

These examples represent just a fraction of the potential impact of emerging VR technologies across industries. As these technologies continue to advance and become more accessible, we can expect to see further integration and innovation in various sectors, transforming the way we work, learn, and experience the world.

Role of haptic feedback on virtual reality hardware

Haptic feedback is a key technology that is fundamentally changing the way we experience VR. Simulating the sense of touch and providing tactile sensations, haptic feedback adds realism and immersion to VR experiences. It enables us to feel the texture, weight, and physical properties of virtual objects, enhancing the sense of presence and making virtual interactions more engaging and believable. Haptic feedback also improves spatial awareness, allowing users to perceive the boundaries of objects and their position in the virtual environment. Through its ability to provide realistic tactile interactions and feedback, haptic feedback revolutionizes the way we interact with virtual worlds, making VR more intuitive, interactive, and impactful than ever before.

Evolution of haptic feedback

Haptic feedback, also known as tactile feedback, has a fascinating history that spans several decades. Its evolution has seen remarkable advancements in technology and applications. Here is a comprehensive overview of the history and evolution of haptic feedback:

- The concept of haptic feedback traces back to the 19th century when scientists began exploring the sense of touch. In the 1860s, Sir Francis Galton and Lord Kelvin developed early devices such as the vibrotactile chair and the aesthetic vibrator to stimulate the sense of touch. However, haptic feedback technology remained in its infancy.
- Fast forward to the 20th century, when haptic feedback gained traction. In the 1950s, Ralph Mosher introduced the Stomatex, an early haptic device that utilized pneumatics to provide tactile sensations. It served as a foundation for future developments. In the 1970s, researchers *Eric Johnson* and *Ivan Sutherland* created DataGlove, a wearable haptic device that tracked hand movements and provided force feedback. This marked a significant step in the evolution of haptic technology.
- The 1990s witnessed the expansion of haptic feedback into the gaming and simulation industries. Companies like Immersion Corporation played a pivotal role in developing force feedback technologies. They introduced products like the Force Feedback Joystick and the TouchSense system, which delivered vibrations and force effects to enhance gaming experiences. Haptic feedback started to become a common feature in gaming peripherals.
- Haptic feedback then extended its reach to consumer electronics in the early 2000s. Mobile phones and gaming consoles began incorporating vibration motors to provide basic tactile feedback for alerts, notifications, and interactions. This integration made haptic feedback a familiar experience for everyday users.

- Advancements in tactile technologies further revolutionized haptic feedback. **Linear resonant actors (LRAs)** and **electroactive polymers (EAPs)** improved the precision and realism of haptic effects. These innovations enabled a wider range of tactile sensations, including textures, vibrations, and localized pressure.
- The emergence of VR has presented new opportunities for haptic feedback. Companies developed haptic gloves, suits, and controllers designed for VR experiences. These devices employed actuators, motors, and sensors to deliver realistic touch sensations, enhancing the immersion and interactivity of virtual environments.
- Ongoing research and development in haptic feedback continue to push boundaries. Scientists are exploring advanced concepts like texture rendering, temperature feedback, and more intricate haptic sensations. These advancements aim to further improve the realism and fidelity of touch-based interactions, paving the way for new gaming, healthcare, education, and beyond applications.

In summary, the history of haptic feedback showcases its evolution from early experiments in the 19th century to becoming an integral part of gaming, consumer electronics, and virtual reality. With continued advancements, haptic feedback holds the promise of enhancing our digital experiences and bridging the gap between the physical and virtual worlds.

Types of haptic feedback

Haptic feedback encompasses a variety of tactile sensations that can be delivered to users through haptic devices. Here are some common types of haptic feedback:

- **Vibration**: Vibration is one of the most basic and widely used forms of haptic feedback. It involves the use of motors or actuators to create rapid oscillations that can be felt by the user. Vibrations can vary in intensity, duration, and frequency, providing cues or notifications in response to events or interactions in virtual or real-world environments.
- **Texture feedback**: Texture feedback aims to simulate the tactile sensation of different surfaces or textures. Modulating the forces or vibrations delivered by haptic devices, users can perceive roughness, smoothness, or variations in surface texture. Texture feedback enhances the realism and immersion of virtual experiences by allowing users to feel the virtual objects they interact with.
- **Force feedback**: Force feedback, also known as haptic force, provides resistance or physical forces to simulate interactions with virtual objects. Haptic devices can exert forces on the user's hand or fingers, creating a sense of pushing, pulling, or resistance. This feedback allows users to perceive the physical properties and responses of virtual objects, making interactions more realistic.

- **Tactile pressure**: Tactile pressure feedback focuses on providing users with the sensation of pressure or touch. Haptic devices can apply pressure or compressive forces to specific areas of the user's skin, mimicking the feeling of contact or physical pressure. Tactile pressure can be utilized to convey information about object shape, size, or stiffness in virtual environments.
- **Haptic text and Braille**: Haptic feedback can be employed to deliver textual information or Braille patterns to users who are visually impaired. Using an array of small actuators or pins, haptic devices can generate patterns and vibrations to represent characters or words. This enables users to read and interact with textual content through touch.
- **Temperature feedback**: Temperature feedback involves simulating hot or cold sensations using haptic devices. Employing heating or cooling elements, haptic feedback systems can create sensations of warmth or coolness on the user's skin. Temperature feedback can enhance immersion and realism in virtual environments where thermal cues are important, such as simulating hot or cold objects or environments.

These are a few examples of the types of haptic feedback that can be implemented in haptic devices. The field of haptics is continually advancing, and researchers are exploring new techniques and combinations of sensations to further enhance the realism, immersion, and communication capabilities of haptic feedback systems.

Benefits and limitations of haptic technology

Haptic technology offers several benefits and advantages, but it also has some limitations. Let us explore both aspects.

Benefits of haptic technology

Let us discuss the benefits of haptic technology:

- **Enhanced user experience**: Haptic feedback enhances the user experience by providing a sense of touch and realism to digital interactions. It adds an additional layer of immersion, making virtual environments feel more tangible and interactive.
- **Improved realism**: Haptic technology enables users to feel textures, forces, vibrations, and other tactile sensations, making virtual objects and environments feel more lifelike. This realism enhances the sense of presence and engagement in virtual experiences.
- **Enhanced communication**: Haptic feedback can convey information and communicate cues and alerts through touch. It enables more intuitive and efficient communication, especially in situations where visual or auditory feedback may be limited or distracting.

- **Skill development and training**: Haptic technology has significant applications in skill development and training scenarios. Simulating real-world physical interactions, haptic feedback allows users to practice and improve their skills in a safe and controlled environment. It is particularly valuable in fields such as medical training, sports training, and simulations for hazardous environments.
- **Accessibility**: Haptic feedback can improve accessibility for individuals with visual impairments. By providing tactile cues and feedback, haptic technology allows visually impaired users to interact with digital content and interfaces, making technology more inclusive.

Limitations of haptic technology

Let us discuss the limitations of haptic technology:

- **Technical limitations**: Haptic technology is still evolving, and there are technical limitations to consider. Haptic devices may have limited accuracy, precision, or range of sensations. Achieving high-fidelity haptic feedback across a wide range of interactions and textures remains a challenge.
- **Cost and availability**: Advanced haptic devices can be expensive, making them less accessible to consumers and smaller businesses. The high cost of development and manufacturing can limit the widespread adoption of haptic technology in various industries.
- **Size and portability**: Some haptic devices, such as full-body suits or large-scale haptic systems, may be bulky and less portable. This limits their usability in certain applications, especially those requiring mobility or on-the-go experiences.
- **Power consumption**: Haptic feedback often requires additional power consumption to operate the actuators or motors. This can affect battery life in portable devices and may limit the duration of haptic feedback experiences.
- **Integration challenges**: Integrating haptic technology into existing systems or devices can be complex. Compatibility issues, software integration, and the need for specialized development and design expertise can pose challenges for seamless integration into various platforms.

While haptic technology offers numerous benefits, it is important to address its limitations and work towards further advancements to maximize its potential in different industries and applications. Continued research and development efforts are necessary to overcome these limitations and refine haptic technology for broader adoption and improved user experiences.

Case studies

We will examine some examples of successful VR hardware, including Oculus Quest and the PlayStation VR, and analyze the design principles that contributed to their success.

Oculus Quest and PlayStation VR are two popular VR platforms that have achieved success in the consumer market. Let us analyze the design principles that have contributed to their success:

- **Immersive and user-friendly design**: Oculus Quest and PlayStation VR prioritize immersive experiences by offering comfortable and user-friendly designs. They are designed to be lightweight, adjustable, and ergonomic, ensuring prolonged usage without discomfort. The headsets are equipped with adjustable straps, cushioned padding, and intuitive controls, making them accessible and easy for a wide range of users.
- **High-quality display and graphics**: Both platforms prioritize high-quality visuals to enhance the VR experience. Oculus Quest and PlayStation VR feature high-resolution displays and optics that deliver crisp and immersive visuals. They leverage advanced display technologies and optics to minimize motion blur and screen door effects, ensuring a more realistic and engaging visual experience.
- **Tracking and motion controllers**: Both platforms incorporate precise tracking systems and motion controllers to enhance user interaction and immersion. They use inside-out or outside-in tracking methods, allowing users to move freely in virtual environments. The motion controllers provide intuitive and natural interaction, enabling users to reach out and manipulate objects within the virtual world.
- **Content ecosystem and developer support**: The success of Oculus Quest and PlayStation VR can be attributed to their robust content ecosystems and strong developer support. Both platforms offer a wide range of VR games, experiences, and applications catering to diverse user preferences. They have cultivated partnerships with developers, fostering a growing library of compelling and high-quality VR content.
- **Wireless and standalone experience (Oculus Quest)**: Oculus Quest's standout design principle is its wireless and standalone experience. Unlike tethered VR systems, the Oculus Quest does not require a PC or external sensors, offering the convenience of untethered mobility. This design freedom allows users to enjoy VR experiences in any room or location, contributing to its popularity and accessibility.
- **Brand reputation and marketing**: Oculus (owned by Meta) and PlayStation (Sony) have strong brand reputations and marketing strategies that have played a significant role in the success of their respective VR platforms. Their established brand presence, along with effective marketing campaigns, has helped generate awareness, build trust, and drive adoption among consumers.
- **Price point and accessibility**: Meta Quest and PlayStation VR have managed to strike a balance between price and performance, making them more accessible to a wider consumer base. They offer different pricing options, including more affordable entry-level packages, allowing users to choose the option that suits their budget and needs.

In conclusion, the success of Oculus Quest and PlayStation VR can be attributed to their immersive and user-friendly designs, high-quality visuals, precise tracking and controllers, robust content ecosystems, strong brand presence, effective marketing, and accessibility. These design principles have enabled them to deliver compelling VR experiences that resonate with consumers, contributing to their popularity and market success.

Refer to *Figure 4.4*:

***Figure 4.4**: Illustration of Meta Quest 3 and handheld devices*

*(**Source**: Meta)*

Refer to *Figure 4.5*:

***Figure 4.5**: Illustration of PlayStation VR 2*

*(**Source**: PlayStation and Sony Interactive Entertainment LLC)*

Conclusion

In this chapter, we tried to take a closer look at the evolution of VR hardware. We learned how VR hardware has evolved. We learned about the history of VR and the first head-mounted displays. We also learned about the rise of consumer-based VR. Then, we deep-dived into the challenges that the VR hardware industry faced. After that, we took a glimpse into the future of VR hardware and what are the emerging technologies. Then, we took a deep dive into haptic feedback technology, its evolution, and its type. Finally, we took two of the most popular VR hardware devices and went through the case study to understand the design principles that contributed to their success.

In the next chapter, we are going to understand how **artificial intelligence** (**AI**) is playing an increasingly important role in VR and **Extended Reality** (**XR**) applications, enabling more realistic and responsive experiences for users.

Points to remember

- Virtual reality hardware is the physical devices and equipment to create immersive virtual reality experiences. This includes headsets, controllers, sensors, and other peripherals that simulate a virtual environment. Understanding the basics of virtual reality hardware is crucial for developers and enthusiasts interested in creating immersive VR applications.
- In recent years, there has been a significant rise in the adoption of consumer virtual reality. Technology advancements and increased affordability have made VR devices more accessible to the general public. This widespread adoption has led to a surge in VR content creation across various industries, including gaming, education, healthcare, and entertainment.
- Designing virtual reality hardware presents several challenges. High-quality graphics, low latency, and seamless motion tracking are essential for a convincing VR experience. Additionally, ensuring comfort, ease of use, and affordability for consumers are key considerations for hardware designers. Overcoming these challenges is vital to delivering immersive and user-friendly VR products.
- The future of virtual reality hardware is promising, with ongoing research and development focusing on enhancing user experiences. Advancements in display technology, such as higher resolutions and wider field-of-view, are expected to provide more realistic visuals. Moreover, tracking systems and gesture recognition innovations are anticipated to improve immersion further. As technology continues to evolve, VR hardware is likely to become more sophisticated, compact, and integrated into everyday life.
- Haptic feedback plays a crucial role in virtual reality hardware by providing users with tactile sensations, enhancing the sense of presence and realism. Haptic feedback technologies, such as vibration motors and force feedback mechanisms, simulate touch and texture, allowing users to feel virtual objects and interactions. Integrating precise and responsive haptic feedback enhances immersion, enabling users to engage more deeply with the virtual environment.

CHAPTER 5
The Role of AI in AR, VR, and XR

Introduction

Artificial intelligence (**AI**) is playing an increasingly important role in **Augmented Reality** (**AR**), **Virtual Reality** (**VR**) and **Extended Reality** (**XR**) applications, enabling more realistic and responsive experiences for users. In this chapter, we will explore the intersection of AI and AR/VR/XR, looking at how AI is being used to improve everything from graphics rendering to user interaction. We will discuss the current state of technology, emerging trends, and the future possibilities for AI in immersive technologies.

Structure

In this chapter, we will discuss the following topics:

- Introduction to AI in AR/VR
- Graphics rendering
- Natural language processing
- User interaction
- Predictive analytics

Objectives

At the end of this chapter, you will be able to know how AI plays an important role in VR applications. We will learn how AI improves the realism and detail of AR/VR graphics, making it possible to render more complex scenes and environments. We will discuss natural language processing technology, such as voice assistants. We will understand how AI can improve user interaction with augmented or virtual reality applications.

Finally, we will end up with some predictive analytics, where we will learn how AI can analyze user behavior and predict their needs, enabling more personalized and responsive experiences.

Introduction to AI in AR/VR/XR

First, we will learn how AI can be used in VR or AR. We will get an overview of the technology and its applications in these fields.

AI and its usage in VR/AR

AI is utilized in various ways to enhance the capabilities and experiences within VR and AR environments. Here are some examples:

- **Realistic simulations**: AI algorithms are employed to create realistic virtual environments, including dynamic physics simulations, object interactions, and realistic rendering of virtual objects and characters. This helps to improve the immersion and believability of the Immersive experience.
- **Graphic rendering**: AI supports graphic rendering in Virtual Real applications by enhancing visual quality, reducing artifacts, and improving overall performance. Through techniques like upscaling and super-resolution, AI algorithms can analyze and enhance low-resolution content, resulting in sharper and more detailed visuals within the virtual environment. By leveraging AI's computational power and intelligent algorithms, graphic rendering in VR/AR is enhanced, resulting in more immersive and realistic virtual experiences.
- **Natural language processing (NLP)**: AI-powered NLP allows users to interact with virtual environments using voice commands and speech recognition. This enables more intuitive and immersive communication with virtual characters or control of virtual objects within the Extended Reality (XR/VR/AR) space.
- **Computer vision**: AI-based computer vision techniques enable object recognition, tracking, and gesture detection within extended/virtual real environments. This allows users to interact with virtual objects using hand gestures or body movements, enhancing the sense of presence and interactivity.

- **Intelligent avatars**: AI algorithms are employed to create intelligent virtual avatars that can understand and respond to human emotions, gestures, and speech. These avatars can provide more engaging and interactive experiences within immersive environments, simulating realistic social interactions.
- **Personalized experiences**: AI algorithms can analyze user data, preferences, and behavior to create personalized Augmented Reality experiences. By adapting content, visuals, and interactions based on individual preferences, AI enhances the immersion and relevance of the virtual environment.
- **Adaptive learning**: AI can track user behavior and performance within AR/VR applications and adapt the content or difficulty level accordingly. This allows for personalized and adaptive learning experiences, making education and training more effective.
- **Content generation**: AI algorithms can assist in generating and populating virtual worlds with realistic and diverse content. This includes generating procedural landscapes, virtual characters, and realistic textures, reducing the manual effort required to create expansive, immersive environments.
- **Predictive analytics**: AI can analyze user behavior and interaction patterns within virtual real environments to gain insights and improve future experiences. This data-driven approach helps understand user preferences, optimize content, and refine the future virtual real experience.

These are a few examples of how AI is integrated into VR/XR applications. Combining AI and AR/VR technologies opens numerous possibilities for creating more immersive, interactive, and personalized virtual experiences.

Graphic rendering

AI supports graphic rendering in VR/XR by enhancing visual quality, reducing artifacts, and improving overall performance. Through techniques like upscaling and super-resolution, AI algorithms can analyze and enhance low-resolution content, resulting in sharper and more detailed visuals within the virtual environment. AI also assists in reducing aliasing artifacts and smoothing jagged edges through techniques like temporal anti-aliasing, providing cleaner and more visually appealing images. Additionally, AI can optimize rendering processes by dynamically adjusting rendering settings based on user interactions and hardware capabilities, ensuring a smooth and responsive experience. By leveraging AI's computational power and intelligent algorithms, graphic rendering in AR/VR/XR is enhanced, resulting in more immersive and realistic virtual experiences.

AI for improving realism and details

AI can significantly improve the realism and level of detail in Virtual Reality graphics.

Here are a few ways AI can enhance the graphics in these immersive experiences:

- **Upscaling and super-resolution**: AI algorithms, such as deep learning-based super-resolution models, can enhance the resolution of the graphics. These algorithms analyze low-resolution images or textures and generate high-resolution versions, resulting in more detailed and sharper visuals.
- **Procedural generation**: AI techniques, such as procedural generation and **Generative Adversarial Networks (GANs)**, can create realistic and diverse virtual environments. By training AI models on large datasets, developers can generate natural-looking terrains, vegetation, buildings, and other objects in real-time, enhancing the level of detail and variety in these immersive experiences.
- **Texture synthesis and reconstruction**: AI algorithms can analyze and reconstruct existing textures at higher resolutions or synthesize entirely new textures. This can be particularly useful for generating detailed and visually appealing surfaces for objects, landscapes, and characters within virtual real environments.
- **Realistic lighting and shadows**: AI algorithms can simulate realistic lighting and shadows in Extended/Virtual real environments, creating more immersive and visually stunning experiences. Machine learning techniques can analyze the lighting conditions and scene geometry to generate accurate reflections, refractions, and shadows, enhancing realism and depth perception.
- **Facial animation and expression**: AI-based facial animation techniques can bring more realistic and expressive characters to Augmented/Virtual experiences. By leveraging facial recognition algorithms and deep learning models, developers can capture and replicate facial expressions, emotions, and lip movements, enhancing the believability of virtual characters and avatars.
- **Real-time object interaction**: AI algorithms can improve the realism of object interaction within Immersive environments. Using physics-based simulations and machine learning, virtual objects can exhibit more accurate and dynamic responses to user interactions, such as collisions, deformations, and realistic object behaviors.
- **Adaptive graphics optimization**: AI can be used to optimize graphics rendering in real time based on the capabilities of the hardware. By analyzing the performance metrics and limitations of the user's device, AI algorithms can dynamically adjust the level of detail, texture quality, and rendering effects to ensure smooth and visually appealing experiences.

It is important to note that while AI can enhance the realism and details of AR/VR or XR graphics, it is not a one-size-fits-all solution. The implementation and effectiveness of AI techniques depend on factors such as the available computational resources, the quality of training data, and the specific requirements of the Immersive application.

Rendering complex scenes and environments

AI enables rendering more complex scenes and environments in AR/VR through various techniques and approaches. Here are a few ways AI contributes to handling the challenges of rendering complexity:

- **Level of Detail (LoD) optimization**: AI algorithms can dynamically adjust the level of detail in a scene based on the user's viewpoint and the available computational resources. By utilizing machine learning techniques, the system can analyze the scene complexity, user behavior, and rendering performance to render only the necessary level of detail for each object or part of the environment. This optimization helps maintain high visual fidelity while ensuring smooth frame rates and efficient resource utilization.

- **Occlusion culling**: AI algorithms can assist in occlusion culling, which involves identifying objects or parts of the environment hidden or occluded from the user's view. The system can predict which objects will be occluded by employing machine learning models based on the scene geometry, user perspective, and movement patterns. This allows for efficient rendering by excluding occluded objects from the rendering process, reducing the computational burden, and enabling the rendering of more complex scenes.

- **Scene reconstruction and depth estimation**: AI can aid in reconstructing the 3D geometry of scenes and estimating depth information from input data, such as images or depth sensors. This capability is particularly useful in XR environments where the user's surroundings must be captured and rendered. AI algorithms, such as structure-from-motion and **Simultaneous Localization And Mapping (SLAM)** techniques, can analyze the input data and generate a more accurate representation of the scene geometry, enabling the rendering of complex and realistic environments.

- **Real-time ray tracing**: AI-accelerated real-time ray tracing is a technique that uses machine learning algorithms to approximate ray-tracing calculations. Ray tracing can accurately simulate light interactions, reflections, and shadows, producing highly realistic graphics. However, it is computationally intensive and challenging to achieve in real-time. AI-based methods, such as denoising and upsampling, can help reduce computational requirements and enable real-time ray tracing, allowing for more complex and visually stunning scenes in VR/XR.

- **Machine learning-based anti-aliasing**: Anti-aliasing techniques smooth out jagged edges and reduce visual artifacts in rendered images. AI algorithms can be trained on large datasets of high-quality images to learn and apply anti-aliasing filters in real-time. VR/XR graphics can benefit from more advanced anti-aliasing techniques using machine learning models, resulting in sharper and more detailed visuals, even in complex scenes.

These AI techniques help alleviate the computational demands and optimize the rendering process, enabling VR/XR applications to handle more intricate and visually rich scenes and environments while maintaining real-time performance and high levels of realism.

Natural language processing

NLP, combined with AI, has the potential to revolutionize the way we interact with Virtual Real environments. By integrating speech recognition, natural language understanding, and dialogue systems, NLP enables users to communicate with virtual environments using natural language. Users can give voice commands, ask questions, or engage in conversations with virtual characters or assistants, creating a more immersive and interactive experience. NLP algorithms can interpret and extract meaning from spoken or written input, allowing for intelligent responses and adaptive behavior. This technology opens new possibilities for intuitive and hands-free interactions, enhancing the accessibility and usability of immersive applications while bringing them closer to natural human-computer communication.

Popularity of other natural language processing

Voice assistants and other NLP technologies are increasingly prevalent in VR and AR applications. As voice recognition and NLP algorithms continue to advance, they provide more seamless and natural ways for users to interact with VR/XR environments. Voice assistants integrated into VR/AR applications enable users to navigate, control, and interact with virtual worlds using voice commands. Users can ask questions, get information, perform actions, or engage in conversations with virtual characters, enhancing the immersion and interactivity of the experience. These technologies make VR/AR more accessible to a broader range of users, eliminating the need for complex controllers or cumbersome interfaces. As voice assistants and NLP technologies evolve, we expect even more sophisticated and intuitive interactions that will further blur the line between the virtual and real worlds.

NLPs contribution in natural and intuitive interaction

Enabling more natural and intuitive interaction between users and virtual environments through technologies like NLP significantly enhances the Immersive experience. By incorporating NLP, users can communicate and engage with virtual environments in ways that mimic real-life interactions. This opens various possibilities, such as conversing with virtual characters, asking questions, and receiving contextual responses. NLP also enables seamless voice commands, allowing users to navigate and control the environment effortlessly. This natural and intuitive interaction fosters a sense of presence and immersion, making AR/VR/XR applications more accessible and engaging for users of all backgrounds and technical expertise. It reduces the learning curve and eliminates the need for complex controllers or input devices, making the experience more user-friendly. Ultimately, by enhancing user interaction and virtual environments, NLP-driven technologies enrich the overall quality and enjoyment of these immersive applications.

User interaction

AI enhances user interaction in AR/VR/XR by enabling natural language processing for intuitive communication, gesture recognition for hands-free interaction, and intelligent avatars that respond intelligently to user inputs. Additionally, computer vision enables VR/AR systems to understand the real-world environment, personalize experiences based on user preferences, and provide intelligent assistance through virtual assistants. AI also analyzes users' emotions and behaviors, allowing for adaptive content and generating appropriate responses.

Overall, AI's contributions in VR/AR facilitate seamless and immersive user interactions, making the experiences more engaging, personalized, and intuitive.

Improved UI with gesture recognition and eye tracking

AI is crucial in improving user interaction in Immersive environments through gesture recognition and eye tracking. By leveraging AI techniques, these technologies offer users more intuitive and seamless interactions.

Gesture recognition utilizes AI algorithms to analyze users' hand movements and gestures. This allows these systems to interpret and respond to these actions, enabling users to interact with virtual objects or environments without needing physical controllers. AI algorithms can accurately recognize and interpret a wide range of gestures, making interactions more natural and immersive.

Eye tracking, another AI-enabled technology, involves tracking users' eye movements and gaze direction. Employing AI algorithms, Immersive systems can precisely monitor and analyze eye movements, enabling a deeper understanding of user intent and focus. This information can be utilized to enhance user experiences in various ways. For example, AI can enable foveated rendering, where high-resolution graphics are rendered only in the user's central field of view, resulting in more efficient resource utilization. AI can also enable gaze-based interaction, allowing users to interact with objects or menus simply by looking at them.

By combining gesture recognition and eye tracking, AI can offer more powerful user interaction experiences. For instance, AI can interpret users' hand gestures with their gaze direction, enabling more precise and context-aware interactions. This fusion of gesture recognition and eye tracking allows for more immersive and intuitive user interactions, as users can seamlessly combine physical gestures with their visual focus to interact with virtual environments.

AI-driven gesture recognition and eye tracking significantly enhance user interaction in AR/VR/XR-based applications. These technologies provide more natural, intuitive, and immersive experiences, ultimately making virtual and extended reality environments more accessible and enjoyable for users.

Predictive analytics

Predictive analytics uses historical data, statistical algorithms, and machine learning techniques to predict future outcomes or behaviors. It involves analyzing patterns and trends within data to identify and forecast potential outcomes. When applied to AR, VR predictive analytics can enhance the user experience by leveraging historical user data and behavior patterns to make real-time predictions and adaptations within the virtual environment. By understanding user preferences, actions, and interactions, predictive analytics algorithms can dynamically adjust the immersive experience, personalize content, optimize visuals, and anticipate user needs. This integration enables more immersive, tailored, and engaging experiences, as these virtual real environments can adapt in real time based on predictive insights derived from user data, providing a more interactive and responsive virtual reality or extended reality experience.

Role of predictive analytics for better user experience

Predictive analytics is utilized in various ways within Immersive applications to enhance user experiences and drive insights. Here are some examples:

- **Personalized recommendations**: Predictive analytics algorithms analyze user behavior and preferences within AR/VR/XR environments to provide personalized recommendations. By understanding user interactions, content preferences, and past choices, predictive analytics can suggest relevant AR/VR/XR experiences, virtual objects, or immersive content that aligns with the user's interests.

- **Adaptive environments**: Predictive analytics algorithms can analyze real-time user data within immersive environments to dynamically adapt and optimize the virtual experience. By monitoring user actions, preferences, and performance, predictive analytics can make real-time adjustments to visuals, audio, difficulty levels, or storyline, creating a customized and engaging experience that aligns with the user's needs and capabilities.

- **User engagement prediction**: Predictive analytics can analyze user interactions and behavior patterns within immersive applications to predict engagement levels. Predictive analytics can forecast user engagement by analyzing factors such as time spent in specific environments, interactions with virtual objects, or social engagement and identify potential areas for improvement or optimization within the immersive experience.

- **Performance and training optimization**: In Virtual/Augmented reality-based training applications, predictive analytics can analyze user performance data and identify patterns correlating with successful outcomes or learning progress. This information can be used to optimize training programs, provide personalized feedback, and identify areas where users may require additional support or guidance, thereby improving training effectiveness within immersive environments.
- **Predictive maintenance**: In applications that simulate real-world environments or equipment, predictive analytics can be used to anticipate maintenance needs. By analyzing data collected from virtual sensors, predictive analytics can identify patterns indicative of potential equipment failures or maintenance requirements. This enables proactive maintenance planning, minimizing downtime, and optimizing the performance of virtual assets.
- **User behavior analysis**: Predictive analytics can analyze user behavior within extended real environments to gain insights into user preferences, decision-making patterns, and engagement levels. This information can be used to optimize user interfaces, streamline user flows, and design more intuitive and user-friendly immersive experiences.

Overall, predictive analytics in AR/VR/XR applications enables personalized experiences, adaptive environments, performance optimization, and data-driven insights, enhancing the overall user engagement, satisfaction, and effectiveness of immersive experiences.

Conclusion

In this chapter, we tried to take a closer look at the role of AI in Immersive technologies like AR, VR, and XR. We learned about AI's use and various applications of AR/VR/XR.

We understood graphics rendering, how AI improves the realism and detailing within AR/VR/XR graphics, and how complex scenes and environments are rendered. We also learned about NLP and how voice assistants and other NLP technologies are becoming more common in AR/VR/XR applications. Companies are enabling more natural and intuitive interaction between users and their respective virtual environments. We also took a deep dive into how AI can improve user interaction. Finally, we understood predictive analytics. We explored the ways predictive analytics is used in AR/VR/XR applications.

In the next chapter, we will examine the business landscape of AR/VR/XR, exploring the trends, challenges, and opportunities facing companies working in these fields.

Points to remember

- AI plays a crucial role in enhancing graphics rendering in Immersive environments.
- Real-time rendering techniques powered by AI algorithms improve the visual quality of virtual worlds, providing more immersive experiences.

- Techniques like ray tracing, deep learning-based super-resolution, and denoising contribute to realistic and detailed virtual scenes.
- Integrating NLP with AR VR enables natural and intuitive interactions between users and virtual environments.
- AI-powered voice recognition and language understanding facilitate seamless verbal communication and control within virtual worlds.
- NLP-driven chatbots and virtual assistants enhance user engagement and provide personalized experiences.
- AI-driven gesture recognition and body tracking enable more natural and expressive user interactions in VR and AR.
- Machine learning algorithms analyze user movements and behavior to create lifelike avatars or optimize gameplay experiences.
- AI-driven predictive analysis enhances the performance and efficiency of VR and AR applications.
- AI algorithms can analyze user behavior and preferences to deliver personalized content and recommendations in real time.
- Predictive analysis helps optimize rendering settings, reducing computational load and enhancing user experiences.

CHAPTER 6
Business Landscape of AR, VR, and XR

Introduction

Augmented Reality, Virtual reality (**VR**), and **Extended Reality** (**XR**) technologies are rapidly evolving, and their potential applications extend far beyond gaming and entertainment. In this chapter, we will examine the business landscape of Immersive technologies, exploring the trends, challenges, and opportunities facing companies working in these fields. From funding and monetization to user adoption and regulation, we will discuss the key factors driving the growth of AR/VR and the strategies companies are using to succeed in this space.

Structure

In this chapter, we will discuss the following topics:

- Introduction to the business of VR/XR
- Funding and investment
- Monetization strategies
- User adoption and marketing
- Technology challenges
- Case studies

Objectives

At the end of this chapter, you will come to know about how business landscapes are getting affected by VR/AR. This chapter provides a comprehensive overview and analysis of the current state and prospects of the VR and AR, collectively referred to as VR/AR, industry within the XR umbrella. This chapter explores the various aspects of the business landscape surrounding VR/AR, including market trends, key players, technological advancements, investment opportunities, and challenges businesses operating in this domain face. By examining the business ecosystem of VR/XR, this chapter intends to equip readers with a deeper understanding of the opportunities and risks associated with the adoption and utilization of VR/AR technologies, thereby facilitating informed decision-making and strategic planning for businesses seeking to enter or expand their presence in this rapidly evolving industry.

Introduction to business of VR/XR

The introduction to the business of VR and AR, collectively known as VR/AR, sets the stage for understanding the dynamic landscape of this emerging industry. In recent years, immersive technologies have transformed from science fiction concepts to real-world applications that revolutionize various sectors, including entertainment, gaming, healthcare, education, architecture, and more.

This chapter delves into the business aspect of VR/AR, exploring the opportunities, challenges, and trends that define this rapidly evolving market. The convergence of technological advancements, increased accessibility, and growing consumer interest have created fertile ground for businesses to leverage VR/XR technologies and create immersive experiences for their customers.

By the end of this chapter, readers will have a solid foundation in the business landscape of VR/AR. They will gain a comprehensive understanding of the market dynamics, key players, emerging trends, and potential challenges, empowering them to make informed decisions when considering VR/AR adoption or investment within their respective industries.

Current state and evolution of VR/AR industry

The current state of the VR/XR industry showcases a landscape of rapid growth, technological advancements, and expanding applications across various sectors. Over the past decade, VR/XR has evolved from a niche technology to a mainstream phenomenon, driven by advancements in hardware, software, and increased accessibility.

One significant indicator of the industry's growth is the increasing market size. According to market research reports, the global VR/XR market is projected to reach a market size of several billion dollars by 2026, driven by the rising demand for immersive experiences and applications across industries.

According to recent data from Grand View Research, the XR market is expected to reach USD 463.7 billion by 2026, growing at a CAGR of 45.0% from 2021. The COVID-19 pandemic has, in a way, accelerated this growth as businesses increasingly seek digital and immersive solutions to stay connected and deliver services. The growth of the XR market is being driven by several factors, including the increasing availability of affordable hardware, the growing popularity of mobile gaming, and the increasing demand for immersive experiences in a variety of industries.

(Source: https://www.grandviewresearch.com/industry-analysis/virtual-reality-vr-market)

Business landscape and key trends

The VR/XR industry is continuously evolving, driven by advancements in technology, changing consumer preferences, and emerging trends. Let us explore how the business landscape of the VR/XR industry is evolving, including the major players and key trends shaping the industry:

- **Major players:**
  - **Meta (Oculus)**: Facebook's acquisition of Oculus has positioned it as a major player in the VR industry. Oculus Rift and Oculus Quest headsets have gained significant market share, and the company continues to invest in content development and platform expansion.
  - **HTC Vive**: HTC Vive is known for its high-end VR headsets and has established a strong presence in the market. They offer VR solutions for consumers and enterprise customers and collaborate with partners to develop innovative VR experiences.
  - **Sony PlayStation VR**: Sony's PlayStation VR has leveraged its existing gaming console user base to become a prominent player in the VR market. With its PlayStation VR headset, Sony focuses on delivering immersive gaming experiences.
  - **Microsoft**: Microsoft's Windows Mixed Reality platform has attracted attention in the VR/XR space. They collaborate with hardware manufacturers to offer a range of VR/XR headsets and provide support for developers through Windows Mixed Reality.
  - **Google**: Google has invested in both VR and AR. While Google Cardboard aimed to make VR more accessible, Google's AR efforts have focused on ARCore for smartphones. They continue to explore new opportunities in the immersive technology space.
  - **Apple**: Apple is relatively new to the AR/VR industry. Apple recently launched Apple Vision Pro, which is one of the most advanced VR headsets.

- **Magic Leap**: Magic Leap specializes in AR and has developed a wearable AR headset. They aim to seamlessly blend digital content with the real world, offering unique AR experiences.

- **Key trends shaping the industry:**
  - **Wireless and standalone devices**: The industry is moving towards wireless and standalone VR/XR devices, eliminating the need for external sensors or PC connections. This trend enhances mobility, ease of use, and accessibility for users.
  - **Enterprise applications**: VR/XR is increasingly being adopted in enterprise settings for training, simulations, and design applications. Industries such as healthcare, manufacturing, architecture, and education are leveraging the immersive nature of VR/XR to enhance productivity and improve outcomes.
  - **Social and collaborative experiences**: The industry is witnessing a shift towards social and collaborative VR/XR experiences. Platforms are being developed where users can interact with others in virtual spaces, enabling shared experiences and collaboration across distances.
  - **Content creation and experiences**: High-quality and engaging content remains a key driver for VR/XR adoption. Content creators are focusing on developing compelling experiences, games, and applications across various sectors, catering to the diverse interests of users.
  - **Integration with AI and IoT**: Integration of VR/XR with other emerging technologies, such as artificial intelligence and the **Internet of Things (IoT)**, is gaining momentum. This integration enables personalized and context-aware experiences, expanding the capabilities and applications of VR/XR.
  - **Accessibility and affordability**: Efforts are being made to make VR/XR more accessible and affordable to a wider audience. From lower-cost headsets to smartphone-based solutions, these advancements aim to remove barriers to entry and drive adoption.
  - **Cross-platform and cross-device experiences**: With the proliferation of different VR/XR platforms and devices, there is a growing focus on enabling cross-platform compatibility and seamless experiences across multiple devices, ensuring users can access and enjoy content regardless of the hardware they own.
  - **Location-based experiences**: Location-based VR/XR experiences, such as VR arcades and immersive theme parks, are gaining popularity. These venues offer unique and immersive experiences that go beyond what can be achieved at home, attracting a broader audience.

- **Health and wellness applications**: VR/XR is being explored for health and wellness applications, including mental health, therapy, rehabilitation, and pain management. This emerging trend holds promise for the industry to contribute to overall well-being.
- **Evolution of the VR/AR industry**: The VR/AR industry continues to evolve rapidly, with advancements in hardware, software, and user experiences driving growth and innovation. The major players are continuously investing in technology, content development, and partnerships to shape the future of the industry and capitalize on emerging opportunities.

Funding and investment

Funding and investment are crucial for the growth, innovation, and sustainability of an industry. In the case of the VR/XR industry, they play a pivotal role in driving research and development, advancing technology, fostering content creation, and expanding market reach. Adequate funding allows companies to invest in cutting-edge hardware and software, enabling technological advancements and pushing the boundaries of immersive experiences. Investment also fuels content creation, driving the development of compelling VR/XR experiences across various sectors. Additionally, funding supports marketing efforts, distribution channels, and strategic partnerships, facilitating market penetration and user adoption. Overall, funding and investment provide the necessary resources for the VR/XR industry to flourish, driving innovation, expanding market opportunities, and delivering immersive experiences to a broader audience.

Funding and its challenges for VR/XR industry

Indeed, VR/XR is a capital-intensive field, and securing funding can be a significant challenge for companies operating in this space. There are several reasons why funding can be difficult to obtain in the VR/XR industry:

- **High development costs**: Developing VR/XR hardware, software, and content requires significant investment. The costs associated with research, design, prototyping, testing, and production can be substantial. Companies may need to invest in specialized equipment, talent, and resources, adding to the overall development costs.
- **Technological uncertainty**: The VR/XR industry is constantly evolving, with new hardware, software, and content innovations emerging frequently. Investors may perceive the technology as being in a relatively early stage, making them cautious about committing substantial funds. The rapid pace of technological advancements and uncertain market trends can create hesitancy among investors.
- **Limited market adoption**: While VR/XR has gained momentum in recent years, market adoption is still growing, particularly outside of the gaming sector.

Investors may be concerned about the market size, user adoption rates, and revenue potential of VR/XR products and services. This uncertainty can make it challenging for companies to attract significant funding.

- **Lack of revenue models**: Monetization strategies in the VR/XR industry are still evolving. Companies often face challenges in defining sustainable revenue models, particularly for non-gaming applications. The absence of proven revenue streams can make potential investors hesitant to commit capital.
- **Risk perception**: The VR/XR industry involves inherent risks, including technological advancements, market competition, and changing consumer preferences. Investors may perceive the risks associated with developing and commercializing VR/XR products as higher compared to more established industries, which can make securing funding more challenging.

Despite these challenges, there are avenues for VR/XR companies to secure funding. Some potential sources include venture capital firms specializing in emerging technologies, strategic partnerships with established companies, government grants and subsidies, crowdfunding platforms, and participation in startup accelerators or incubators. Over time, as the industry continues to mature and demonstrates strong growth potential, funding opportunities may expand.

Moreover, companies can work on showcasing a clear and compelling business plan, highlighting the market potential, differentiation, and revenue-generating opportunities. Demonstrating traction through user adoption, partnerships, and successful pilot projects can also instill confidence in potential investors. As the VR/XR industry continues to evolve and demonstrate its value across multiple sectors, securing funding may become relatively easier for innovative and promising companies in this space.

Funding options and investment-securing strategies

In the VR/AR industry, securing funding and investment requires a thoughtful approach and consideration of various options. Here are some funding options and investment-securing strategies that companies in the VR/XR space can explore:

- **Venture Capital (VC) funding**: VC firms that specialize in emerging technologies can be a viable source of funding for VR/XR companies. These firms are often interested in innovative and high-growth potential ventures. For example, VC firms like Super Ventures specialize in getting AR projects funded. Their previous ventures are Gravity Sketch, cognitive3D, Fringefy, and so on. Another one is Accel, which is a Venture Capital fund that invests in people and their companies from early stages throughout all the phases of growth. Accel has invested in businesses like Emergent VR, Spotify, and so on.

- **Strategic partnerships**: Forming strategic partnerships with established companies can provide access to funding and resources. This can involve collaboration with hardware manufacturers, software developers, content creators, or industry-specific companies. Strategic partnerships not only bring financial support but also provide expertise, market access, and credibility. For example, automobile companies can collaborate to fund us so that we can provide them with AR-based rear-view camera images or 360-degree views from the top.

- **Government grants and subsidies**: Many governments and organizations offer grants, subsidies, or funding programs to support innovation and technology development. Companies in the VR/AR industry can explore various incubators, research institutes, and labs, which can be particularly beneficial in early-stage development or research initiatives. For example, MIT Labs is one of the budding grounds for all such major developments.

- **Crowdfunding**: Crowdfunding platforms provide an avenue for companies to raise funds directly from the public. VR/AR companies can leverage platforms like Kickstarter or Indiegogo to showcase their projects, gather community support, and secure funding. Crowdfunding campaigns also serve as effective marketing tools, generating awareness and building a user base.

- **Accelerators and incubators**: Participating in VR/XR-focused startup accelerators or incubator programs can provide funding, mentorship, and networking opportunities. These programs offer support in business development, product refinement, and investor introductions, increasing the chances of securing investment.

- **Angel investors**: Angel investors are individuals who provide capital to startups in exchange for equity. VR/AR companies can seek out angel investors with an interest in immersive technologies. Networking events, industry conferences, and online platforms that connect entrepreneurs with angel investors can be valuable resources.

- **Industry-specific grants and competitions**: Some industries or organizations offer grants or competitions specifically tailored to VR/XR innovations. These opportunities not only provide funding but also offer exposure, recognition, and validation for companies. Keeping an eye on industry associations, research institutions, or corporate-sponsored competitions can uncover such funding prospects.

- **Revenue generation and proof of concept**: Generating revenue through VR/XR products or services can demonstrate market viability and attract potential investors. Companies can focus on securing contracts or partnerships that provide revenue streams, validating their business model, and attracting investor interest.

- **Investor pitch and business plan**: Crafting a compelling investor pitch and business plan is crucial for securing funding. Companies should highlight the market opportunity, competitive advantage, monetization strategies, and growth potential. Demonstrating a deep understanding of the industry, a strong team, and a clear path to profitability can instill confidence in potential investors.
- **Demonstrating traction**: Building a track record of success can be influential in securing investment. This includes showcasing user adoption, revenue growth, partnerships with key industry players, successful pilot projects, and achievements in product development. Demonstrating traction and market demand can build investor confidence and increase the likelihood of securing funding. For example, companies like Swipetouch Edutech Pvt. Ltd. prove themselves via their product. Within two years, it received market acceptance. Similarly, for any new technology like AR/VR, we need to provide acceptance.

It is important for VR/XR companies to explore multiple funding options, tailor their approach to investors' interests, and leverage industry networks and events to connect with potential investors. Additionally, seeking guidance from experienced advisors or consultants can provide valuable insights and increase the chances of securing funding in the competitive VR/XR landscape.

Monetization strategies

Monetization strategies in the VR/XR industry are still evolving, but there are several approaches companies can consider. One common strategy is selling hardware, such as VR headsets or AR glasses, to consumers or enterprise customers. Companies can also generate revenue through licensing or selling software applications, games, or content. In-app purchases and subscription models offer opportunities for additional revenue streams within VR/XR experiences. Another avenue is partnering with brands for advertising and sponsored content within VR/XR applications. Enterprise solutions, such as providing VR/XR training or simulation services to businesses, can also be a lucrative monetization strategy. Furthermore, partnerships with content creators, merchandising, location-based experiences, and offering premium or exclusive content are avenues to explore in the VR/XR industry. As the industry continues to mature, companies will likely experiment with and refine monetization strategies to maximize revenue while delivering value to users.

Monetization challenges in VR/XR industry

Making money in the VR/XR industry can indeed be challenging due to the combination of high development costs and a limited user base. Here are some key reasons why monetization can be difficult:

- **High development costs**: Developing VR/XR hardware, software, and content can require substantial investment. The cost of research, design, prototyping, testing, and production can be significant, often requiring specialized skills and resources. These high development costs can put pressure on profitability and make it challenging for companies to recoup their investments. For example, a very basic VR/AR developer would cost around $100-$150 per hour.

- **Limited user base**: While immersive technology is growing in popularity, the user base remains relatively small compared to other established platforms or industries. Limited user adoption can restrict revenue opportunities, as companies may struggle to reach a critical mass of users to generate substantial returns on investment.
- **Price sensitivity**: The cost of VR, AR, or XR hardware and accessories, such as headsets and controllers, can be a barrier for potential users. Higher price points can deter widespread adoption, particularly among budget-conscious consumers. Finding the right balance between affordability and profitability becomes crucial for companies seeking to attract a larger user base.
- **Content availability and quality**: The success of VR/XR relies heavily on compelling content and experiences. However, developing high-quality content can be costly and time-consuming. Limited availability of engaging and diverse content can impact user engagement, repeat usage, and overall demand for VR/AR/XR experiences.
- **Market fragmentation and compatibility**: The immersive technology market is characterized by multiple platforms, devices, and operating systems, leading to fragmentation. This fragmentation can pose challenges for developers and content creators, requiring them to invest in adapting their products to various platforms and ensuring compatibility across different devices. This complexity can increase development costs and limit the reach of content.
- **Perception and education**: Many potential users may still have limited awareness or understanding of VR/AR technology and its potential applications. Educating consumers about the benefits and possibilities of VR/AR experiences can be a slow process. Overcoming skepticism or misconceptions and building a strong user base may require significant marketing and educational efforts.

To overcome these challenges, VR/XR companies should focus on optimizing costs, diversifying revenue streams, targeting niche markets, forging strategic partnerships, and prioritizing user engagement and retention. Additionally, addressing price sensitivity, expanding the user base through marketing and education efforts, and staying adaptable to evolving market dynamics can contribute to long-term profitability in the VR/XR industry.

Pros and cons of various monetization models

Let us discuss some of the monetization models commonly used in the VR/XR industry, along with their advantages and disadvantages:

- **Paid content/software**
  - **Advantages**
    - Direct revenue generation through one-time purchases or paid downloads.
    - Provides a straightforward and transparent monetization model.
    - Offers a clear value proposition to users.
    - Can be appealing for developers who have high-quality and unique content.
  - **Disadvantages**
    - May deter potential users who are unwilling to pay upfront.
    - Relies on a smaller user base willing to make a purchase.
    - Requires continuous development of new content to sustain revenue flow.
- **In-app purchases**
  - **Advantages**
    - Offers an opportunity for additional revenue beyond the initial app download.
    - Allows developers to offer premium features, upgrades, or virtual goods.
    - Encourages user engagement and repeat usage.
    - Can be appealing to users who prefer a free initial experience with the option to enhance it.
  - **Disadvantages**
    - Users may feel the pressure to make repeated purchases to fully enjoy the experience.
    - Balancing the pricing and perceived value of in-app purchases can be challenging.
    - Potential backlash if the in-app purchase system is perceived as pay-to-win or unfair.
- **Subscription models**
  - **Advantages**
    - Provides recurring revenue and predictable cash flow.
    - Encourages user loyalty and long-term engagement.

   - Can foster a sense of community and exclusivity for subscribers.
   - Allows for continuous content updates and improvements.
- **Disadvantages**
   - Requires a robust and ongoing stream of valuable content to justify the subscription cost.
   - Users may be reluctant to commit to long-term subscriptions without a proven track record of quality content.
   - Can be challenging to compete with other subscription services and justify the added cost to users.

- **Advertising**
   - **Advantages**
      - Offers potential for revenue generation through partnerships with advertisers.
      - Can provide a free or lower-cost experience for users.
      - Can be lucrative if VR/XR experiences attract a large and engaged user base.
      - Opportunities for targeted advertising based on user behavior and preferences.
   - **Disadvantages**
      - Intrusive or poorly implemented advertising can negatively impact the user experience.
      - Balancing ad placements without compromis-ing immersion can be challenging.
      - Difficulty attracting advertisers without a large user base or established track record.
- **Sponsorships and brand partnerships**
   - **Advantages**
      - Can provide a significant source of revenue through partnerships with brands or sponsors.
      - Offers opportunities for product placement, brand integration, or exclusive content.
      - Can provide financial support for development and marketing efforts.
      - Adds credibility and endorsement to the VR/XR experience.

- **Disadvantages**
  - Requires establishing relationships and negotiating partnerships, which can be time-consuming.
  - Risk of compromising the user experience if sponsorships or brand integrations are too intrusive or unrelated to the content.
  - Dependence on maintaining sponsor relationships for sustained revenue.
  - It is important for VR/XR developers to evaluate their target audience, content offerings, user engagement, and long-term sustainability when selecting a monetization model. A combination of these models or hybrid approaches can be employed to diversify revenue streams and optimize the monetization potential in the VR/XR industry.

User adoption and marketing

User adoption and effective marketing play critical roles in driving the success and widespread acceptance of VR/XR technologies. User adoption relies on several factors, including providing a user-friendly and comfortable experience, offering high-quality and diverse content, ensuring affordability and accessibility, and educating the public about the potential of VR/XR. To achieve these goals, marketing efforts should focus on building awareness, creating compelling messaging, and showcasing the unique benefits and immersive experiences of VR/XR. This can involve targeted advertising campaigns, partnerships with influencers or content creators, leveraging social media platforms, organizing events and demonstrations, and collaborating with industry stakeholders. By effectively marketing the value proposition and addressing potential barriers, companies can attract and engage users, drive user adoption, and propel the growth of the VR/XR industry.

VR/XR's adoption challenges among users

Adoption challenges for VR/XR technology, considering its niche market status, can be attributed to several factors, which we already discussed in earlier topics, such as:

- **High cost**: Due to expensive hardware.
- **Limited content availability**: While the VR/XR content library has been expanding, it still lags other established platforms. Limited availability of high-quality, diverse, and engaging content can hamper user adoption.
- **Motion sickness and discomfort**: VR/AR experiences can cause motion sickness or discomfort for some users, especially during extended usage or when content is not optimized for comfort. This can create apprehension and reluctance to adopt the technology.

- **Lack of awareness and understanding**: The general public's limited awareness and understanding of VR/AR technology can hinder adoption
- **Fragmented ecosystem and compatibility**: The VR/AR ecosystem is fragmented, with multiple hardware platforms, software frameworks, and compatibility issues.
- **Social acceptance and social integration**: Immersive technology can still face social acceptance challenges, with some individuals perceiving it as isolating or disconnected from real-world interactions. Encouraging social integration within VR/XR experiences, facilitating shared experiences, and highlighting the potential for collaboration and community-building can help overcome these challenges.
- **Technological barriers**: Although significant advancements have been made, immersive technology continues to face technical challenges, such as resolution limitations, processing power requirements, and wireless connectivity. Continued technological progress and addressing these barriers can enhance the user experience and drive adoption.

Overcoming these challenges requires concerted efforts from industry players, including hardware manufacturers, content creators, developers, and marketers. Collaboration, investment in content development, user education, and addressing user concerns will be key to expanding the VR/XR user base and driving adoption in the broader market.

Marketing strategies of the companies for VR/XR

Here are some strategies that companies in the VR/XR industry are using to market their products:

- **Social media marketing**: Social media platforms provide an effective channel for reaching and engaging with potential users. Companies leverage platforms like Facebook, Instagram, Twitter, and YouTube to showcase VR/XR experiences, share promotional content, highlight user testimonials, and provide updates on new releases or features. Social media marketing enables direct interaction with users, encourages user-generated content, and fosters a community around VR/XR experiences.
- **Influencer marketing**: Collaborating with influencers who have a significant following and influence in the gaming, tech, or entertainment space can amplify brand visibility and product awareness. Influencers can create content featuring VR/XR experiences, provide reviews and recommendations, and share their firsthand experiences with their audience. This helps generate excitement, trust, and interest among their followers, potentially leading to increased user adoption.
- **Experiential marketing**: Creating immersive and interactive experiences for potential users through live events, pop-up activations, or demonstrations is an effective strategy in the VR/XR industry. Companies set up booths or dedicated areas at industry conferences, trade shows, or public spaces where users can try

VR/XR experiences firsthand. This allows people to experience the technology and its capabilities, fostering curiosity and creating memorable encounters that drive interest and word-of-mouth promotion.

- **Content marketing**: Companies leverage content marketing strategies to educate, engage, and build brand authority in the VR/XR industry. This can involve creating informative blog posts, tutorials, videos, and case studies that highlight the benefits and applications of VR/XR technology. Content marketing helps generate organic traffic, build trust, and position companies as thought leaders in the industry.
- **Partnerships and collaborations**: Collaborating with other brands, developers, or content creators can expand reach and tap into existing communities. Partnerships can involve joint marketing efforts, co-creation of content, or cross-promotions. By leveraging the reach and influence of partners, companies can extend their marketing reach to new audiences and gain credibility within the industry.
- **Digital advertising**: Digital advertising campaigns, including display ads, video ads, and search engine marketing, can help raise awareness and drive targeted traffic to VR/XR products. Companies can optimize their advertising strategies by targeting specific demographics, interests, and relevant keywords to reach potential users actively searching for VR/XR experiences.
- **Public relations and media outreach**: Engaging with industry-specific media outlets, tech publications, and journalists is essential to gaining media coverage and press mentions. Companies can send out press releases, provide review units to journalists or content creators, and pitch stories or case studies showcasing the innovative use of VR/XR technology. Positive media coverage helps build credibility, generate buzz, and increase brand visibility.
- **Community building and user engagement**: Building and nurturing a community around VR/XR experiences is crucial for long-term success. Companies actively engage with users through forums, social media groups, and dedicated communities where users can share experiences, provide feedback, and interact with fellow enthusiasts. Community building fosters brand loyalty, encourages user-generated content, and strengthens the user adoption cycle.

By implementing a combination of these marketing strategies, companies in the VR/XR industry can effectively promote their products, increase brand awareness, and drive user adoption in the market. It is important to continuously adapt and experiment with different approaches to find the most effective marketing mix for their target audience.

Technology challenges

In the complex and rapidly evolving field of VR/XR, staying abreast of the latest technology advancements can be a significant challenge for companies. The industry undergoes continuous innovation, with new hardware, software frameworks, and content creation tools constantly emerging. Companies must invest in ongoing research and development, closely monitor industry trends, and actively engage in collaborations and partnerships to keep up with the latest technological developments. This requires a dedicated commitment to staying informed about cutting-edge technologies, attending industry conferences and events, fostering relationships with hardware manufacturers and software developers, and actively participating in industry forums and communities. Additionally, maintaining a talented and adaptable workforce with expertise in the latest technologies is crucial for companies to navigate the challenges and seize opportunities in this dynamic VR/XR landscape.

Technological challenges for VR/XR industry

The VR/XR industry faces ongoing technology challenges as it strives to advance and meet the evolving demands of users and industries. Some key technology challenges include:

- Hardware advancements
- Content creation tools
- Standardization and interoperability
- Motion sickness and comfort
- Wireless and mobile solutions
- Artificial intelligence and machine learning

Overcoming these technology challenges requires ongoing research, collaboration, and innovation from hardware manufacturers, software developers, content creators, and industry stakeholders. Continued investment in research and development, combined with industry-wide standardization efforts, will drive the advancement of VR/XR technology and pave the way for its broader adoption and integration into various sectors.

Case studies

We will examine some of the successful companies in the VR/XR industry. Let us take a closer look at two prominent companies in the VR/XR industry: Oculus and Magic Leap.

Oculus case study

Oculus, founded in 2012 by Palmer Luckey, gained significant attention with its Oculus Rift VR headset. The company's dedication to developing high-quality VR experiences propelled it to success. In 2014, Oculus launched a highly successful Kickstarter campaign that helped fund the development of the Oculus Rift. This attracted the attention of Facebook, which acquired Oculus in 2014 for $2 billion

(*Source*: **cnbc.com**).

Oculus' success can be attributed to several factors, including some of the latest updates in the Quest 3 product:

- **Boundary-free mixed reality**: No Quest boundary is necessary for Mixed Reality, meaning you can take your puzzle anywhere in your house.
- **Automated mixed reality launch at home**: If your home environment is in Mixed Reality, the game will launch in Mixed Reality, too (unless you manually change this in the game's settings).
- **Developer community**: Oculus actively engaged with developers, providing **Software Development Kits** ( ) and fostering a robust developer community. This helped create a wide range of content, from games to educational experiences, enhancing the appeal and adoption of Oculus devices.
- **Strategic partnerships**: Oculus formed partnerships with leading game developers, ensuring a strong lineup of VR games and experiences at launch. This helped create a vibrant ecosystem around the Oculus platform and drove user adoption.
- **Market reach**: Facebook's acquisition of Oculus provided the company with the resources and reach to accelerate market penetration. Facebook's strong presence and distribution channels allowed Oculus to reach a broader audience.

Magic Leap case study

Magic Leap, founded in 2010 by *Rony Abovitz*, aimed to revolutionize AR with its Magic Leap One AR headset. The company garnered attention with its promises of highly immersive and spatial computing experiences. Magic Leap attracted significant investments, raising over $2 billion from renowned investors like Google and Alibaba.

(*Source*: **cnbc.com**)

Magic Leap's success factors include:

- **Technological innovation**: Magic Leap focused on creating advanced AR technology, combining computer vision, light field technology, and spatial mapping to deliver realistic and interactive AR experiences. The Magic Leap One headset offered a wide field of view and seamless integration of virtual content with the real world.
- **Content creation and partnerships**: Magic Leap invested in content creation and established partnerships with major brands and developers. These collaborations resulted in a range of AR applications, from gaming and entertainment to enterprise and healthcare solutions, enhancing the value proposition of Magic Leap devices.
- **Developer support**: Magic Leap provided developer tools and resources to encourage the creation of AR content. The company fostered a developer community and launched initiatives like the Magic Leap Independent Creator

Program, which supported independent developers in creating innovative AR experiences.

- **Enterprise applications**: Magic Leap positioned itself as a provider of AR solutions for enterprise use cases. By targeting industries such as healthcare, manufacturing, and retail, Magic Leap sought to leverage the potential of AR technology for business applications.

Both Oculus and Magic Leap demonstrate the importance of technological advancements, developer support, strategic partnerships, and market reach in the success of companies in the VR/XR industry. These companies have played significant roles in driving the adoption and evolution of VR and AR technologies, contributing to the growth and potential of the broader VR/XR industry.

Conclusion

In this chapter, we tried to take a closer look into the business landscape of the VR/XR Industry. VR and XR technologies are rapidly evolving, and their potential applications extend far beyond gaming and entertainment. We explored the trends, challenges, and opportunities the companies are facing in this field. From funding and monetization to user adoption and regulation, we discussed the key factors driving the growth of VR/AR and the strategies companies are using to succeed in this space. In the end, we also went through the case studies of Oculus and Magic Leap and analyzed the strategies that contributed to their success.

In the next chapter, we are going to learn about the applications of VR/XR in healthcare.

Points to remember

- Explore the historical development and growth of VR, AR, and XR technologies.
- Gain insights into the current state of the AR/VR/XR industry, major players, and emerging trends shaping the business landscape.
- Identify key areas and use cases attracting significant investments in the AR/VR/XR sector.
- Understand the types of investors involved, including venture capitalists, angel investors, and corporate funding.
- Explore various revenue streams such as hardware sales, software licensing, subscription models, and in-app purchases.
- Analyze successful monetization strategies employed by leading AR/VR/XR companies and learn from their business models.

- Examine factors influencing user adoption, including content quality, user experience, and accessibility.
- Explore effective marketing strategies tailored to the unique challenges of promoting immersive technologies to diverse consumer and enterprise markets.
- Delve into challenges related to hardware capabilities, including processing power, display technology, and form factor.
- Understand the complexities of creating immersive experiences, addressing issues like content creation, software optimization, and cross-platform compatibility.

CHAPTER 7
Applications of AR, VR, and XR in Healthcare

Introduction

Immersive Technologies like **Augmented Reality (AR)**, **Virtual Reality (VR)**, and **Extended Reality (XR)** have enormous potential in the healthcare industry, enabling more effective training, diagnosis, treatment, and rehabilitation. In this chapter, we will explore the applications of these technologies in healthcare, discussing the latest research, the challenges, and the opportunities for healthcare professionals, patients, and caregivers.

Structure

In this chapter, we will discuss the following topics:

- Introduction to AR, VR, and XR in healthcare
- Diagnosis and treatment
- Rehabilitation and physical theory
- Medical education and training
- Patient education and engagement
- Case studies

Objectives

At the end of this chapter, you will come to know about how the healthcare industry is being impacted by immersive technologies. This chapter provides a comprehensive overview and analysis of how VR/XR plays a crucial role in the diagnosis and treatment. You will also learn how VR/XR can be used to create immersive environments for rehabilitation, physical therapy, and various latest research in this area.

Then, we will take a deep dive and see how immersive technologies can be used for realistic simulation for medication education and training and enable students and healthcare professionals to learn in a safe and controlled environment. We will explore some of the latest research in this field.

Then, we will go through patient education and engagement and find out how immersive technologies can educate patients and engage them in their healthcare. Finally, we will go through case studies, where we will examine some examples of successful applications of AR, VR, and XR in healthcare.

Introduction to AR, VR, and XR in healthcare

In recent years, the field of healthcare has been witnessing a remarkable transformation with the integration of cutting-edge technologies. Among the most promising and revolutionary innovations are AR and VR. VR, in its immersive and interactive nature, allows individuals to step into computer-generated worlds, while XR encompasses a broader spectrum that includes AR and **Mixed Reality** (**MR**). In this chapter, we delve into the captivating world of AR, VR, and XR in healthcare and explore how these transformative technologies are redefining medical training, patient care, pain management, rehabilitation, and patient education.

The allure of these immersive technologies lies in their ability to transport users beyond the confines of reality, opening doors to endless possibilities in the healthcare domain. Medical professionals are embracing these technologies as a powerful tool to enhance their training and education. By simulating realistic medical procedures and surgeries in safe, virtual environments, aspiring physicians and seasoned practitioners can gain invaluable experience, refine their skills, and increase their confidence before stepping into the operating room. These immersive training experiences not only contribute to improved patient outcomes but also revolutionize the way medical education is conducted.

Beyond the realm of medical professionals, patients themselves are benefiting from the transformative impact of these technologies. One of the most compelling applications lies in pain management and distraction during medical interventions. By immersing patients in calming and captivating virtual worlds, Immersive technologies can effectively reduce anxiety and alleviate the perception of pain during uncomfortable procedures. Patients can find solace in serene landscapes, drawing their focus away from the medical setting and fostering a sense of relaxation and comfort.

As we venture further into this chapter, we will explore the challenges and potential future advancements of AR/VR/XR in healthcare.

Current state of AR, VR, and XR in healthcare and its evolution

VR and XR technologies have made considerable advancements in healthcare. Medical training and education have been revolutionized, with VR/XR simulations providing immersive and risk-free experiences for medical professionals to practice complex procedures. These technologies have found applications in pain management, distraction therapy, physical and cognitive rehabilitation, and mental health treatment, offering innovative and effective therapeutic interventions. Patient education and engagement have also been enhanced, with VR/XR providing interactive and informative experiences that empower patients to make informed decisions about their healthcare. Additionally, the integration of VR/XR in telemedicine and remote collaboration has facilitated virtual consultations and real-time data visualization, enabling healthcare professionals to work together seamlessly across distances. While accessibility, data integration, and regulatory considerations remain points of development, the current state of VR/XR in healthcare holds great promise for the future of medicine.

Evolution of VR/XR in healthcare:

- **Increased accessibility:** As VR/XR hardware and software become more affordable and user-friendly, they will likely become more accessible to a broader range of healthcare facilities, from large hospitals to smaller clinics.
- **Advancements in simulation realism:** Advancements in VR/XR technology, such as haptic feedback and realistic graphics, will continue to improve the accuracy and realism of medical simulations, making them even more valuable for medical training and surgical practice.
- **Data integration and interoperability:** VR/XR platforms will likely become more integrated with **Electronic Health Records (EHRs)** and other healthcare systems, allowing for seamless data sharing and interoperability. This integration will facilitate personalized patient care and data-driven decision-making.
- **Customization for specific medical specialties:** The development of specialized VR/XR applications tailored to various medical specialties, such as cardiology, neurology, and orthopedics, will likely increase, enabling healthcare providers to address specific needs within their fields.
- **Research and evidence-based practice**: As more healthcare institutions incorporate VR/XR into their practice, there will be an increased focus on research and evidence-based studies to validate the effectiveness of these technologies in different medical contexts.

- **Regulatory guidelines and standards**: With the growing adoption of VR/XR in healthcare, regulatory bodies may develop specific guidelines and standards to ensure patient safety, data privacy, and ethical use of these technologies.
- **Collaboration with Artificial Intelligence (AI) and Big Data**: The integration of VR/XR with AI and big data analytics may unlock new opportunities for personalized patient care, treatment optimization, and predictive healthcare.

In conclusion, VR/XR technologies have made significant strides in healthcare, enhancing medical training, patient care, therapy, and patient education. As technology continues to evolve and become more accessible, we can expect even more profound transformations in healthcare, with VR/XR playing a pivotal role in shaping the future of medicine. However, it is essential to monitor ongoing research, regulatory developments, and industry collaborations to ensure safe and effective integration in healthcare practices.

Major players and some of the key trends

Healthcare has witnessed the emergence of several major players and notable trends. While the landscape may have evolved since then, some key players and trends during that time included:

- **Major players:**
    - **AccuVein**: AccuVein is known for its AR-based vein visualization technology, helping healthcare professionals locate veins for intravenous access and blood draw procedures, improving patient comfort, and reducing the number of needle sticks.
    - **Osso VR**: Osso VR specializes in immersive surgical training simulations for medical professionals, offering realistic and hands-on experiences to improve surgical skills and knowledge.
    - **Surgical theater**: Surgical theater develops VR-based platforms for surgical planning and patient engagement. Their solutions allow surgeons to visualize and plan complex surgeries using patient-specific 3D virtual models.
    - **MedyMatch (now MaxQ AI)**: MedyMatch leveraged AI and XR technology to provide real-time decision support for radiologists, assisting in the detection and diagnosis of critical neurological conditions, such as strokes.
    - **MindMaze**: MindMaze focuses on VR-based neurorehabilitation solutions to aid in the recovery of patients with neurological disorders and injuries.
- **Key trends:**
    - **Telemedicine and remote collaboration**: The COVID-19 pandemic accelerated the adoption of telemedicine, leading to an increased interest in immersive technologies for remote consultations and collaborative

medical practices. These immersive technologies help facilitate real-time visualization of patient data and enable healthcare professionals to work together, regardless of geographical barriers.

- **Personalized medicine and patient-specific interventions**: Technologies have enabled the creation of patient-specific simulations and interventions, allowing healthcare providers to tailor treatment plans and surgical procedures according to each patient's unique anatomy and condition.
- **Integration with AI and big data**: Integrating immersive technologies with AI and big data analytics has allowed for advanced data processing and predictive capabilities. This integration has the potential to enhance patient outcomes through personalized treatment recommendations and improved diagnostics.
- **Remote patient monitoring and home healthcare**: Immersive technologies have shown potential in remote patient monitoring and home healthcare settings. Patients can receive personalized rehabilitation exercises and therapies in the comfort of their homes, with real-time feedback and guidance from healthcare professionals.
- **Digital therapeutics and mental health interventions**: AR/VR/XR-based digital therapeutics have gained traction for treating various mental health conditions, including anxiety disorders, **Post Traumatic Stress Disorder** (**PTSD**), and depression. These immersive therapies offer a safe and controlled environment for patients to confront and manage their psychological challenges.
- **Standardization and regulatory guidelines**: As immersive technologies become more widespread in healthcare, there is an increasing focus on developing industry standards and regulatory guidelines to ensure patient safety, data privacy, and ethical use of these technologies.

Note: The information provided is based on the situation up to September 2021, and the VR/XR landscape in healthcare may have evolved further since then.

Diagnosis and treatment

AR, VR, and XR have revolutionized diagnosis and treatment in healthcare by providing innovative and immersive solutions for medical professionals and patients alike. In the realm of diagnosis, these technologies enable healthcare providers to visualize medical imaging data in 3D environments, facilitating accurate and detailed assessments of complex anatomical structures. Surgeons leverage this for preoperative planning, creating patient-specific 3D models to simulate procedures and enhance surgical precision. Remote consultations using VR/XR enable specialists to collaborate in real-time across geographical barriers, optimizing patient care. Moreover, VR/XR aids in diagnostic simulations and assessments of neurological conditions and visual impairments, streamlining the diagnostic process. In treatment, immersive technologies serve as a powerful tool for pain management and distraction during medical procedures, reducing patient anxiety and discomfort. It enhances physical and cognitive rehabilitation by offering interactive exercises and real-time feedback, motivating patients and improving rehabilitation outcomes. VR/XR-based exposure therapy is employed for treating phobias, anxiety, and PTSD, while mental health interventions leverage virtual environments for relaxation and coping techniques. As immersive technology advances, its integration into healthcare continues to shape a patient-centric approach with personalized and effective diagnostic and treatment modalities.

Diagnosis using AR/VR/XR:

- **Medical imaging visualization**: AR/VR technologies enable healthcare professionals to visualize medical imaging data in immersive 3D environments. This immersive experience allows for a more comprehensive understanding of complex anatomical structures, facilitating accurate and detailed diagnosis.
- **Preoperative planning**: Surgeons can use AR/VR to create patient-specific 3D virtual models based on imaging data. This assists in preoperative planning, allowing surgeons to practice and simulate surgical procedures, assess potential risks, and determine the best approach for each individual patient.
- **Remote consultations**: VR/XR facilitates remote consultations, enabling specialists to visualize patient data and collaborate with on-site medical teams in real-time, even if they are located in different geographical areas. This enhances access to expertise and enables multidisciplinary discussions for complex cases.
- **Diagnostic simulations**: In some cases, VR/XR can be used for diagnostic simulations, such as assessing visual impairments or neurological conditions. These simulations provide a controlled environment to observe and analyze patient responses, aiding in the diagnostic process.

Doctors and nurses practice and refine skills using AR, VR, or XR

Immersive technologies have proven to be a valuable tool in medical training and education, particularly in simulating medical procedures. By creating realistic and interactive virtual environments, doctors, nurses, and other healthcare professionals can practice and refine their skills without any risk to real patients. This approach offers several advantages:

- **Risk-free training**: VR/XR simulations provide a safe and controlled environment for medical professionals to practice high-risk procedures without the potential consequences of errors on real patients. This helps build confidence and competence before performing procedures in a clinical setting.

- **Repetitive practice**: Healthcare professionals can repeat AR/VR simulations as many times as needed to perfect their techniques and master complex procedures. This repetitive practice fosters muscle memory and procedural fluency, leading to improved performance in real-world scenarios.
- **Variability in scenarios**: AR/VR allows the creation of various medical scenarios with different levels of complexity. This flexibility enables medical professionals to train in a wide range of cases, from routine procedures to rare and critical situations.
- **Real-time feedback**: Many AR/VR/XR medical simulation platforms provide real-time feedback and performance metrics. Medical professionals can receive immediate assessments of their actions, allowing them to identify areas for improvement and adjust their approach accordingly.
- **Team training**: AR/VR/XR simulations can facilitate team-based training, allowing doctors, nurses, and other healthcare team members to practice their roles collaboratively. This enhances communication, coordination, and teamwork, which are vital in complex medical procedures.
- **Continuing Medical Education (CME)**: AR/VR/XR provides an interactive and engaging approach to CME, enabling healthcare professionals to update their skills and knowledge regularly, keeping pace with advancements in medical practice.

Overall, the use of VR/XR for simulating medical procedures is a transformative approach that enhances medical training and contributes to improved patient care outcomes. As technology continues to advance and become more accessible, its integration into medical education is expected to expand further, benefiting healthcare professionals and patients alike.

Use of AR/VR in various healthcare areas

Let us delve deeper into the latest research in the field of VR/XR, focusing on its applications in surgical training, pain management, and mental health treatment:

- **Surgical training**: In recent years, there have been some significant advancements in the use of VR/XR for surgical training. Studies have demonstrated that VR-based simulations can effectively improve surgical skills and shorten the learning curve for trainees. Surgical residents who underwent VR/XR training displayed enhanced technical proficiency and a higher level of confidence in performing surgical procedures.

  Orthopedics and Neurosurgery are two distinct parts of medical specialties; orthopedics primarily deals with musculoskeletal issues, including bones and joints, and neurosurgery focuses on surgical interventions related to the nervous system. Both specialties play crucial roles in the overall healthcare system, addressing a wide range of medical conditions to improve patients' mobility, function, and overall quality of life. VR/XR platforms are designed for specific surgical specialties, such as in the field of orthopedics neurosurgery.

Even laparoscopy, also known as minimally invasive surgery, is a surgical technique that involves making small incisions in the abdominal wall through which a thin, flexible tube with a camera and light source (laparoscope) is inserted. This allows surgeons to view the inside of the abdomen or pelvis and perform various surgical procedures without the need for a large incision.

VR can be used to create realistic surgical simulations, allowing surgeons to practice and refine their skills in a virtual environment. This helps in training both novice and experienced surgeons, providing a safe and controlled space to learn and improve techniques. Even AR can be used to overlay virtual information, such as 3D reconstructions of a patient's anatomy or critical structures, onto the surgeon's view during preoperative planning. This aids in better understanding the patient's anatomy and planning the surgery more effectively.

- **Pain management**: The latest research in pain management has continued to support the effectiveness of VR/XR as a non-pharmacological intervention for pain reduction. Distraction therapy by immersive technologies has been studied extensively and has demonstrated positive outcomes in various medical settings, such as burn wound care, chemotherapy administration, and dental procedures. Patients who engaged in distraction reported reduced pain intensity, decreased anxiety, and a more positive perception of the medical procedure. Furthermore, research has explored the neurobiological mechanisms underlying the analgesic effects of VR/XR, providing insights into its potential applications in chronic pain management. As the opioid crisis continues to be a major concern in healthcare, VR/XR offers a promising alternative for pain relief, potentially reducing the reliance on opioids and improving patient experiences during painful interventions.
- **Mental health treatment**: Recent research has expanded the use of VR/XR in mental health treatment, particularly in exposure therapy for anxiety disorders, phobias, and PTSD. Studies have shown that VR/XR-based exposure therapy is as effective as traditional in vivo exposure, offering a safe and controlled environment for patients to confront their fears. Beyond exposure therapy, VR/XR has been explored in the treatment of other mental health conditions, such as depression, addiction, and eating disorders. VR environments have been utilized in mindfulness-based interventions and relaxation techniques to reduce stress and improve emotional well-being. The versatility of VR/XR in mental health treatment allows for personalized and immersive interventions catering to the specific needs of each individual. Ongoing research in this area aims to further refine and validate the efficacy of VR/XR-based interventions and to expand their accessibility in mental healthcare settings.

Rehabilitation and physical therapy

The use of immersive technologies like AR, VR, and XR in rehabilitation and physical therapy has opened up exciting possibilities for patient care and treatment. These immersive technologies offer personalized and engaging experiences, enhancing motivation and adherence to therapy programs. Through interactive exercises and simulations, patients can target specific impairments and work on mobility training in safe virtual environments. AR, VR, or XR provides real-time feedback, allowing patients to adjust their movements and improve technique during therapy sessions. Furthermore, these technologies enable therapists to track patients' progress more effectively, enabling data-driven treatment modifications. Gamified rehabilitation exercises in VR/XR add an element of enjoyment to the therapy process, leading to improved functional outcomes and quality of life. Additionally, VR/XR facilitates home-based rehabilitation, empowering patients to continue their exercises remotely. As these technologies continue to advance, they hold great promise in revolutionizing rehabilitation and physical therapy practices, providing patients with innovative and effective tools for their recovery journey.

AR, VR, and XR for rehabilitation and physical therapy

VR and XR technologies are making significant contributions to rehabilitation and physical therapy, transforming the way patients recover from injuries, surgeries, and neurological conditions. These immersive technologies offer a range of benefits that improve patient engagement, motivation, and treatment outcomes:

- **Personalized therapy programs**: These technologies enable therapists to create customized therapy programs based on each patient's specific needs and impairments. This tailored approach allows for targeted exercises that address individual challenges, promoting more efficient and effective rehabilitation.
- **Enhanced engagement and adherence**: Traditional therapy exercises can sometimes become monotonous, leading to reduced patient motivation and adherence. AR, VR, and XR introduce a novel and interactive element to therapy, making it more enjoyable and engaging. As a result, patients are more likely to adhere to their treatment plans, leading to better rehabilitation outcomes.
- **Realistic simulations**: These technologies provide realistic simulations of various activities and environments, allowing patients to practice functional movements in a safe and controlled setting. This is particularly beneficial for patients relearning how to walk, climb stairs, or perform other daily tasks.
- **Balance and proprioception training**: Immersive technologies can challenge patients' balance and proprioception, helping them improve their stability and

reduce the risk of falls. Virtual environments provide a safe space to work on these skills, gradually increasing difficulty as patients progress.

- **Pain management**: Distraction therapy can be used as a non-pharmacological method for pain management during physical therapy sessions. Immersing patients in soothing and calming virtual environments can reduce pain perception and anxiety, making therapy more comfortable.
- **Feedback and progress tracking**: VR/XR platforms offer real-time feedback on patient movements and techniques during exercises. This instant feedback helps patients make necessary adjustments, while therapists can track progress more effectively, guiding treatment decisions based on objective data.
- **Home-based rehabilitation**: Immersive technologies are getting more portable and accessible, enabling patients to continue their therapy at home. Home-based rehabilitation programs through VR/XR empower patients to stay engaged in their treatment and maintain progress between in-person therapy sessions.
- **Gamified rehabilitation**: Many VR/XR applications incorporate gamification elements into rehabilitation exercises. These VR games not only make therapy enjoyable but also encourage patients to work on their rehabilitation with enthusiasm.

Overall, VR/XR for rehabilitation and physical therapy offers a holistic and patient-centered approach to recovery. These immersive technologies enhance therapy experiences, optimize treatment outcomes, and provide patients with a sense of empowerment and progress throughout their rehabilitation journey. As VR/XR continues to evolve, it is likely to become an indispensable tool in modern rehabilitation practices, benefiting patients of all ages and conditions in achieving their rehabilitation goals.

Use of VR/XR for stroke and other injuries

VR and XR have emerged as promising technologies in the latest research for stroke rehabilitation, **Traumatic Brain Injury** (**TBI**), and **Spinal Cord Injuries** (**SCI**). These immersive technologies offer innovative solutions to address the complex challenges associated with these neurological conditions, providing patients with personalized and effective rehabilitation interventions.

In stroke rehabilitation

Recent research in stroke rehabilitation has demonstrated the efficacy of VR/XR in promoting motor recovery and functional improvement. VR/XR platforms can create virtual environments that simulate real-life activities, enabling stroke patients to engage in repetitive and task-specific exercises. These virtual simulations encourage neuroplasticity, where the brain forms new neural connections to compensate for damaged areas. Studies have shown that VR/XR-based interventions result in better outcomes in motor function, balance, and activities of daily living compared to conventional therapy. The use of haptic feedback in VR/XR also enhances sensory feedback, aiding in the recovery of sensory-motor functions. VR/XR is also useful for home-based rehabilitation, enabling patients to continue their therapy remotely and promoting long-term adherence to treatment plans.

In traumatic brain injury

For individuals with traumatic brain injuries, VR/XR has shown promise in cognitive rehabilitation and functional recovery. VR/XR exercises can be tailored to address specific cognitive deficits, such as attention, memory, and executive function. These interactive simulations provide a controlled environment for patients to practice cognitive tasks, allowing therapists to monitor progress and customize interventions accordingly. Additionally, VR/XR applications are increasingly used to assess and treat balance and gait impairments in TBI patients. The use of immersive environments provides a safe space for patients to practice balance and walking exercises, promoting mobility and reducing the risk of falls.

VR/XR in spinal cord injuries

As per the research conducted by the National Library of Medicine, part of the **National Center for Biotechnology Information (NCBI)**. In the context of spinal cord injuries, VR/XR plays a crucial role in facilitating neurorehabilitation and enhancing functional recovery. These technology platforms offer patients with SCI the opportunity to engage in intensive and task-specific therapies that target the upper and lower extremities. These immersive therapies focus on motor relearning and strengthening, fostering neural plasticity and encouraging the reconnection of neural pathways. Additionally, VR/XR-based balance training helps SCI patients improve postural control and stability. VR simulations of real-life environments enable patients to practice navigating through different terrains, enhancing their confidence and independence.

The latest study suggests that stroke rehabilitation, traumatic brain injury, and spinal cord injuries indicate that VR/XR technologies hold immense potential in neurorehabilitation and functional recovery. These immersive technologies offer a safe, engaging, and personalized approach to rehabilitation, enabling patients to achieve meaningful progress in their recovery journey. As technology continues to advance and research in this field grows, VR/XR is likely to become an integral part of standard rehabilitation protocols, benefiting a wide range of patients with neurological conditions.

(*Source*: **https://www.ncbi.nlm.nih.gov/pmc/articles/PMC7564926/**)

Medical education and training

Medical education and training benefit significantly from VR and XR technologies. These immersive technologies offer realistic and interactive simulations of medical scenarios, allowing students and trainees to practice in safe yet lifelike environments. Learners can engage in hands-on experiences, performing virtual surgeries, diagnosing patients, and managing complex medical cases, leading to improved clinical skills and decision-making. VR/XR facilitates personalized learning, allowing individuals to progress at their own pace and focus on areas where improvement is needed. Moreover, these technologies enable remote and distance learning, expanding access to high-quality medical education globally. With VR/XR, medical education becomes more engaging, efficient, and accessible, empowering healthcare professionals with the necessary skills and knowledge to provide better patient care.

Use of AR, VR, and XR for medical education

VR/XR technologies offer a revolutionary approach to medical education and training by providing realistic simulations in a safe and controlled environment. Here are some key benefits of using VR/XR for medical education and training:

- **Realistic and immersive learning**: VR/XR simulations create lifelike medical scenarios, allowing students and healthcare professionals to experience situations as if they were in a real clinical setting. This immersive learning experience enhances their understanding of complex medical procedures and patient care.
- **Risk-free practice**: With AR and VR, learners can practice medical procedures without any risk to patients. This risk-free environment enables them to make mistakes, learn from them, and gain confidence before performing procedures on real patients.
- **Hands-on experience**: Immersive technologies provide hands-on experience, enabling learners to interact with virtual patients, medical equipment, and surgical tools. This interactivity improves muscle memory and procedural skills, leading to better performance in real-world scenarios.
- **Customizable learning scenarios**: Educators can create customized VR/XR scenarios to cater to specific learning needs. Learners can choose the level of difficulty, practice repeatedly, and receive feedback, fostering a personalized learning experience.
- **Collaboration and teamwork**: AR and VR allow multiple learners to participate in the same simulation simultaneously, promoting collaboration and teamwork. This collaborative learning approach simulates real clinical environments where healthcare professionals work together to achieve better patient outcomes.
- **Remote training**: VR/AR makes medical training accessible remotely. Learners can access simulations from anywhere, breaking geographical barriers and making high-quality education available to a broader audience.
- **Continuous skill improvement**: Learners can track their progress and performance in immersive simulations, identifying areas for improvement. This continuous feedback loop supports ongoing skill development and competence enhancement.
- **Expanding learning opportunities**: VR/XR can simulate rare and complex medical cases that may not be readily available for traditional training. Learners

can experience a broader range of scenarios, preparing them for diverse medical challenges.

- **Ethical training**: AR/VR/XR allows learners to practice ethical decision-making in medical situations involving patient care, privacy, and consent. This training enhances their understanding of ethical principles and professionalism.

In conclusion, AR, VR, and XR have revolutionized medical education and training by offering realistic simulations, risk-free practice, and immersive learning experiences. As the technology continues to advance, VR/XR will play an increasingly critical role in shaping well-prepared and competent healthcare professionals, ultimately improving patient care and safety in the medical field.

Immersive technologies for some other areas of medical education

Let us explore some of the latest research in the field of VR/XR, focusing on its applications in anatomy and physiology education, surgical training, and emergency response training:

- **For anatomy and physiology education**: Recent research has demonstrated the effectiveness of AR, VR, and XR in enhancing anatomy and physiology education. VR applications allow students to explore detailed 3D models of the human body, organs, and systems. Learners can dissect and interact with virtual anatomical structures, gaining a deeper understanding of complex spatial relationships. VR/XR-based anatomy education provides a more engaging and immersive learning experience compared to traditional 2D textbooks or diagrams. Studies have shown that students exposed to VR/XR anatomy education exhibit improved retention, spatial reasoning, and overall comprehension of anatomical concepts.

- **For surgical training**: VR/XR has emerged as a powerful tool for surgical training, providing medical professionals with realistic and risk-free simulations of surgical procedures. Surgeons can practice complex surgeries in a virtual environment, refining their skills and techniques without endangering real patients. Recent research has shown that AR, VR, and XR-based surgical training leads to faster skill acquisition, increased confidence, and improved surgical outcomes. Additionally, these platforms are being developed for specialty-specific training, such as minimally invasive surgeries and robotic-assisted procedures. The integration of haptic feedback in AR/VR/XR further enhances the training experience by simulating tactile sensations during surgery.

- **For emergency response training**: In emergency response training, AR, VR, and XR are increasingly utilized to create realistic and high-stress scenarios. First responders and medical personnel can practice their critical decision-making skills and teamwork in simulated emergencies. VR/XR training offers a safe space to experience and manage high-pressure situations, such as mass casualty incidents, natural disasters, and terrorist attacks. Studies have shown that VR/XR-based emergency response training improves participants' ability to assess situations, make rapid decisions, and communicate effectively during crisis situations.

In conclusion, the latest research in VR/XR applications in anatomy and physiology education, surgical training, and emergency response training underscores the transformative potential of these technologies in medical and healthcare education. VR/XR offers unparalleled immersive experiences, enhancing learning outcomes, skill development, and preparedness of medical professionals. As the technology continues to evolve and become more accessible, its integration into medical education and training is expected to further revolutionize the way healthcare professionals are trained and equipped to provide quality patient care.

Patient education and engagement

VR and XR offer valuable tools to revolutionize patient education and engagement in healthcare. By immersing patients in interactive and personalized experiences, VR/XR enhances communication and understanding of medical conditions and treatment options. Patients can visualize complex anatomical structures and medical procedures in 3D virtual environments, leading to better comprehension and informed decision-making. Interactive learning experiences enable patients to actively engage with healthcare information, making the educational process more enjoyable and memorable. VR/XR can also help manage patient anxiety and pain by providing calming virtual environments during medical procedures. Additionally, remote patient education becomes possible with VR/XR, ensuring that patients in remote or underserved areas have access to high-quality healthcare information. Overall, VR/XR empowers patients, promotes better adherence to treatment plans, and fosters a collaborative patient-caregiver relationship, ultimately leading to improved patient outcomes and a more patient-centered healthcare experience.

Use of immersive technology in patient education

AR, VR, and XR technologies have the potential to revolutionize patient education and engagement in several ways:

- **Visual and immersive learning**: VR/XR enables patients to experience medical information in a visual and immersive manner. Instead of relying solely on abstract explanations, patients can interact with 3D models of their medical conditions, anatomy, and treatment procedures. This visual learning experience enhances understanding and retention of complex medical concepts.

- **Personalized education**: Healthcare professionals can create customized VR/XR content based on each patient's specific medical condition and needs. This personalized approach ensures that patients receive relevant and targeted information, increasing engagement and relevance.

- **Empowerment through decision-making**: VR/XR allows patients to explore different treatment options and their potential outcomes in virtual simulations. This empowers patients to make informed decisions about their healthcare, leading to increased involvement and satisfaction in the treatment process.
- **Anxiety and pain management**: VR/XR can help manage patient anxiety and pain during medical procedures. By immersing patients in calming and distraction-based virtual environments, VR/XR reduces stress and pain perception, enhancing overall patient comfort and experience.
- **Rehabilitation and physical therapy**: VR/XR can be used in rehabilitation and physical therapy to engage patients in interactive exercises and simulations. The gamified nature of VR/XR exercises motivates patients to actively participate in their therapy, leading to better adherence and improved rehabilitation outcomes.
- **Telehealth and remote education**: VR/XR technologies enable remote patient education, making healthcare accessible to patients in remote or underserved areas. Patients can receive personalized education and support through virtual telehealth sessions, eliminating the need for physical visits.
- **Continued learning and monitoring**: VR/XR can support ongoing patient education and monitoring after discharge from the hospital. Patients can access virtual resources and educational materials to continue learning about their conditions and self-management strategies.
- **Enhanced patient-provider communication**: VR/XR facilitates better communication between patients and healthcare providers. Through shared virtual experiences, patients and providers can discuss medical information more effectively, leading to improved patient understanding and compliance with treatment plans.

Overall, VR/XR technologies offer patient-centered and engaging solutions that promote better patient education, involvement, and empowerment in their healthcare journey. As these technologies continue to advance, they are expected to become integral components of patient education, fostering improved patient outcomes and a more positive healthcare experience.

Case studies

Here, we are going through the case studies about successful applications of VR/XR in Healthcare. For example, Osso VR and Medical Realities.

VR and XR technologies have gained traction in the healthcare industry, offering innovative solutions to enhance medical training, patient education, and surgical simulations. Two successful examples of VR/XR applications in healthcare are Osso VR and Medical Realities. In this case study, we will analyze the design principles that contributed to their success and examine the impact they have had on medical education and patient care.

Osso VR

Osso VR is a medical training platform that utilizes VR technology to improve surgical training and proficiency among healthcare professionals. It offers realistic simulations of surgical procedures, allowing surgeons to practice and refine their skills in a risk-free and immersive environment.

Design principles

The following are the design principles for Osso VR:

- **Realism and immersion**: Osso VR's success can be attributed to its realistic and immersive simulations. The platform uses high-fidelity 3D models, haptic feedback, and precise hand-tracking to replicate surgical scenarios accurately. The immersive experience enhances engagement, leading to improved skill acquisition and muscle memory among surgeons.
- **Task-specific training**: Osso VR focuses on task-specific training, allowing surgeons to practice specific steps and techniques of a surgical procedure. This targeted training approach ensures that surgeons can focus on areas that require improvement, leading to more efficient and effective training.
- **Objective performance assessment**: Osso VR provides objective performance assessment through data analytics and performance metrics. Surgeons receive real-time feedback on their performance, enabling them to track their progress and identify areas for improvement. This data-driven approach enhances the effectiveness of the training program.

Medical realities

Medical Realities is a VR-based medical education platform that focuses on providing immersive and interactive learning experiences for medical students and healthcare professionals. It offers a range of VR content, including surgical procedures, anatomy lessons, and patient case studies.

Design principles

The following are the design principles for medical realities:

- **Interactive learning**: Medical realities' success lies in its interactive learning experiences. Learners can actively engage with VR content, such as participating in virtual surgeries and dissecting 3D anatomical models. This interactive approach fosters a deeper understanding of medical concepts and enhances knowledge retention.
- **Telemedicine and remote learning**: Medical realities utilize VR to enable remote learning and telemedicine. Medical students and professionals can access

educational content from anywhere, breaking geographical barriers and making high-quality medical education accessible globally.

- **Patient empowerment and education**: Medical realities also focus on patient education by creating patient-specific VR content. This approach allows patients to understand their medical conditions better, treatment options, and the surgical procedures they may undergo. Informed patients are more engaged in their care and more likely to adhere to treatment plans.

Osso VR and medical realities are successful examples of how VR/XR technologies can revolutionize healthcare by enhancing medical training, patient education, and surgical simulations. Their design principles, including realism, interactivity, objective assessment, and patient empowerment, have contributed to their success in transforming medical education and patient care. As VR/XR technologies continue to evolve, their impact on healthcare is expected to grow, further improving patient outcomes and the skills of medical professionals.

Conclusion

In this chapter, we tried to take a closer look into the healthcare landscape of the VR/XR industry. VR and XR technologies are rapidly evolving, and their potential applications extend far beyond gaming and entertainment. We learned about the application of VR/XR in the healthcare industry, some of the major players, and the key trends. We then went through the *Diagnosis and treatment* section, and we learned how VR/XR can be used to simulate medical procedures, enabling doctors and nurses to practice and refine their skills in a safe and controlled environment. Then, in the Rehabilitation section, we learned about how VR/XR can be used to simulate medical procedures, enabling doctors and nurses to practice and refine their skills in a safe and controlled environment. Then, in the Rehabilitation and Physical Therapy section, we learned how an immersive environment can be used to create immersive rehabilitation and physical therapy, enabling patients to perform exercises in a fun and engaging way. Then, we found how medical education and training enable students and healthcare professionals to learn in a safe and controlled environment. Then, finally, we touched on patient education and engagement. We also went through the case studies of Osso VR and medical realities and analyzed the design principles that contributed to their success.

In the next chapter, we will explore the latest research on the applications of VR/XR in education.

Points to remember

- **Diagnosis and treatment**: VR/XR can be used to simulate medical procedures, enabling doctors and nurses to practice and refine their skills in a safe and controlled environment. We will explore some of the latest research in this field, including the use of VR/XR in surgical training, pain management, and mental health treatment.

- **Rehabilitation and physical therapy**: VR/XR can be used to create immersive environments for rehabilitation and physical therapy, enabling patients to perform exercises in a fun and engaging way. We learned the bigger significance of VR/XR for stroke rehabilitation, traumatic brain injury, and spinal cord injuries.
- **Medical education and training**: VR/XR can be used to create realistic simulations for medical education and training, enabling students and healthcare professionals to learn in a safe and controlled environment.
- **Patient education and engagement**: VR/XR can be used to educate patients and engage them in their healthcare, enabling them to better understand their conditions and treatments.

CHAPTER 8
Applications of AR, VR, and XR in Education

Introduction

Immersive technologies like **Augmented Reality (AR)**, **Virtual Reality (VR)**, and **Extended Reality (XR)** have enormous potential to revolutionize the education industry by creating immersive, interactive learning experiences that engage and motivate students. In this chapter, we will explore the latest research on the applications of AR/VR in education, discussing the challenges and opportunities they present for students, teachers, and educational institutions.

Structure

In this chapter, we will discuss the following topics:

- Introduction to AR, VR, and XR in education
- Immersive learning environments
- Simulations and training
- Personalized learning
- Collaborative learning
- Case studies

Objectives

At the end of this chapter, you will come to know about how the education industry is impacted by immersive technologies. This chapter provides a comprehensive overview of the role these technologies can play in the education industry. We will start with the current state of these technologies in this industry, and we will also explore the potential of AR, VR, and XR in enhancing learning outcomes and discuss some of the latest research and their efficacy in education.

You will learn how these technologies can be useful in creating immersive learning environments that engage and motivate students by transporting them to different places and times. You will learn about the role that *Simulation and training* can play in this industry. Then, you will dive deep into the *Personalized learning* experience, where you will see how immersive techs can be used to create an experience that adapts to the needs and preferences of individual learners. Then, you will learn some of the latest research in this field, including the use of AR, VR, and XR for adaptive learning, gamification, and personalized assessment.

Then, we will shift our gear and make you aware of *Collaborative learning*, and you will learn what research is taking place in that area. You will explore the usage of these technologies for team building, project-based learning, and group problem-solving.

Finally, we will go through *Case studies*, where we will examine some examples of successful applications of immersive technologies in education.

Introduction to AR, VR, and XR in education

AR, VR, and XR have opened up new frontiers in education, presenting an exciting way to engage and educate students. By immersing learners in lifelike and interactive virtual environments, AR, VR, and XR offer an unparalleled learning experience. Students can explore historical events, conduct scientific experiments, or even practice complex skills in safe and controlled settings. Technology fosters creativity, critical thinking, and collaboration, while its personalized approach caters to individual learning styles. Although challenges such as cost and content quality exist, the potential benefits of integrating these technologies into education are vast, promising to revolutionize the classroom and prepare students for the dynamic future ahead.

Current state of AR, VR, and XR in education and its evolution

Immersive technologies were already making significant strides in the education sector, and their evolution has likely continued since then. Here is an overview of the current state and potential evolution in education:

- **Current state:**
  - **Adoption and integration**: Many educational institutions have started to integrate VR/XR into their curriculum, particularly in fields like science, engineering, healthcare, and vocational training. Technology is being used to supplement traditional teaching methods and create more engaging and interactive learning experiences.
  - **Content development**: The availability of educational VR/XR content has grown steadily, with developers and educators creating a wide range of immersive experiences. For example, there are certain YouTube videos that portray an immersive view of Hawaii or, let us say, of the Himalayas. This produces such an immersive experience that it feels very real. These experiences cover various subjects, from historical events and biology lessons to language learning and soft skills training.
  - **Accessibility**: As VR/XR technology becomes more affordable and accessible, more schools and institutions have been able to adopt it. Furthermore, advancements in standalone VR headsets have reduced the need for expensive computer setups, making VR/XR more viable for educational use.
  - **Research and case studies**: There have been several studies and research papers exploring the effectiveness of VR/XR in education. Let us take an instance of the research published in the ITIF* portal (**https://itif.org**) suggests that VR/XR can enhance student learning outcomes, increase engagement, and improve retention rates compared to traditional methods.

    (*ITIF: International Technology and Innovation Foundation,

    Portal: **https://itif.org/publications/2021/08/30/promise-immersive-learning-augmented-and-virtual-reality-potential/**)
- **Evolution:**
  - **Improved hardware and technology**: VR/XR hardware will continue to advance, offering higher resolution displays, improved tracking systems, and more comfortable and lightweight headsets. Additionally, haptic feedback and other sensory enhancements may become more prevalent, further enhancing immersion.
  - **Expanded content library**: The library of educational VR/XR content will likely continue to grow, covering an even broader range of subjects and topics. This expansion will cater to diverse educational needs and preferences, ensuring there is something valuable for every discipline.
  - **Personalization and adaptive learning**: With advancements in AI and machine learning, VR/XR educational experiences may become more personalized. AI algorithms could analyze student behavior and progress to

adapt content and difficulty levels, optimizing the learning experience for each individual.

- **Collaborative learning**: Future VR/XR applications may enable seamless collaboration among students and teachers, allowing multiple users to interact in the same virtual environment simultaneously. This would foster teamwork and cooperative problem-solving.

- **Integration with emerging technologies**: VR/XR may be integrated with other emerging technologies, such as blockchain for credentialing and assessment or AR for more blended learning experiences, where digital information overlays the real world.

- **Continued research and validation**: As VR/XR becomes more prevalent in education, there will likely be more extensive research to measure its long-term impact on student learning, cognitive development, and skill acquisition. For example, research journals published by the Journal of Computer Assisted Learning and blog posts made at phys.org also support this fact. Hence, they are demonstrating that exposing VR/XR to juniors in K-12 can have a greater impact on their studies than introducing it late.

The evolution of VR/XR in education will depend on factors like technological advancements, content development, cost-effectiveness, and research-backed evidence of its educational benefits. As these technologies continue to mature, they have the potential to transform the education landscape and prepare students for the challenges of the future.

VR/XR impact on education's efficacy

Some of the benefits of VR/XR in education:

- **Enhanced learning experience**: VR/XR enables students to visualize complex concepts and abstract ideas in a more tangible and interactive manner, leading to better comprehension and retention.

- **Real-world simulations**: Students can engage in realistic simulations and experiences that would otherwise be challenging, costly, or unsafe in the real world. For example, exploring historical events, conducting science experiments, or practicing surgical procedures.

- **Personalized learning**: VR/XR allows educators to tailor content based on individual learning preferences and pace, creating a more personalized learning experience.

- **Engagement and motivation**: Immersive experiences captivate students' attention, leading to increased engagement and motivation to learn.

- **Empathy and cultural understanding**: VR/XR can transport students to different locations and time periods, fostering empathy and cultural understanding by experiencing life from different perspectives.
- **Collaboration and social learning**: VR/XR applications can facilitate collaborative learning, where students work together in the virtual environment, promoting teamwork and communication skills.

Immersive learning environment

VR/XR technology has the unique ability to create immersive learning environments that transcend the physical limitations of traditional classrooms. By transporting students to different places and times, educators can provide experiential and engaging learning opportunities that foster motivation and active participation. Here are some ways VR/XR can achieve this:

- **Historical immersion**: Students can virtually visit historical events, ancient civilizations, or important landmarks, allowing them to witness history firsthand and gain a deeper understanding of past events and cultures.
- **Science and exploration**: VR/XR can take students on virtual field trips to outer space, the deep sea, or remote ecosystems, offering a sense of exploration and discovery that traditional lectures cannot match.
- **Language and cultural exchange**: Language learners can practice their skills in real-life scenarios, interacting with virtual native speakers and experiencing different cultures through VR/XR language simulations.
- **Virtual laboratories**: In scientific disciplines, students can conduct experiments in virtual labs, providing a safe and cost-effective way to learn and practice without the risk of physical mishaps.
- **Role-playing and simulations**: VR/XR can facilitate role-playing scenarios, such as historical reenactments, medical simulations, or business management scenarios, enabling students to apply knowledge and skills in a practical setting.
- **Artistic and creative expression**: Students can use VR/XR to explore and create 3D art, architecture, or design, promoting creativity and spatial understanding.
- **Problem-solving and critical thinking**: Immersive learning environments present students with realistic challenges that require problem-solving and critical thinking skills, encouraging active learning and engagement.
- **Virtual mentorship**: VR/XR can enable students to learn from virtual mentors or experts, providing access to specialized knowledge and guidance beyond what is available in the traditional classroom.

By leveraging the power of VR/XR to create these immersive learning experiences, educators can foster a deeper connection between students and the subject matter, making education more enjoyable, memorable, and effective. As technology continues to advance and becomes more accessible, its potential impact on education is bound to grow, providing even more exciting opportunities for transformative learning experiences.

Simulations and training

VR and XR technologies have tremendous potential in education and training by providing realistic simulations and immersive experiences for students to practice and refine their skills in a safe and controlled environment. Here are some ways VR/XR can be utilized for educational purposes:

- **Skill-based training**: VR/XR can be employed to create simulations for various fields, such as medical training (surgery simulations), aviation (flight training), engineering (mechanical simulations), and more. Students can practice their skills in a realistic but risk-free environment, allowing them to make mistakes and learn from them without consequences.
- **Hazardous environments**: For professions that involve working in dangerous or hazardous environments, like firefighting or military training, VR/XR can provide a way for students to experience and learn how to respond to critical situations safely.
- **Historical and cultural exploration**: Students can explore historical events or different cultures by immersing themselves in virtual recreations of significant locations, periods, or events. This interactive approach enhances learning and engagement.
- **Language learning**: Language learners can benefit from immersive language simulations where they interact with native speakers and practice their language skills in real-world scenarios.
- **Soft skills development**: VR/XR can be used to facilitate training in interpersonal skills, leadership, public speaking, and more. Students can engage in realistic simulations that help them build confidence and competence in these areas.
- **Special education**: VR/XR can be tailored to cater to the needs of students with disabilities, providing a more inclusive learning experience.
- **Distance learning**: VR/XR can bridge the gap in distance learning by offering immersive virtual classrooms, making remote education more engaging and interactive.
- **Team collaboration**: VR/XR platforms enable students to collaborate and work together on projects in a virtual space, fostering teamwork and communication skills.

- **Science and exploration**: Students can explore distant planets, the deep ocean, or microscopic worlds through VR/XR, expanding their understanding of science and discovery.

As technology continues to advance and becomes more accessible, educators and institutions are increasingly incorporating VR/XR into their curricula to enhance the learning experience and prepare students for real-world challenges effectively. However, it is essential to continue researching and refining these technologies to optimize their educational benefits fully.

Personalized learning

In the education industry, VR/XR plays a pivotal role in advancing personalized learning experiences for students. By offering immersive and interactive simulations, students can engage with educational content in ways that cater to their individual needs and learning styles. VR/XR technology allows students to explore subjects at their own pace, delve into areas of interest, and receive immediate feedback on their progress. Additionally, these technologies can adapt to a student's skill level and adjust the complexity of content, accordingly, ensuring a challenging yet manageable learning journey. Personalized learning through VR/XR fosters greater student motivation and retention as learners become active participants in their education, leading to a deeper understanding and mastery of concepts. Furthermore, educators can analyze data generated by VR/XR platforms to gain insights into each student's strengths and weaknesses, enabling them to provide targeted support and interventions. As VR/XR technology continues to evolve, it holds significant promise in revolutionizing the education landscape by making learning more individualized, engaging, and effective.

Customized and personalized learning experience

VR/XR technologies offer a unique opportunity to create personalized learning experiences that cater to the specific needs and preferences of individual learners. By harnessing the immersive capabilities of VR/XR, educational content can be presented in diverse and interactive ways, allowing students to engage with the material at their own pace and according to their learning style.

Through adaptive algorithms and data analytics, VR/XR platforms can continuously assess a student's performance, understanding, and progress. This data-driven approach enables the system to dynamically adjust the content and difficulty level to match the student's abilities, ensuring an optimal level of challenge and avoiding unnecessary frustration or boredom.

Furthermore, VR/XR can provide students with choices and pathways to explore subjects based on their interests. Whether it is exploring historical eras, practicing language skills in virtual conversations, or diving into complex scientific simulations, learners can shape their educational journey and focus on areas that resonate with them the most.

By offering personalized learning experiences, VR/XR empowers students to take ownership of their education, leading to increased motivation, engagement, and, ultimately, better learning outcomes. Educators can also benefit from VR/XR data insights, gaining a deeper understanding of each student's learning progress and challenges, which in turn helps them provide targeted support and guidance.

Incorporating VR/XR into personalized learning not only enhances the learning process but also nurtures students' curiosity, creativity, and critical thinking skills. As technology evolves, it has the potential to transform education by making it more student-centered, adaptive, and effective.

VR/XR for adaptive learning, gamification, and assessment

VR/XR research in the education field has been continuously evolving and exploring various applications, including adaptive learning, gamification, and personalized assessments. Since then, there might have been additional advancements and research findings. Here are some key areas of research related to VR/XR in education:

- **Adaptive learning**: Adaptive learning in VR/XR involves using data-driven algorithms and artificial intelligence to tailor educational content to individual learners. **Machine learning (ML)** is also combined with VR/XR to develop more sophisticated adaptive systems that can monitor students' interactions in virtual environments, analyze their performance, and dynamically adjust the difficulty and content to match their progress and abilities. This personalized approach aims to optimize learning outcomes by providing a challenging yet supportive experience for each learner.

- **Gamification**: Gamification techniques, which involve incorporating game elements into educational experiences, are being explored in VR/XR to enhance engagement and motivation. Researchers are investigating how game mechanics, such as rewards, challenges, and interactive storytelling, can be integrated into virtual learning environments to make the educational process more enjoyable and effective.

- **Personalized assessments**: VR/XR is being leveraged to create innovative assessment methods that adapt to each student's unique learning journey. This includes using immersive simulations to assess practical skills, creating scenario-based assessments, and utilizing eye-tracking and motion-capture technologies to gain deeper insights into student responses and behaviors during assessments. These personalized assessment approaches aim to provide a more comprehensive and accurate understanding of a student's capabilities beyond traditional testing methods.

- **Embodied learning**: Embodied learning research explores how VR/XR can enhance learning by engaging the body and spatial cognition. Studies have looked into the impact of immersive experiences on memory retention, understanding complex concepts, and fostering deeper connections with the subject matter.
- **Inclusivity and accessibility**: Researchers are investigating ways to make VR/XR educational experiences more accessible to diverse learners, including students with disabilities. This includes designing interfaces and interactions that accommodate different learning needs and providing alternative modalities for content consumption.
- **Learning analytics**: The use of learning analytics in VR/XR education is gaining attention. Researchers are examining how data collected from student interactions within virtual environments can be analyzed to gain insights into their learning patterns, preferences, and challenges. These analytics can inform educators and designers about the effectiveness of VR/XR experiences and guide continuous improvement.

It is important to note that the field of VR/XR research in education is continuously evolving, and new studies and findings may have emerged beyond my last update. For the latest research, we recommend checking academic journals, conference proceedings, and reports from reputable educational technology organizations and research institutions.

Collaborative learning

The impact of VR/XR in collaborative learning has been transformative, revolutionizing the way students interact and engage in educational settings. By creating immersive virtual environments, VR/XR fosters a profound sense of presence, enabling students to collaborate as if they were physically together. This heightened sense of immersion enhances engagement, motivation, and participation in collaborative activities. Learners can engage in group projects, discussions, and problem-solving tasks, benefitting from diverse perspectives and collective problem-solving. VR/XR's ability to transcend geographical boundaries allows students from different locations to collaborate seamlessly, promoting cross-cultural understanding and global collaboration. Moreover, this technology facilitates experiential learning, where students can collectively explore complex scenarios and simulations, leading to a deeper understanding of the subject matter. Through real-time feedback and interactions, VR/XR empowers students to refine their communication and teamwork skills, preparing them for success in a collaborative and interconnected world. The inclusivity and accessibility offered by VR/XR ensure that all students can participate on an equal footing, promoting a supportive and inclusive collaborative learning environment. Overall, VR/XR's impact on collaborative learning transcends traditional boundaries, fostering dynamic, engaging, and effective educational experiences.

Benefits of collaborative learning using VR/XR

VR/XR offers a powerful platform to create collaborative learning experiences that bring students together in a shared virtual space. By leveraging the immersive capabilities of VR/XR, students can engage in teamwork, discussions, and problem-solving activities as if they were physically present in the same room. Here are some ways VR/XR enables collaborative learning experiences:

- **Virtual classrooms**: VR/XR can simulate traditional classroom settings, allowing students and teachers to interact, share content, and conduct lectures virtually. This fosters an engaging and interactive learning environment that encourages participation and collaboration among students.
- **Group projects**: Students can collaborate on group projects within a virtual space, sharing ideas, assigning tasks, and working together to achieve shared goals. VR/XR's immersive nature makes the collaboration more compelling and facilitates seamless communication among team members.
- **Problem-solving simulations**: VR/XR can create realistic scenarios where students must collaborate to solve complex problems. This interactive approach to problem-solving encourages critical thinking, creativity, and teamwork.
- **Distance collaboration**: VR/XR enables students from different locations to collaborate effectively, overcoming geographical barriers. This opens up opportunities for cross-cultural collaboration and diverse perspectives.
- **Role-playing and interactive storytelling**: Collaborative VR/XR experiences can involve role-playing and interactive storytelling, where students work together to navigate through scenarios and make decisions that impact the outcome of the story. This cultivates empathy and encourages collective decision-making.
- **Scientific and engineering simulations**: In fields like science and engineering, students can work collaboratively on virtual experiments and simulations. This hands-on approach allows them to explore concepts in a safe and controlled environment.
- **Collaborative feedback and reflection**: VR/XR platforms can facilitate collaborative feedback sessions, where students can review and discuss each other's work, providing constructive criticism and reflections on their learning journey.

By enabling collaborative learning experiences, VR/XR not only enhances student engagement and motivation but also nurtures essential 21st-century skills such as communication, teamwork, problem-solving, and adaptability. As technology continues to evolve, the potential for VR/XR in collaborative education grows, offering exciting possibilities for immersive and effective learning experiences.

Utilizing VR/XR for team building and project learning

However, we can provide an overview of some of the general trends and directions in the use of VR/XR for team building, project-based learning, and group problem-solving based on information available up to that point:

- **Team building**: Research in the education domain has explored how VR/XR can be used to foster team building and collaboration among students. Virtual team-building activities and simulations have been designed to promote trust, communication, and cooperation within groups. VR/XR's immersive nature allows students to feel more connected and engaged during team-building exercises, leading to improved interpersonal relationships and better group dynamics.

- **Project-based learning**: VR/XR has been integrated into **Project-Based Learning (PBL)** pedagogies to enhance student learning experiences. By creating interactive and realistic virtual environments, students can work collaboratively on complex projects and solve real-world problems. PBL in VR/XR empowers students to apply theoretical knowledge to practical situations, encouraging critical thinking, creativity, and teamwork.

- **Group problem-solving**: The use of VR/XR in group problem-solving activities has been studied to understand its impact on student engagement and problem-solving skills. Virtual simulations and scenarios challenge students to collaborate, communicate effectively, and find solutions together. This trend is very similar to earlier team building/project-based learning.

- **Immersive learning environments**: The benefits of immersive learning environments created by VR/XR technologies. Immersive experiences can increase student motivation and interest in collaborative learning tasks. VR/XR's ability to create realistic and interactive settings can make learning more engaging and impactful.

- **Inclusivity and accessibility**: Studies have shown how VR/XR can address inclusivity and accessibility in collaborative learning. By providing customizable interfaces and accommodating different learning needs, VR/XR can make collaborative experiences more accessible to diverse learners, including those with disabilities.

- **Teacher training and professional development**: VR/XR has also been studied as a tool for teacher training and professional development in collaborative learning approaches. Educators can use VR/XR to practice facilitating group activities, receive feedback, and refine their instructional strategies.

It is important to note that the field of VR/XR in education is continuously evolving, and there may have been significant advancements in research beyond our last update.

To explore the latest developments, we recommend looking into academic journals, conference proceedings, and publications from reputable research institutions and educational technology organizations that focus on VR/XR applications in collaborative learning.

Case studies

VictoryXR is an educational VR company that focuses on creating immersive learning experiences for students. They offer a wide range of virtual reality content, including interactive science, math, history, and language lessons. One successful application of VictoryXR is in the field of science education, where they have created detailed and realistic virtual laboratories and simulations. These VR experiences allow students to perform experiments and explore scientific concepts in a safe and engaging environment.

Design principles contributing to success:

- **Immersive content**: VictoryXR's success is attributed to its focus on creating highly immersive and interactive content. By leveraging the full potential of VR, they offer realistic and engaging learning experiences beyond traditional classroom settings.
- **Curriculum alignment**: The company ensures its VR content aligns with educational standards and curriculum requirements. This approach makes their virtual experiences valuable supplements to classroom learning and ensures relevance to academic goals.
- **Engaging and safe experiences**: VictoryXR prioritizes student engagement and safety in their VR experiences. They design content encouraging active participation, critical thinking, and problem-solving while maintaining a secure and age-appropriate environment.

Refer to the following figure:

***Figure 8.1**: Illustration of VictoryXR virtual class of human organs*

The success of educational VR experiences, such as those designed by VictoryXR, often hinges on the effective implementation of design principles that enhance learning outcomes and user engagement. Here are some design principles that may contribute to the success of VictoryXR's educational VR:

- **Learning-centered design**: VictoryXR likely prioritizes designing VR experiences with a focus on educational goals and outcomes. The content should align with learning objectives and support the curriculum.
- **Engagement and motivation**: Designing immersive and interactive experiences helps capture learners' attention and motivation. VictoryXR may employ gamification elements or scenarios that inherently motivate users to explore and learn.
- **User Experience (UX) and interface design**: A user-friendly interface is crucial for success. VictoryXR may emphasize intuitive controls, easy navigation, and a seamless overall user experience to ensure learners can concentrate on the educational content.
- **Interactivity and hands-on learning**: By incorporating interactive elements and hands-on learning experiences, VictoryXR can simulate real-world scenarios, providing learners with practical skills and reinforcing theoretical concepts.
- **Adaptive learning paths**: VictoryXR's success may be attributed to the incorporation of adaptive learning paths. VR experiences may adapt to individual learner progress, providing tailored content to address specific needs and pacing.
- **Realism and immersion**: Creating realistic and immersive environments enhances the effectiveness of the learning experience. VictoryXR may utilize VR technology to simulate scenarios that are difficult or impossible to replicate in traditional classrooms.
- **Feedback and assessment**: Timely and constructive feedback is critical for learning. VictoryXR likely integrates feedback mechanisms within the VR experiences, helping learners understand their performance and providing guidance for improvement.
- **Collaborative learning**: Encouraging collaboration and social interaction within VR environments promotes a sense of community and shared learning. VictoryXR may design experiences that allow users to collaborate on tasks or projects.
- **Inclusivity and accessibility**: Success may be attributed to designing VR experiences that are accessible to a diverse range of learners. VictoryXR might consider factors such as accessibility features, language options, and compatibility with different devices.
- **Analytics and continuous improvement**: The incorporation of data analytics enables VictoryXR to track user interactions and performance. This data can be used

to assess the effectiveness of the VR experiences, identify areas for improvement, and refine future content.

- **Curriculum integration**: Aligning VR content with educational curricula contributes to success. VictoryXR's design principles likely involve ensuring that the VR experiences complement and enhance traditional learning objectives.
- **Scalability and flexibility**: Designing VR experiences that can scale across different educational settings and adapt to evolving technologies ensures long-term success. VictoryXR may prioritize flexibility in content delivery and compatibility with various VR platforms.

These design principles collectively contribute to the success of educational VR experiences by creating engaging, effective, and inclusive learning environments. Keep in mind that the specific strategies employed by VictoryXR may evolve, and checking their latest documentation or updates would provide the most accurate information.

It is important to note that the success of these applications is not solely based on the technology but also on their pedagogical approach, content quality, ease of use, and alignment with educational objectives. Additionally, since the education technology landscape is continuously evolving, we recommend checking the latest updates and reviews to see how VictoryXR and Nearpod VR have continued to evolve and innovate in the educational VR/XR.

Conclusion

In this chapter, we tried to look at how VR and XR technologies are rapidly evolving, and their potential applications extend far beyond gaming and entertainment. These technologies have emerged as transformative tools in the education industry, offering unparalleled opportunities to revolutionize the learning experience. From immersive simulations and personalized learning to collaborative environments and experiential training, VR/XR's impact on education is vast and promising.

The application of VR/XR in education has redefined the way students engage with content, fostering deeper understanding and knowledge retention. By transporting learners to virtual worlds and creating interactive scenarios, VR/XR provides experiential learning opportunities that bridge the gap between theory and practice. Collaborative learning takes on a new dimension with VR/XR, breaking geographical barriers and encouraging students to collaborate, problem-solve, and communicate effectively in shared virtual spaces.

The integration of VR/XR in teacher professional development further enhances instructional strategies and empowers educators to create engaging and immersive learning environments. By leveraging data-driven insights, teachers can tailor instruction to meet the unique needs of each student.

While the potential of VR/XR in education is evident, successful implementation relies on careful consideration of content design, pedagogical approaches, and accessibility. Additionally, ongoing research and innovation are crucial to refine and expand VR/XR applications to address evolving educational needs and challenges.

As the education industry embraces technology's transformative power, VR/XR promises to revolutionize education, empowering learners and educators alike to embrace new horizons in knowledge acquisition and skills development.

In the next chapter, we will learn how VR/XR/AR has the potential to transform our lives in many positive ways, but they also raise a range of ethical concerns that must be addressed.

Points to remember

- **Immersive learning experiences**: VR/XR technologies offer immersive and interactive learning experiences beyond traditional classroom settings. Students can engage with educational content in realistic virtual environments, enhancing their understanding and retention of complex subjects.
- **Personalized learning**: VR/XR allows personalized learning experiences tailored to individual students' needs and learning styles. Adaptive algorithms can adjust the content and difficulty level based on each student's progress, ensuring optimal challenges and support.
- **Experiential learning**: VR/XR facilitates experiential learning by providing hands-on and practical experiences. Students can explore historical events, conduct virtual experiments, or visit distant locations, enriching their learning with real-world applications.
- **Collaborative learning**: VR/XR fosters collaboration and teamwork among students. Learners can work together in shared virtual spaces, engaging in group projects, discussions, and problem-solving activities, regardless of geographical location.
- **Inclusivity and accessibility**: VR/XR promotes inclusivity by accommodating diverse learning needs. Customizable interfaces and features cater to students with disabilities, ensuring equal access to educational opportunities.
- **Engagement and motivation**: The immersive nature of VR/XR captivates students' attention and enhances their motivation to learn. Interactive elements and gamification techniques make learning enjoyable and rewarding.
- **Training and skill development**: VR/XR is used for skill-based training in various fields, such as medical procedures, technical skills, and hazardous environments. Students can practice and refine their skills in safe and controlled virtual settings.

- **Cross-disciplinary learning**: VR/XR supports cross-disciplinary learning, allowing students to explore connections between different subjects and fostering a holistic understanding of complex concepts.
- **Teacher professional development**: VR/XR is utilized for teacher training and professional development, providing educators with new instructional methods and strategies to enhance their teaching practices.
- **Future-ready skills**: Integrating VR/XR in education equips students with 21st-century skills, including critical thinking, problem-solving, communication, and adaptability, preparing them for future challenges.
- **Evolution of VR/XR integration in education**: VR/XR in education is continually evolving, and successful implementation relies on thoughtful integration, appropriate content design, and a student-centered approach to enhance the learning journey.

CHAPTER 9
Ethics in Immersive Technologies

Introduction

Immersive technologies like **Virtual reality** (**VR**) and **Augmented Reality** (**AR**) or **Extended Reality** (**XR**) have the potential to transform our lives in many positive ways, but they also raise a range of ethical concerns that must be addressed. In this chapter, we will examine the ethical considerations surrounding these technologies, including issues related to privacy, safety, and social impact. We will explore the challenges and opportunities presented by these technologies and consider how they can be developed and deployed to benefit society as a whole.

Structure

In this chapter, we will discuss the following topics:

- Introduction to ethics in immersive technologies
- Privacy and data protection
- Safety and physical health
- Psychological and emotional impact
- Case studies

Objectives

At the end of this chapter, you will learn about the ethical challenges immersive technologies pose. We will discuss the importance of ethical considerations in the development and deployment of these technologies. Then, you will understand the role of *Privacy and data protection* in the vast amount of personal data. We will examine the legal and ethical frameworks that govern data collection and use and discuss best practices for protecting user privacy and ensuring data security.

Then, you will learn about users' physical health and safety, such as motion sickness or eyestrains that can happen due to wearing the head mounts or VR/AR/XR hardware.

We will shift our gear, and you will take a deep dive into the *Psychological and emotional impact* on users and concerns about addiction, desensitization, and manipulation.

Finally, we will go through *Case studies*, where we will examine some examples of ethical challenges in the development and deployment of VR and XR technologies and analyze the design principles that contributed to their success or failure.

Introduction to ethics in immersive technologies

Ethics in Immersive technologies like AR, VR, or XR is a pressing concern as these immersive technologies gain widespread adoption. VR and XR offer transformative experiences in entertainment, education, and various industries, but they also bring forth ethical challenges. Privacy and data security issues arise due to the vast amounts of user data collected, demanding transparent practices and secure handling. Psychological impacts, potential addiction, and virtual harassment necessitate responsible content creation and user support. Ensuring representation, inclusivity, and accessibility is imperative for equitable user experiences. Moreover, differentiating between virtual and real-world contexts and addressing the ownership of virtual property adds further complexity. As VR and XR continue to evolve, anticipating and addressing unforeseen ethical consequences becomes essential to shaping a virtuous and sustainable digital landscape.

Overview of the ethical challenges posed by VR and AR

VR and AR technologies have revolutionized the way we perceive and interact with the digital world, blurring the boundaries between the virtual and physical realms. While these immersive technologies offer exciting opportunities, they also present a range of ethical challenges that need careful consideration. Here are some key ethical concerns:

- **Privacy and data security**: VR and AR applications often collect extensive user data to provide personalized experiences. This data includes behavioral patterns, preferences, and even biometric information. Ensuring user privacy, obtaining informed consent, and safeguarding sensitive data from potential breaches or misuse is crucial.

- **Psychological impact**: The immersive nature of VR and AR experiences can have profound psychological effects on users. Content that involves violence, trauma, or explicit material may lead to emotional distress or even trigger post-traumatic reactions. Ethical considerations arise around responsibly managing content to minimize potential harm.
- **Addiction and dependency**: VR and AR technologies can be highly immersive and addictive, especially in gaming or social experiences. Ethical concerns include promoting responsible usage, providing support for individuals struggling with addiction, and avoiding exploitative practices.
- **Virtual harassment and bullying**: Virtual environments may not be physically real, but the emotional impact of harassment and bullying experienced in VR or AR can be significant. Developers must implement measures to prevent and address virtual harassment, creating safe reporting systems and fostering respectful communities.
- **Representation and inclusivity**: VR and AR content creators must be mindful of representation and inclusivity. Ensuring diverse and inclusive content can lead to positive experiences for all users and avoid perpetuating stereotypes or biases.
- **Accessibility**: Making VR and AR experiences accessible to users with disabilities is an ethical responsibility. Developers should consider providing alternative ways of interaction and design experiences that are inclusive and cater to different needs.
- **Reality versus illusion**: As VR and XR experiences become increasingly realistic, users may struggle to differentiate between virtual and real-world contexts. Ethical concerns involve clearly delineating between the two to prevent confusion and potential negative consequences.
- **Virtual property and ownership**: In virtual worlds, users can create, buy, and sell virtual property and goods. Ethical issues arise concerning the ownership and control of virtual assets, as well as the potential for fraud or exploitation.
- **Impact on social interaction**: Immersive technologies can reshape social interactions, potentially leading to isolation and detachment from the physical world. Ethical considerations include promoting responsible usage to maintain healthy social relationships.
- **Unforeseen consequences**: As Immersive technologies continue to advance, there may be unforeseen ethical implications that emerge over time. Ethical frameworks must remain flexible and adaptable to address emerging challenges.

Addressing these ethical challenges in VR and AR technologies is essential for ensuring responsible and beneficial use, promoting positive user experiences, and fostering a technology-driven future that upholds ethical principles and values.

Importance of ethical consideration in VR and AR

The importance of ethical considerations in the development and deployment of VR and AR technologies cannot be overstated. As these immersive technologies become more prevalent in various aspects of our lives, it is crucial to prioritize ethical principles to guide their responsible and beneficial use.

Ethical considerations play a pivotal role in the realm of Immersive Technologies, influencing their development, deployment, and societal impact. First and foremost, ethical guidelines are essential for building and maintaining user trust. Users are more likely to embrace immersive technologies when they feel confident that their well-being and privacy are prioritized.

Additionally, ethical frameworks help mitigate potential harms associated with these technologies, ranging from psychological effects to physical risks. In a landscape where extensive data collection is commonplace, ethical practices ensure the protection of user privacy, guiding responsible data handling and usage.

Inclusivity and diversity are promoted through ethical considerations, steering developers away from biased or discriminatory content and fostering a more inclusive digital environment. Transparency and informed consent are critical components, empowering users to make informed decisions about their engagement with immersive experiences.

Furthermore, ethical guidelines address the social and cultural impact of immersive technologies, aiming to prevent the propagation of harmful ideologies and ensure a positive influence on societal values.

Ultimately, ethical considerations contribute to the long-term sustainability of immersive technologies by enhancing public perception, reducing regulatory risks, and steering the responsible evolution of these transformative tools.

In conclusion, ethical considerations are integral to the responsible and sustainable development and deployment of VR and AR technologies. By incorporating ethical principles into the design, content creation, and usage policies, we can harness the potential of these immersive technologies for the benefit of individuals and society as a whole while safeguarding against potential harm and negative consequences.

Privacy and data protection

Privacy and data protection play a critical role in the responsible development and use of VR and AR technologies. As these immersive experiences collect extensive user data, including personal preferences, biometric information, and behavioral patterns, safeguarding user privacy is paramount. Ethical and legal obligations require VR and AR developers to implement robust data protection measures, such as obtaining informed consent for data collection, ensuring secure storage and transmission of data, and providing clear and transparent privacy policies. By prioritizing privacy, developers can establish trust with users, mitigating concerns about data misuse or breaches. Additionally, adhering to stringent data protection standards fosters a more ethical and sustainable VR and AR ecosystem, promoting the safe and responsible integration of these technologies into various aspects of our lives.

Privacy of personal data and safeguard

Indeed, VR and AR technologies have the capability to gather a significant amount of personal data about users. The immersive nature of these experiences allows for the collection of data on user movements, interactions, preferences, biometric information, and even emotional responses. While this data can enhance the user experience and enable personalized content, it raises legitimate concerns about privacy and data protection.

One of the main concerns is the potential for unauthorized access or misuse of this sensitive data. As VR and AR applications often connect to the internet or cloud services, there is a risk of data breaches, leading to the exposure of personal information to malicious actors. Additionally, the sharing of user data with third parties, such as advertisers or data brokers, without explicit consent can result in user profiling and invasion of privacy.

To address these concerns, developers and companies in the VR and AR industry must prioritize privacy and data protection. Implementing strong data encryption and security measures, obtaining clear and informed consent for data collection, and providing users with transparent privacy policies are essential steps to safeguard user information. Furthermore, adhering to relevant privacy laws and regulations, such as the **General Data Protection Regulation** (**GDPR**) in Europe, can help ensure compliance and accountability.

As VR and AR technologies continue to evolve and become more integrated into our daily lives, it is crucial for all stakeholders to be vigilant in protecting user privacy. By proactively addressing privacy and data protection concerns, the industry can build trust with users and promote the responsible and ethical use of these immersive technologies.

Legal and ethical framework that governs data collection

Let us discuss legal and ethical frameworks one by one:

- **Legal frameworks**
    - **GDPR**: The GDPR is a comprehensive data protection regulation in the **European Union** (**EU**) that sets strict rules for the collection, processing, and storage of personal data. It gives individuals greater control over

their data and requires explicit consent for data collection, as well as the provision of transparent privacy policies.

  - **California Consumer Privacy Act (CCPA)**: The CCPA is a privacy law in California that grants California residents certain rights regarding the collection and sale of their personal information. It requires businesses to inform consumers about the types of data collected and gives individuals the right to opt out of data sharing with third parties.

  - **Personal Information Protection and Electronic Documents Act (PIPEDA)**: PIPEDA is a Canadian law that governs the collection, use, and disclosure of personal information by private sector organizations. It establishes rules for obtaining consent and ensuring data security.

- **Ethical frameworks**

  - **Privacy by design**: It is an ethical approach that emphasizes integrating privacy measures into the design of VR and AR technologies from the outset. This ensures that privacy considerations are embedded in the development process rather than added as an afterthought.

  - **Informed consent**: Respecting user autonomy and providing clear, concise, and understandable information about data collection practices fosters ethical data usage. Users should have the option to give informed consent to data collection, knowing the purpose and scope of data processing.

  - **Data minimization**: Ethical data collection involves collecting only the necessary data for the intended purpose. Minimizing data collection helps reduce the risk of data breaches and potential misuse.

Let us discuss best practices for protecting user privacy and data security:

- **Anonymization and pseudonymization**: Employ techniques like anonymization and pseudonymization to protect user identities and ensure that data cannot be linked back to specific individuals.

- **Secure data storage**: Use robust encryption and secure storage methods to protect user data from unauthorized access or breaches.

- **Regular security audits**: Conduct regular security audits and risk assessments to identify vulnerabilities and address potential data security issues promptly.

- **Data access controls**: Implement strict access controls to limit data access to authorized personnel only.

- **Data retention policies**: Establish clear data retention policies to retain user data only for as long as necessary and delete it when no longer needed.

- **Transparent privacy policies**: Provide users with transparent and easily accessible privacy policies that clearly state the purpose and scope of data collection and usage.
- **Regular training and awareness**: Educate employees and stakeholders about privacy and data security best practices to foster a culture of data protection within the organization.

By adhering to both legal regulations and ethical principles, VR and AR developers can ensure that user privacy is protected, data is handled responsibly, and trust in these technologies is upheld. Balancing the benefits of data-driven experiences with user privacy rights is key to creating a sustainable and ethical future for Immersive technologies.

Safety and physical health

Safety and physical health considerations are of utmost importance in the development and use of AR, VR, or XR technologies. The immersive nature of these experiences can lead to potential risks and challenges that need careful attention. VR, in particular, may cause motion sickness and discomfort due to discrepancies between the virtual and physical movements. Therefore, developers must focus on minimizing motion sickness through optimized tracking, low-latency rendering, and smooth locomotion techniques.

Additionally, ensuring a safe physical environment is crucial as users may be immersed in the virtual world and unaware of their surroundings, leading to collisions or accidents.

Implementing boundary systems and warning mechanisms can help users navigate the real world while engaged in VR or AR experiences.

By adhering to safety standards, conducting thorough user testing, and continuously improving hardware and software, the industry can create more user-friendly and physically safe VR and AR environments.

Physical effect on users due to VR and AR technologies

VR and AR technologies can indeed have physical effects on users, and certain safety risks need to be considered. Here are some key factors to be aware of:

- **Motion sickness**: VR experiences can lead to motion sickness or discomfort, commonly referred to as cybersickness. This occurs when there is a discrepancy between the motion perceived by the user in the virtual environment and their physical motion. Developers need to optimize VR experiences to minimize motion sickness by reducing latency, improving frame rates, and using smooth locomotion techniques.

- **Eyestrain and fatigue**: Extended use of VR and AR devices can cause eyestrain and visual fatigue due to the proximity of screens to the eyes and the prolonged focus on virtual content. Proper design choices, such as adjustable **Interpupillary Distance (IPD)** settings and incorporating breaks during extended use, can help alleviate these issues.
- **Physical hazards**: Users immersed in VR may become less aware of their physical surroundings, leading to potential collisions with objects or people. This is especially concerning in open or crowded spaces. Implementing clear boundaries and warning systems within VR experiences can help users navigate their physical environment more safely.
- **Tripping and falls**: Users engaged in VR or AR experiences might walk or move around in the real world while their attention is focused on the virtual environment. This can lead to tripping or falling hazards, especially if the physical space is cluttered or hazardous. Ensuring that users have sufficient room to move safely and providing guidance for safe usage can mitigate these risks.
- **Simulator sickness**: In AR experiences, where virtual objects are overlaid in the real world, users might experience simulator sickness due to conflicts between the virtual and real environments. Addressing issues like lag, inaccurate tracking, or poorly integrated virtual elements can reduce the occurrence of this type of discomfort.

To ensure user safety, educating users about potential risks and best practices for safe usage should contribute to a more responsible and secure adoption of VR and AR technologies.

Measures are taken to ensure user safety

Ensuring user safety in VR and AR experiences involves implementing various measures, including ergonomic design and the appropriate use of warning labels. Here are some key steps:

- **Ergonomic design**: Design VR and AR hardware with ergonomics in mind to minimize physical discomfort and fatigue. This includes creating comfortable headsets with adjustable straps, weight distribution, and breathable materials to reduce pressure on the face and head.
- **Eye comfort**: Consider the comfort of users' eyes using high-quality displays with adjustable IPD settings to match the user's inter-pupillary distance. Employ anti-glare coatings and flicker-free screens to reduce eyestrain and fatigue.
- **Motion sickness mitigation**: Implement design strategies that reduce the likelihood of motion sickness. This includes maintaining consistent frame rates, minimizing latency, and avoiding sudden camera movements or jarring transitions.

- **Clear boundaries**: In VR experiences, provide users with visual and auditory cues to establish clear boundaries within the virtual environment. This helps users stay aware of their surroundings and reduces the risk of colliding with objects or people.
- **Warning labels**: Use warning labels or notifications to alert users about potential risks, such as motion sickness, eye strain, and the need for breaks during extended usage. Communicate any safety guidelines or precautions to users before they begin their VR or AR experiences.
- **Age restrictions**: Consider age-appropriate content and apply age restrictions to experiences that may not be suitable for young children. Provide parental controls and ensure that content is labeled accordingly.
- **Educate users**: Offer guidance and instructions on the safe use of VR and AR devices. Provide users with information on how to adjust the headset properly, take breaks, and be mindful of their surroundings.
- **Physical environment checks**: Encourage users to create a safe physical environment for VR usage by removing tripping hazards and ensuring sufficient space for movement.

By integrating these safety measures into the design and the usage of VR and AR technologies, developers can enhance user safety and create more enjoyable and comfortable experiences.

Psychological and emotional impact

The integration of Immersive technologies and hardware has brought transformative experiences across various domains, but it has also raised concerns about potential psychological and emotional impacts.

The immersive nature of VR, AR, or XR can evoke intense emotions and create a powerful sense of presence, blurring the lines between reality and the virtual world. While this can lead to heightened engagement and therapeutic applications, it also carries the risk of causing disorientation, motion sickness, and even a detachment from actual reality. Prolonged exposure to VR/XR environments might result in altered perceptions, impacting users' mental well-being and contributing to issues such as simulation sickness, VR addiction, and exacerbation of existing psychological conditions.

As these technologies continue to evolve, a comprehensive understanding of their psychological implications is crucial to harness their benefits while mitigating potential harm.

Psychological and emotional impact due to immersive technology

We are trying to highlight important points regarding the potential psychological and emotional impact caused by AR, VR, or XR technologies. The immersive and interactive nature of immersive technology experiences can indeed lead to a range of psychological effects:

- **Addiction**: The captivating nature of VR and AR can potentially lead to excessive usage, resulting in behavioral addiction. Users may become so engrossed in these alternate realities that they struggle to disengage, leading to neglect of real-world responsibilities and relationships.
- **Desensitization**: Exposure to intense or repetitive VR/AR experiences, particularly those involving violent or distressing content, could lead to desensitization. Users might become less sensitive to real-life emotional cues and situations, impacting their empathy and emotional responses.
- **Manipulation**: The immersive qualities of VR and AR can make users more susceptible to persuasion and manipulation. Advertisers or creators may exploit this vulnerability, potentially leading to changes in users' behaviors, beliefs, or perceptions without their conscious awareness.

To ensure the responsible and ethical adoption of these technologies, it is crucial to address these concerns through guidelines, regulations, and user education. Additionally, ongoing research into the psychological effects of VR and AR will help us better understand their impact and implement appropriate safeguards.

Potential risks of AR, VR, and XR technologies

Let us discuss the risks of AR, VR, and XR technologies:

- **Health concerns**: Prolonged VR usage can lead to issues like motion sickness, eye strain, and headaches due to the sensory disconnect between visual and physical movement. Additionally, VR may trigger seizures in individuals with photosensitive epilepsy.
- **Psychological impact**: As discussed earlier, VR/AR can have psychological effects like addiction, desensitization, and manipulation, particularly when not used responsibly.
- **Social isolation**: Excessive immersion in virtual environments can potentially lead to isolation from the real world, impacting real-life relationships and social interactions.

- **Privacy concerns**: AR technologies that gather real-time data from users' surroundings can raise concerns about privacy breaches, as well as the potential for unauthorized surveillance.
- **Ethical dilemmas**: The line between reality and virtuality can become blurred, raising ethical questions about how VR/AR content is created, shared, and consumed. Misuse, misinformation, and manipulation can be especially problematic.
- **Physical safety**: VR/AR users can become disoriented or unaware of their surroundings, leading to accidents and injuries. This is especially relevant when using these technologies when users are walking, moving, or operating machinery.

Balancing these benefits and risks requires careful consideration, research, and regulation. As VR/AR technologies evolve, it is crucial to prioritize user safety, ethical practices, and the responsible development of these immersive experiences.

VR, AR, or XR and their impact to promote well-being and mental health

VR and AR have shown significant potential to positively impact well-being and mental health in various ways:

- **Exposure therapy**: VR can create controlled and safe environments for exposure therapy, helping individuals confront and overcome phobias, anxiety disorders, and PTSD. It allows therapists to gradually expose patients to triggering stimuli while monitoring and guiding their reactions.
- **Stress reduction**: VR experiences designed to promote relaxation and stress reduction can transport users to tranquil environments, offering an escape from the pressures of daily life. Mindfulness apps and serene landscapes can help individuals manage stress and anxiety.
- **Pain management**: VR has been employed as a distraction technique to alleviate pain during procedures or treatments in medical settings. Engaging patients' senses with immersive experiences can reduce their perception of pain.
- **Cognitive rehabilitation**: VR/AR can aid in cognitive rehabilitation for individuals recovering from brain injuries or cognitive impairments. Customized tasks and exercises in virtual environments can help improve cognitive function.
- **Social interaction**: VR can counter social isolation by enabling users to interact with others in virtual spaces, making it particularly beneficial for individuals with limited mobility or who face barriers to socializing.

- **Empathy building**: VR experiences that place users in the shoes of others, allowing them to experience different perspectives, can foster empathy and understanding, ultimately contributing to improved interpersonal relationships.
- **Mindfulness and meditation**: AR applications can guide users through meditation and mindfulness exercises by overlaying soothing visuals and auditory cues onto their physical surroundings.
- **Therapeutic creativity**: VR/AR can serve as outlets for creative expression, enabling users to create art, music, or immersive stories that serve as therapeutic outlets for emotional expression and self-discovery.

However, it is important to proceed cautiously and responsibly when using VR/AR for well-being and mental health purposes. Designers and developers should consider potential negative effects like simulation sickness or exacerbation of existing conditions. Additionally, professional guidance and research-backed approaches are crucial to ensuring that these technologies genuinely contribute to improved mental health outcomes.

Case studies

Case study: How ethics were challenged in the AR-based game Pokémon GO

Challenge: Pokémon GO, a popular AR mobile game, faced ethical challenges related to players' safety and privacy. The game encourages users to explore real-world locations to find virtual creatures, sometimes leading players to trespass on private property, engage in risky behavior, or enter dangerous locations.

Design principles:

- **User education**: The developers added safety reminders and informational screens when players launched the game, encouraging them to be aware of their surroundings and respect private property.
- **Geo-fencing**: Niantic, the developer of Pokémon GO, introduced geo-fencing to restrict virtual creatures' appearances in sensitive areas like hospitals and public buildings, addressing safety and privacy concerns.
- **Location designation**: Users can request removal of in-game locations near their property, allowing players to report problematic locations for review.
- **Outcome**: By implementing these design principles, Niantic addressed some ethical challenges and promoted player safety. However, the game still faced incidents where players ignored warnings, emphasizing the ongoing need for user education and responsible use of AR technology.

Case study: VR violence and desensitization

Challenge: Using violent and graphic content in VR simulations raises ethical concerns about potential desensitization and negative real-world consequences, particularly in training scenarios like military simulations.

Design principles:

- **Content regulation**: Developers should carefully curate and regulate the content within VR experiences, avoiding gratuitous violence or extreme realism that might contribute to desensitization.
- **Ethical narratives**: VR experiences can include narratives emphasizing violent actions' ethical and moral implications, encouraging users to critically engage with their choices.
- **Professional guidance**: Collaborating with experts in psychology, ethics, and the specific field (military, law enforcement) can help ensure that VR simulations are responsibly designed and aligned with the intended training outcomes.
- **Outcome**: By adhering to these design principles, VR simulations can mitigate the risk of desensitization and promote ethical training without glorifying violence.

These case studies highlight the importance of user education, content curation, responsible location-based features, and collaboration with experts to navigate ethical challenges in developing and deploying VR and AR technologies. Balancing innovation with responsible use and ethical considerations is crucial to ensuring the long-term positive impact of these technologies.

Conclusion

In this chapter, we tried to look at the ethical challenges of VR and AR technologies. You saw the importance of ethical considerations in developing and deploying these technologies. Then you studied our concern about how the vast amount of personal data we captured is protected, and you saw the legal and ethical frameworks governing the data collection and use. Also, we took a look into the best practices of data protection.

Under the *Safety and physical health* section, you took a deep dive into the physical effects on physical and mental health due to VR/XR. Then, you will explore the measures that can be taken to ensure user safety, including ergonomic design and appropriate use of warning labels.

Under the *Psychological and emotional impact* section, you understood how VR and AR can profoundly impact users and raise concerns about addiction, desensitization, and manipulation. There, we discussed the potential risks and benefits of these technologies and considered how they could be used to promote well-being and mental health.

Finally, there was a case study where we examined some examples of ethical challenges in developing and deploying VR and AR technologies and analyzed the design principles that contributed to their success or failure.

In the next chapter, we will delve into the technical aspects of VR and AR, exploring the hardware and software considerations that underpin these technologies. We will also examine the design principles that guide the creation of immersive experiences, from 3D modeling to user interface design.

Points to remember

- **User safety first**: Prioritize user safety by implementing design features that prevent accidents and promote responsible behavior while using VR/AR technologies.
- **Informed consent**: Obtain explicit user consent before collecting personal data or using location-based services to ensure transparency and respect for privacy.
- **Content curation**: Curate VR/AR content responsibly to avoid promoting violence, harm, or desensitization. Incorporate ethical narratives that encourage critical engagement.
- **User education**: Provide clear guidelines and reminders for users to be aware of their surroundings, especially in AR experiences that blend virtual and real environments.
- **Respect for privacy**: Implement measures to protect user privacy, preventing unauthorized data collection and ensuring user control over their information.
- **Diversity and inclusion**: Create VR/AR experiences that are inclusive and respect cultural, social, and individual differences, avoiding content that perpetuates stereotypes or biases.
- **Location-based features**: Use geo-fencing and location-based limitations to prevent AR experiences from causing unintended disruptions or encroachments on private property.
- **Regulation and compliance**: Adhere to existing laws and regulations related to data privacy, content ratings, and safety standards, ensuring ethical alignment with legal frameworks.
- **Sensitivity to vulnerable populations**: Consider the impact of VR/AR experiences on vulnerable populations, such as children, people with disabilities, or those with mental health conditions.
- **Long-term impact**: Anticipate the potential long-term psychological, societal, and cultural effects of VR/AR experiences, aiming for positive contributions to well-being.
- **User empowerment**: Empower users to make informed choices about their engagement with VR/AR technologies, allowing them to customize experiences and settings.
- **Ethical frameworks**: Utilize established ethical frameworks, such as utilitarianism, deontology, and virtue ethics, to guide decision-making in VR/AR development.
- **Ethical considerations in VR/AR integration**: Remember that ethical considerations in VR/AR extend beyond technical aspects, encompassing user experience, societal impact, and the broader implications of these technologies. Balancing innovation with ethical responsibility is essential for the sustainable and positive integration of VR/AR in various domains.

Chapter 10
3D Modeling and User Interface Design

Introduction

Virtual reality (**VR**) and **Augmented Reality** (**AR**) technologies rely on sophisticated hardware and software systems to create immersive experiences for users. In this chapter, we will delve into the technical aspects of VR and AR, exploring the hardware and software considerations that underpin these technologies. We will also examine the design principles that guide the creation of immersive experiences, from 3D modeling to user interface design.

Structure

In this chapter, we will discuss the following topics:

- Introduction to 3D modeling
- Modeling techniques
- Animating 3D models
- Real-time 3D and game engines
- User interface design principles
- UI design software and workflow
- Implementing UIs in 3D environments

Objectives

At the end of this chapter, you will be introduced to the exciting world of 3D modeling. There you will be exposed to various modeling techniques. You will learn how we can animate 3D models. After that, we will go through real-time 3D and game engine concepts and their usability.

In the later part of the chapter, we will shift our bases toward user interface design principles. Then you will learn about UI design software and its workflow. Finally, you will learn about how we can implement these UIs and respective 3D environments.

Introduction to 3D modeling

3D modeling refers to the process of developing a mathematical representation of any three-dimensional surface or object via specialized software. 3D models can be created using various techniques including polygonal modeling, spline modeling, subdivision surfaces, procedural modeling, implicit surfaces, **Non-uniform rational B-spline (NURBS)**, constructive solid geometry, or dynamic tessellation. The 3D model typically consists of points in 3D space connected by various geometric entities such as triangles, lines, curved surfaces, and so on.

Refer to the following figure:

Figure 10.1: *Illustration of 3D modelling, combining AR with Interactive display*

Immersive environments refer to VR, AR, or mixed reality systems that aim to immerse the user in a computer-generated 3D environment. In immersive 3D modeling, the designer interacts with the virtual 3D model in real time using specialized hardware devices. This allows the designer to inspect the model from all angles, walk around and through it, and manipulate it with their hands or motion controllers. Immersion provides a greater understanding of spatial relationships, scale, and aesthetics compared to traditional 3D modeling on a 2D monitor.

Key concepts

The following are the key concepts of 3D modeling:

- **Three-dimensional space**: Traditional design and media have often been confined to two-dimensional surfaces. 3D modeling, however, introduces the concept of three-dimensional space, enabling the creation of objects with depth, height, and width. This adds realism and depth to virtual experiences, making them more engaging and interactive.

- **VR and AR**: VR immerses users in entirely virtual worlds, blocking out the physical surroundings. AR overlays digital content onto the real world, enhancing it with additional information or interactions. 3D modeling is pivotal in both these realms, as it allows designers to craft the virtual elements users interact with.

- **Creation of assets**: In immersive environments, 3D models serve as assets that populate the virtual space. These models can range from simple objects like furniture to complex characters, vehicles, architecture, and landscapes. Designers use specialized software to create and manipulate these models, ensuring they align with the desired user experience.

- **Realism and interaction**: High-quality 3D models contribute to the realism of immersive environments. Realism, in turn, enhances user engagement and immersion. Additionally, these models are often designed with interactivity in mind, allowing users to manipulate or explore objects within the virtual space.

- **Spatial awareness**: 3D modeling plays a crucial role in spatial awareness within immersive environments. Objects need to be accurately represented in terms of size, scale, and distance to provide users with a sense of depth and perspective, which is vital for realistic and intuitive interactions.

- **Collaboration and iteration**: Creating immersive environments is often a collaborative effort involving designers, developers, artists, and other specialists. 3D models can be shared and iterated upon, allowing for refinements and adjustments as the project progresses.

- **Challenges**: 3D modeling for immersive environments comes with challenges, such as optimizing models for real-time rendering to ensure smooth experiences, addressing compatibility across various devices and platforms, and managing file sizes and data transfer in bandwidth-sensitive scenarios.

Applications: The applications of 3D modeling in immersive environments are vast. From entertainment (video games, movies, and interactive experiences) to education (simulations, virtual classrooms) and industries like architecture, healthcare, and engineering (virtual prototypes and training simulations), 3D modeling transforms the way we visualize and interact with digital content.

Modeling technique

In the realm of immersive environments, where VR, AR, and interactive simulations flourish, the techniques used to create 3D models play a pivotal role in shaping the quality and realism of the user experience. These techniques are a blend of artistic skill, technical knowledge, and a deep understanding of how humans perceive and interact with digital content within these immersive spaces.

Key aspects:

- **Polygonal modeling**: This is the most common technique used for creating 3D models in immersive environments. It involves constructing models by connecting vertices, edges, and faces to form polygons. These polygons collectively create the surface of the object. Artists manipulate vertices and edges to shape objects. Low-polygon models are often used for real-time rendering to optimize performance, while high-polygon models offer greater detail. Refer to the following figure:

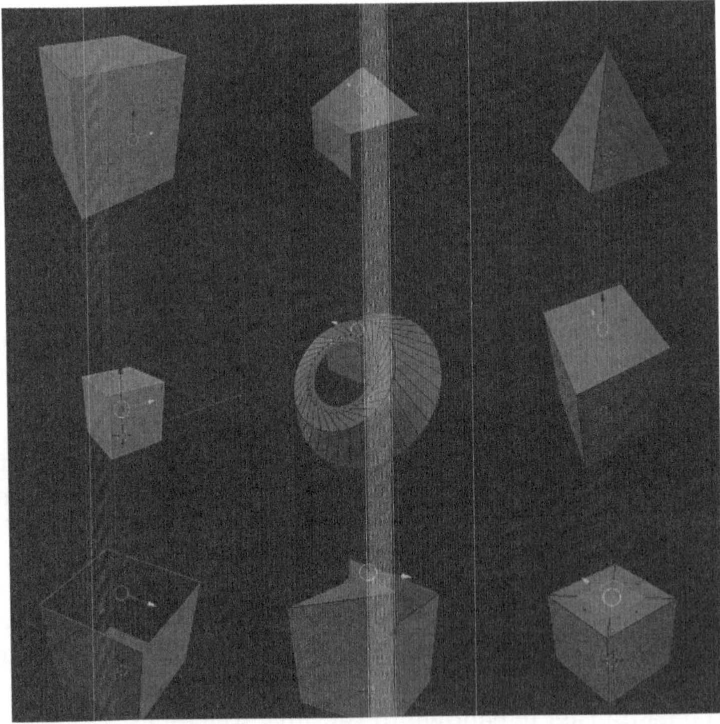

***Figure 10.2**: Illustration of polygonal modeling*

- **Subdivision surface modeling**: Also known as Sub-D modeling, this technique begins with a simple polygonal mesh and iteratively subdivides it into smoother and more detailed shapes. It is used to create organic forms, characters, and objects that require smooth curves and surfaces. Refer to the following figure:

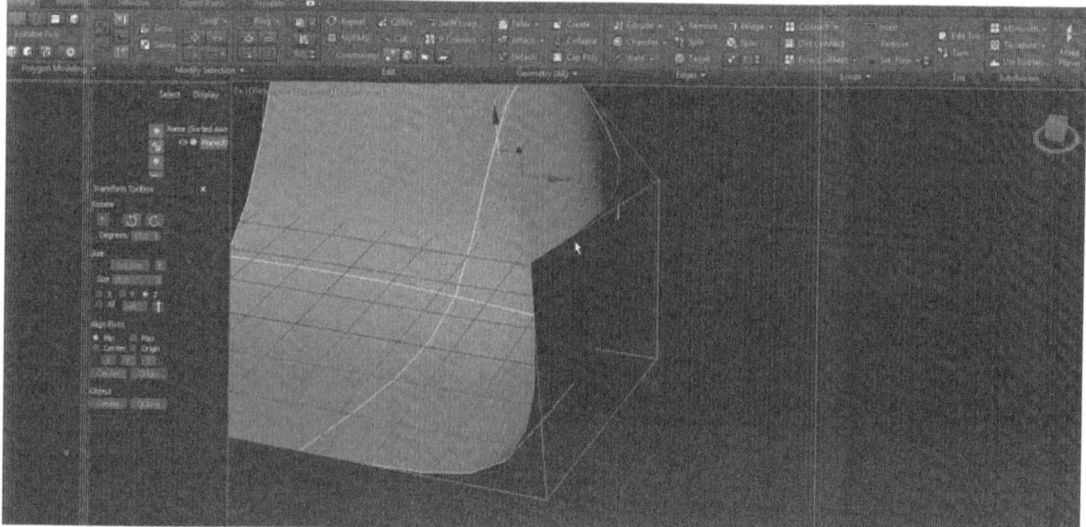

***Figure 10.3**: Illustration of surface modeling*

- **Sculpting**: Sculpting involves digitally sculpting the model's surface using brushes and tools, akin to sculpting with clay. It is particularly useful for creating highly detailed characters, creatures, and natural elements like terrain. The details added in this process enhance realism. Refer to the following figure:

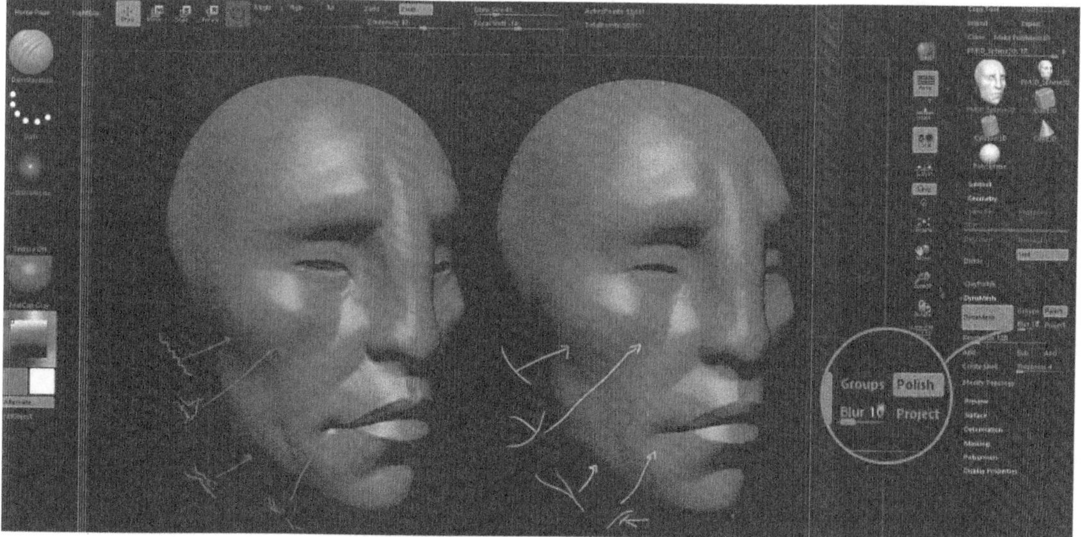

***Figure 10.4**: Illustration of sculpting modeling technique*

- **Parametric modeling**: This technique involves defining the model's properties and shapes using mathematical equations and parameters. It is often used in engineering and architecture for creating precise models with adjustable parameters.
- **Procedural modeling**: In this technique, models are generated algorithmically based on predefined rules and parameters. It is useful for creating complex structures, terrains, and patterns. Procedural modeling can save time and offer diversity in environments.
- **Photogrammetry**: This technique involves capturing the real world through photographs and transforming them into 3D models. Photogrammetry is used to create realistic assets, such as environmental props and textures, by capturing real-world details. Refer to the following figure:

***Figure 10.5**: Illustration of photogrammetry modeling technique*

- **Animation and rigging**: In immersive environments, models often need to be animated. Rigging is the process of adding a digital skeleton to a model, allowing it to be posed and animated realistically. Techniques like inverse kinematics and blend shapes enhance the complexity of animations. Refer to the following figure:

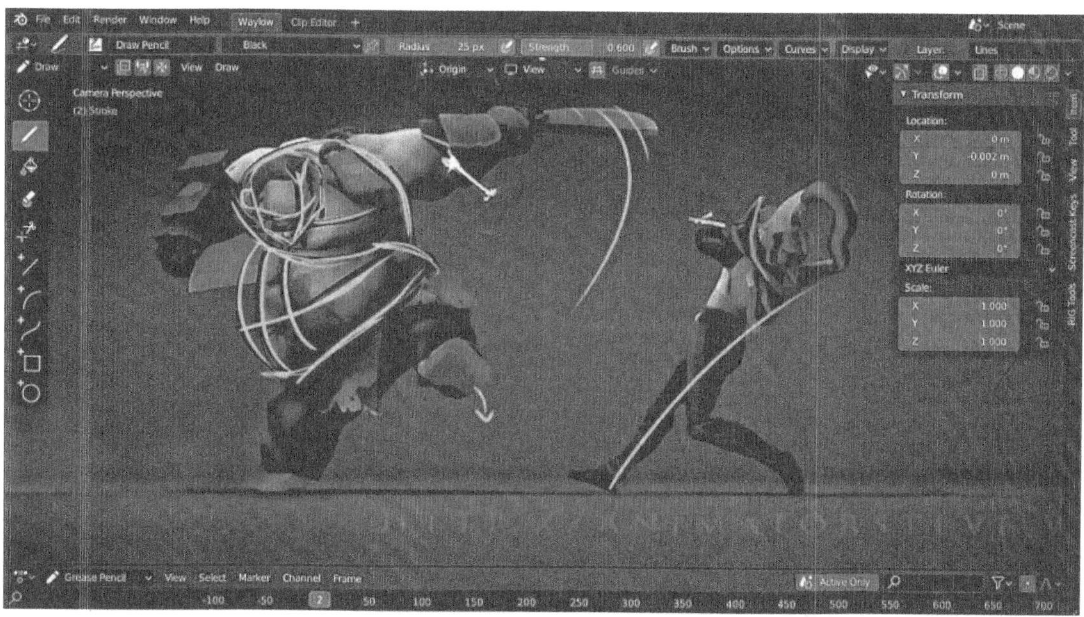

Figure 10.6: Illustration of animation and rigging modeling technique

- **Texturing and materials**: Adding textures and materials to models is crucial for enhancing realism. Techniques include UV mapping (unwrapping the 3D model onto a 2D surface for texture application), normal mapping (faking high-detail geometry), and physically based rendering (creating materials that respond to light in a physically accurate way). Refer to the following figure:

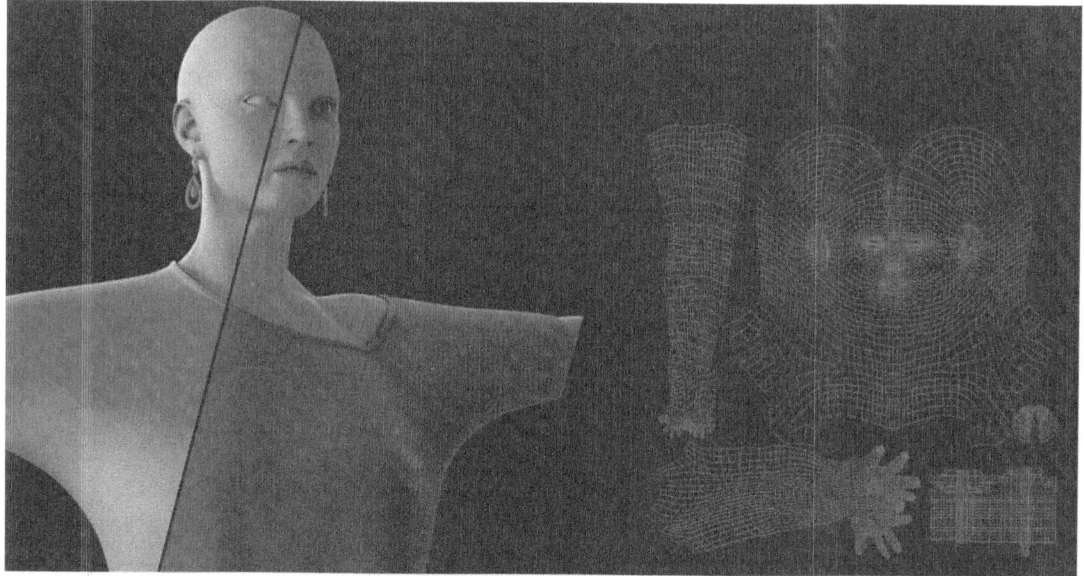

Figure 10.7: Illustration of texturing and material modeling technique

- **Optimization**: Immersive environments often require real-time rendering, demanding efficient models. Optimization techniques involve reducing polygon counts, creating levels of detail, and using texture atlases to minimize memory and processing requirements.

Artistic and technical balance

Creating 3D models for immersive environments is a fusion of artistic expression and technical expertise. Artists must consider aesthetics, visual appeal, and storytelling, while also accounting for the limitations and requirements of the technology and platform. The aim is to strike a balance between high-quality visuals and smooth performance, ensuring that users are both visually immersed and interactively engaged.

Animating 3D models

In the realm of immersive environments, the ability to bring 3D models to life through animation is a key factor in creating captivating and interactive experiences. Whether it is a VR game, an AR application, or a simulation, animating 3D models adds depth, realism, and engagement to the virtual world. This comprehensive overview delves into the techniques, challenges, and importance of animating 3D models within immersive environments.

Importance of animation and techniques

Animation enriches immersive environments by infusing them with movement, emotion, and narrative. It enables objects, characters, and elements to behave naturally, enhancing user engagement and suspension of disbelief. The dynamic nature of animation allows users to interact with and respond to the virtual world, leading to a more memorable and impactful experience.

Techniques for animating 3D models:

- **Keyframe animation**: This classic technique involves defining specific keyframes (significant moments) in an animation sequence. The software then interpolates between keyframes to create smooth motion. Keyframe animation is versatile and used for a wide range of motions, from simple movements to complex actions.

- **Inverse Kinematics (IK)**: IK animation involves manipulating a model's end-effector (such as a hand or foot) and letting the software calculate the joint rotations needed to achieve that position. This technique is valuable for creating natural and believable character movements.

- **Blend shapes and morph targets**: Commonly used in facial animation, blend shapes involve creating a set of pre-defined facial expressions and smoothly transitioning between them. This technique imparts emotions and realism to characters.

- **Physics-based animation**: Physics simulations can create dynamic and natural movements. Objects can react to gravity, collisions, wind, and other forces just as they would in the real world. This technique is especially useful for creating realistic environments and interactions.

- **Rigging and skinning**: Rigging involves creating a digital skeleton for a 3D model. Skinning assigns vertices of the model to specific bones of the skeleton. When the bones move, the model deforms accordingly. This is crucial for character animation.

- **Motion capture**: Motion capture involves recording real-world movements and applying them to 3D models. This technique ensures lifelike and authentic animations, especially for characters.

Challenges in animating for immersive environments

The following are the challenges in animating for immersive environments:

- **Realism**: Achieving realism in animation involves meticulous attention to detail, from lifelike physics interactions to subtle facial expressions. Even the slightest inconsistencies can break immersion.

- **Performance optimization**: Immersive environments often require real-time rendering. Animations must be optimized for smooth playback and interaction, which can involve techniques like **Level of Detail (LoD)** and efficient use of resources. To be precise LoD in computer graphics, refers to the complexity of a 3D model representation. LoD can be decreased as the model moves away from the viewer or according to other metrics such as object importance, viewpoint-relative speed or position. LoD techniques increase the efficiency of rendering by decreasing the workload on graphics pipeline stages, usually vertex transformations. The reduced visual quality of the model is often unnoticed because of the small effect on object appearance when distant or moving fast. Although most of the time LoD is applied to geometry detail only, the basic concept can be generalized.

- **User interaction**: Animations in immersive environments should respond to user inputs and interactions. This dynamic aspect requires careful synchronization between user actions and animations.

- **Motion sickness**: Poorly executed animations can induce motion sickness in users. Jerky or overly fast movements can disrupt the user's sense of balance and orientation.

- **Storytelling and emotion**: Animations play a crucial role in storytelling within immersive environments. Through movement, characters convey emotions, environments tell stories, and interactions communicate intent. Skillful animation adds depth and emotional resonance to the user's experience, making it more memorable and impactful.

Real-time 3D and game engines

The convergence of real-time 3D graphics and game engines has revolutionized the way we experience immersive environments, offering a seamless blend of interactive virtual worlds and creative possibilities. This in-depth exploration delves into the concepts, significance, and applications of real-time 3D graphics and game engines in the context of immersive environments.

Understanding real-time 3D graphics

Real-time 3D graphics refer to the ability to render and display 3D content instantaneously, as opposed to pre-rendering frames. This real-time aspect is crucial for maintaining interactivity and responsiveness in dynamic virtual spaces, such as video games, simulations, and virtual experiences. With real-time rendering, the content adapts and reacts to user input in the moment, providing a fluid and immersive user experience.

Game engines: The heart of immersive environments

Game engines are software frameworks that provide tools and resources for creating interactive applications, often centered around video games but extending to various immersive environments. They offer a suite of functionalities, including:

- **Rendering**: Game engines use rendering techniques to transform 3D models, textures, and effects into visually appealing scenes. Real-time rendering capabilities ensure that the content responds to changes in lighting, environment, and user interactions.
- **Physics simulation**: Engines simulate physics to create realistic interactions between objects, including gravity, collisions, and momentum. This enhances the authenticity of immersive experiences.
- **Animation**: Game engines facilitate animation by providing tools for character rigging, keyframing, procedural animation, and more. Animations bring life to characters and objects within the environment.
- **Scripting and logic**: Logic and scripting tools allow developers to define behaviors, interactions, and rules in the virtual world. This scripting layer enables the creation of complex interactions and scenarios.

- **Asset management**: Game engines handle the organization and management of assets like 3D models, textures, audio, and scripts. This streamlines the development process and ensures efficient use of resources.
- **User Interface (UI)**: Game engines include UI tools for creating user interfaces that enable interactions, menus, and information display within the immersive environment.

Applications of game engines

The following are the applications of game engines:

- **Video games**: Game engines are the backbone of modern video game development, offering the framework to create complex gameplay, stunning visuals, and immersive storytelling.
- **VR and AR**: Game engines power VR and AR experiences by rendering and adapting content in real time as users interact with their environment. This allows for the creation of engaging and interactive virtual worlds.
- **Simulations**: From flight simulators to medical training scenarios, game engines simulate real-world experiences for training and educational purposes.
- **Architectural visualization**: Game engines aid architects and designers in creating interactive 3D walkthroughs of architectural projects, enabling clients to explore spaces before construction.
- **Entertainment and media**: Game engines are used to create interactive exhibits, immersive art installations, and even real-time visual effects in movies.

The democratization of immersive content creation

The accessibility and user-friendly interfaces of modern game engines have democratized content creation. Artists, designers, and developers with varying levels of expertise can harness the power of these engines to bring their visions to life, expanding the potential for creativity and innovation.

In conclusion, real-time 3D graphics and game engines are the backbone of immersive environments. They enable the creation of interactive and dynamic virtual spaces that captivate, educate, entertain, and challenge users. As these technologies continue to evolve, they will undoubtedly reshape how we perceive and interact with the digital world, blurring the lines between reality and imagination.

User interface design principles

Designing UI for AR, VR, and XR environments present unique challenges and opportunities. The fusion of the physical and digital worlds demands a thoughtful approach that enhances immersion, interaction, and usability. This comprehensive exploration delves into the principles that guide effective UI design in AR/VR/XR:

- **Spatial awareness and context**: AR/VR/XR interfaces exist within 3D space. Designers must consider users' physical environment, providing contextual cues and visual feedback to guide interactions. Elements should fit seamlessly into the user's surroundings, maintaining a sense of presence.
- **Minimalism and simplicity**: In immersive environments, less is often more. A clean and minimalist UI reduces visual clutter and distractions, allowing users to focus on the experience. Designers should prioritize essential information and interactions while avoiding overwhelming users with unnecessary elements.
- **Natural gestures and interactions**: Leverage users' familiarity with real-world gestures and interactions. Intuitive gestures, like pointing or swiping, should align with users' expectations. Mapping actions to natural movements enhances usability and reduces the learning curve.
- **Hierarchy and depth**: Hierarchy remains crucial even in 3D UI. Elements closer to the user should receive more prominence, while those farther away can appear smaller. This depth perception enhances visual organization and guides users' attention.
- **Feedback and animation**: Incorporate responsive animations and feedback to provide a tangible connection between user actions and system responses. These cues clarify interactions and make the UI feel more responsive and engaging.
- **Consistency and familiarity**: Build on users' existing knowledge by adopting familiar design patterns and icons. Consistency in UI elements across different parts of the experience ensures a cohesive and intuitive journey.
- **User-centric adaptation**: Design for a range of users and environments. AR/VR/XR interfaces should adapt to different devices, screen sizes, and user preferences while maintaining usability and accessibility.
- **Visual comfort**: Considering the potential for motion sickness and eye strain, design UIs with visual comfort in mind. Avoid rapid movements, flickering elements, and overly complex visuals that might contribute to discomfort.
- **Contextual information presentation**: Information should be presented contextually. In AR, overlay relevant data directly onto the user's physical surroundings. In VR, create information displays that are easily accessible without pulling users out of the experience.

- **Spatial sound and audio cues**: Sound is a powerful tool for guiding attention and providing feedback in immersive environments. Use spatial audio cues to direct users' focus and enhance their understanding of their surroundings.
- **User testing and iteration**: User testing is essential to validate design choices. Iterate based on user feedback, observing how users naturally interact with the interface and refining the design accordingly.

User interface design software and workflow

Designing UI for immersive systems such as AR, VR, and XR involves a distinct set of tools and workflows. This comprehensive exploration delves into the software and processes that enable designers to create intuitive and engaging UIs for these cutting-edge technologies.

Understanding the workflow

Here is a step-by-step guide to help you navigate the intricate world of 3D UI design:

1. **Conceptualization**: Just like traditional UI design, the process begins with ideation. Understand the project goals, target audience, and the context in which the UI will operate. Sketch out initial ideas and concepts.
2. **Prototyping**: Immersive UIs often involve 3D elements. Start with low-fidelity prototypes to visualize the UI's spatial arrangement and interactions. Tools that offer 3D prototyping capabilities are invaluable in this stage.
3. **3D modeling**: Create 3D models of UI elements, considering their placement and interaction within the immersive environment. Tools like Blender, Maya, or Unity's built-in 3D tools can help model buttons, panels, and other components.
4. **Visual design**: Apply visual design principles to your 3D UI elements. Use software like Adobe XD, Figma, or Sketch for designing textures, colors, and visual effects. Consider how these elements will look in both static and dynamic states.
5. **Interaction design**: Map out user interactions within the 3D space. Define how users will navigate, select, and manipulate UI elements. Tools like ProtoPie, Adobe XD, or Unity's animation features can help create interactive prototypes.
6. **User testing**: Conduct usability testing with prototypes to gather feedback on interactions and visual comfort. Iterate based on user insights to refine the UI's functionality and usability.
7. **3D animation**: Animate UI elements to respond to user input and system feedback. Use animation software (such as Maya or Blender) or animation features in game engines like Unity or Unreal Engine.

8. **Integration**: Integrate the UI into the immersive environment using game engines. Unity and Unreal Engine offer tools for importing 3D assets, creating interactions, and testing the UI within virtual space.
9. **Optimization**: Ensure that the UI runs smoothly in real time within the immersive environment. Optimize textures, polygon counts, and animations for optimal performance.
10. **User feedback loop**: Continuously gather feedback from users as the immersive experience is tested. Adjust based on real-world user interactions and observations.

Tools of the trade

The following are the tools that empower designers to craft immersive interfaces:

- **3D modeling and animation**: Software like Blender, Autodesk Maya, and Cinema 4D allow designers to create and animate 3D assets.
- **UI/UX design**: Adobe XD, Figma, Sketch, and ProtoPie offer tools for creating UI mockups, prototypes, and interactive designs.
- **Game engines**: Unity and Unreal Engine provide robust platforms for developing and testing immersive UIs, complete with interaction scripting and real-time rendering.
- **Spatial design**: Tools like Gravity Sketch enable designers to work directly in 3D space, which is especially valuable for XR environments.

Challenges and considerations

Let us delve into some of the key aspects when crafting immersive user experiences:

- **Spatial awareness**: UIs in immersive environments must seamlessly integrate with physical surroundings, requiring a shift from traditional 2D screen design.
- **User interaction**: Designers must anticipate and accommodate natural gestures and movements that users would employ in AR/VR/XR spaces.
- **Performance**: UI elements must be optimized for real-time rendering without sacrificing visual quality or responsiveness.

In conclusion, designing UIs for immersive systems demands a blend of traditional UI/UX design principles and a deep understanding of 3D space. The right software tools and a thorough workflow enable designers to craft interfaces that seamlessly merge digital and physical worlds, offering users truly immersive and intuitive experiences. As AR, VR, and XR continue to evolve, so will the tools and techniques used to create captivating user interfaces.

Implementing UIs in 3D environment

Creating UIs in three-dimensional environments for AR, VR, and XR requires a unique approach that merges interactivity with immersive experience. This detailed exploration unveils the intricacies of implementing UIs within these immersive systems.

Design principles and considerations

The key aspects that can significantly enhance the user's interaction with the digital environment are as follows:

- **Spatial context**: Design UI elements with the environment's spatial context in mind. UI components should exist naturally within the user's surroundings, enhancing immersion.
- **Depth and hierarchy**: Utilize depth and scale to convey hierarchy and prioritize elements. Elements closer to the user's viewpoint should be more prominent, simulating real-world perceptions.
- **Interaction design**: Intuitive interaction is crucial. Leverage gestures, gaze, and controllers to enable users to interact with UI elements. Consider real-world interactions for a seamless experience. Interactions in VR are more important than in flat screen development, simply because players expect to be able to act in-game the same way they would in real life. For instance, if there's a panel with a lot of buttons to push, you want to be able to push all these buttons.
- **Visual clarity**: UI elements should be visually clear and legible. Choose appropriate font sizes, colors, and contrast levels to ensure readability, even in dynamic environments.
- **Feedback and animation**: UI elements should provide responsive feedback to user actions. Use animations to visualize interactions, making the experience more engaging and informative.

Implementation workflow

Let us explore the essential steps in crafting an effective and immersive UI within immersive environments:

1. **Choose a development platform**: Select a platform or game engine that supports AR/VR/XR development, such as Unity or Unreal Engine. These engines offer tools for creating immersive environments, importing 3D models, and scripting interactions.
2. **Design UI components**: Create 3D models for UI elements, including buttons, panels, menus, and icons. Design textures, animations, and visual effects that suit the overall aesthetic of the immersive experience.

3. **Spatial placement**: Determine where UI elements will appear in the 3D space. Ensure they do not obstruct the user's view or interfere with the primary experience. Consider the user's gaze direction and hand/controller positions.

4. **User interaction**: Implement interactions based on the platform's input methods. This could involve hand gestures, gaze-based selection, or handheld controllers. Make interactions intuitive and responsive.

5. **Animation and transition**: Animate UI elements to respond to user actions. Use animations for button presses, transitions between states, and visual feedback. Smooth animations enhance user engagement.

6. **Integration with environment**: Integrate UI elements seamlessly with the 3D environment. Ensure that lighting, shadows, and reflections interact realistically with the UI components.

7. **Testing and iteration**: Test the implemented UI within the immersive environment. Gather user feedback to refine interactions, placement, and visual design. Iteratively improve the UI based on user insights.

8. **Performance optimization**: Optimize the UI's performance for real-time rendering. Balance visual quality with frame rates to ensure a smooth and immersive experience.

9. **Accessibility**: Consider accessibility aspects, such as adjusting font sizes for legibility, providing alternative input methods, and ensuring color contrast for users with varying visual capabilities.

Tools and technologies

Let us explore the key components that empower the creation of these interfaces:

- **Game engines**: Unity and Unreal Engine offer robust platforms for developing immersive UIs. They provide tools for importing 3D assets, scripting interactions, and optimizing performance.

- **3D modeling and animation**: Software like Blender, Autodesk Maya, and Cinema 4D are used for creating 3D UI assets and animations.

- **Interaction libraries**: Platforms often provide interaction libraries and APIs for handling gestures, gaze tracking, and input from controllers.

So, implementing UIs in 3D environments for AR/VR/XR involves a marriage of design principles and technical expertise. By crafting UI elements that blend seamlessly with the immersive experience and ensuring intuitive interactions, designers can create interfaces that enhance immersion while providing users with meaningful engagement and control. As AR, VR, and XR technologies continue to evolve, the implementation of immersive UIs will remain a critical aspect of creating captivating user experiences.

Conclusion

In this chapter, we began with an overview of common 3D modeling paradigms, including polygon modeling, NURBS, sculpting, and procedural techniques. The various strengths and use cases of each approach were discussed. Key factors like optimizing topology for animation rigging and rendering were explored.

Shifting focus to 2D user interface design, core principles and best practices were outlined to equip readers with fundamental UI/UX design skills applicable across domains. Software packages for mocking up and prototyping digital interfaces were explored in order to demystify the workflow from wireframes to high-fidelity interactive prototypes.

Armed with the preceding knowledge, the concluding chapter guided readers through practical considerations in implementing clean, functional UI/UX designs in three-dimensional spaces using the tools introduced earlier in the book. Principles covered apply equally to designing interfaces for VR, AR, and other spatial computing platforms.

By progressing through the interconnected facets of 3D discipline covered in this book, readers have gained a comprehensive, multidisciplinary foundation to pursue their goals and passions, whether in entertainment, design, or emerging tech fields.

In the next chapter, we will understand and deep dive into Unity **architecture**. We will explore various components that make up the engine. We will create a Unity project and produce scenes, and environments, and produce 3D models, textures, and lightning.

Points to remember

- Polygonal and subdivision surface modeling are common approaches for organic 3D models. Procedural and sculpting techniques facilitate rapid iteration.
- Optimize topology flow for rigging. Re-topologize sculptures for clean animation. Utilize edge loops, good pole placement, and quad faces.
- Keyframe animation involves posing models on keyframes and interpolating between them. Maintain volumes and forms between poses.
- Performance capture tracks motions from actors to rapidly animate. Physics-driven simulation creates natural motion.
- Game engines like Unity and Unreal provide full real-time 3D pipelines. Learning C# or C++ is needed to code interactivity.
- UI/UX design emphasizes understanding users, workflows, and psychology. User-centered design yields better adoption.
- Rapidly iterate interfaces with software like Figma and Adobe XD. Transition from low to high fidelity.

- 3D UI elements must be legible from multiple angles. Utilize motion and depth for spatial interfaces.
- Test UI/UX rigorously in VR headsets. Refine based on user testing feedback. Prioritize performance.
- The skills covered equip you to model, animate, design and implement robust 3D experiences. Apply them diligently in practice.

CHAPTER 11
Building VR Applications with Unity

Introduction

In this chapter, we will introduce Unity, one of the most popular game engines for creating VR applications. We will understand its basic features, architecture, and workflow. We will then explore how Unity can be used to build VR applications, discussing the various components that make up a typical VR project and the key considerations that need to be considered when developing VR.

Structure

In this chapter, we will discuss the following topics:

- Introduction to Unity
- Unity architecture
- Unity workflow
- VR development in Unity
- Creating scenes and environments
- Scripting in Unity
- UI design in VR

Objectives

In this chapter, our objective is to provide a comprehensive understanding of Unity, a powerful game development engine widely used to create **Virtual Reality (VR)** experiences.

We will begin by delving into the fundamentals with an introduction to Unity, exploring its essential features and capabilities. The chapter will then focus on Unity's workflow, guiding readers through the intricate process of developing VR applications seamlessly.

A significant portion of our discussion will be dedicated to VR development in Unity, shedding light on the specialized techniques and considerations required for immersive VR experiences.

Furthermore, we will delve into the art of crafting captivating scenes and environments within Unity, emphasizing the importance of visual aesthetics and user engagement. Scripting, a fundamental aspect of game development, will also be thoroughly explored, enabling readers to comprehend the intricacies of coding within Unity's framework.

Lastly, we will unravel the complexities of UI design specifically tailored to the VR environment, equipping readers with the skills to create intuitive and user-friendly interfaces in their VR projects.

Through this chapter, readers will gain a holistic understanding of Unity's core concepts and its application in the dynamic realm of VR.

Introduction to Unity

In this section, we embark on a journey into the dynamic realm of VR by exploring the foundational aspects of Unity, one of the industry's leading game development engines. Unity stands at the forefront of VR innovation, empowering developers to create immersive and interactive experiences that push the boundaries of reality. Within the virtual landscapes of Unity, the possibilities are limitless, and in this chapter, we will unravel the secrets behind crafting compelling VR applications. These are some of the key concepts that we will deep dive into this unit:

- **Understanding Unity's core concepts**: We will commence by delving into Unity's core concepts, demystifying its interface, and understanding the basic building blocks of game development. Readers will grasp essential notions such as scenes, game objects, components, and assets, laying the groundwork for creating VR environments from scratch. By unraveling Unity's intuitive interface, readers will gain a solid foundation, ensuring a smooth transition into VR development.

- **Navigating the VR landscape**: Next, we will explore Unity's VR-specific functionalities. From integrating VR hardware and configuring input systems to optimizing performance for seamless VR experiences, this section will comprehensively understand the unique considerations involved in VR application development. Readers will learn how to leverage Unity's capabilities to create immersive 3D worlds, design interactive elements, and handle user interactions within VR environments.

- **Hands-on exploration and practical insights**: This chapter offers hands-on exploration and practical insights beyond theory. Through step-by-step tutorials and real-world examples, readers will gain practical experience building VR applications from the ground up. We will cover topics like spatial audio, VR **User Interfaces** (**UI**), and motion tracking, enabling readers to enhance the immersive qualities of their projects. By the end of this section, readers will have a firm grasp of Unity's features, equipping them with the skills to embark on their VR development journeys with confidence.

Unity architecture

In this section, we delve into the intricate architecture of Unity, unraveling the underlying components that form the backbone of this powerful game development engine. At its core, Unity operates through a sophisticated system comprising several vital elements, and this exploration aims to shed light on its inner workings. The following are some of the key components of the Unity architecture:

- **Exploring the game loop**: Central to Unity's functionality is the game loop, a fundamental concept in game development. Here, we dissect the game loop's mechanics, comprehending how Unity handles processes like input, logic, and rendering in a continuous cycle. Understanding this loop is pivotal, as it dictates the flow of gameplay and ensures seamless interactions within the virtual worlds developers create.

- **Scripting and rendering systems**: Within Unity's architecture, scripting and rendering systems play pivotal roles. Scripting empowers developers to breathe life into their creations, enabling them to define behaviors, interactions, and game mechanics. We will delve into the scripting languages supported by Unity, emphasizing their syntax and usage. Simultaneously, the rendering system will be demystified for translating game data into visual experiences. Developers can create visually stunning and performance-efficient applications by understanding rendering techniques and optimizations.

Integration of Unity with 3D modeling and animation

Integrating Unity with other tools and technologies, including 3D modeling and animation software, is crucial for creating immersive and visually appealing games and interactive experiences. Unity offers robust support for various file formats and plugins, making it easier for developers to collaborate and leverage assets from different software programs. Here is how Unity can integrate with 3D modeling and animation tools:

- **Importing 3D models**: Unity supports various 3D model file formats, including FBX, OBJ, and Blender files. Developers can directly import models created in software like Blender, Maya, 3ds Max, or Cinema 4D into Unity. These models can include characters, environments, props, and more.
- **Animation integration**: Animation data created in software like Maya or Blender can be imported into Unity using compatible file formats. Unity supports skeletal animation, blend trees, and state machines, enabling complex animations to be created and controlled within the Unity editor.
- **Physics simulations**: Unity's physics engine can work with 3D modeling software. Developers can import realistic physics simulations created by external tools, ensuring the game objects behave realistically within the Unity environment.
- **Shader integration**: Shaders play a vital role in the visual aesthetics of games. Unity supports shader programming using languages like CG and ShaderLab. Developers can create custom shaders in software like Unity's Shader Graph, Substance Designer, or external shader editors. These shaders can then be integrated into Unity to achieve specific visual effects.
- **Lighting and rendering:** Unity allows for integrating pre-rendered images and lighting data from software like Autodesk's Arnold or Unity's rendering solutions. This integration ensures that complex lighting setups and high-quality rendering can be achieved seamlessly in Unity projects.
- **Collaboration tools**: Unity Collaborate and Unity Teams offer version control and collaboration features. These tools enable teams working with different software to collaborate efficiently.
- **AR and VR integration**: Unity supports integration with AR and VR development platforms. This allows developers to create 3D models and animations in software designed specifically for AR and VR applications and then import these assets into Unity for further development and interaction design.

Let us take one 3D Modelling software, Autodesk® Maya®, and we will see how the Unity Integration tool allows you to effortlessly exchange Assets between Unity and Autodesk® Maya®, Autodesk® Maya LT™ or Autodesk® 3ds Max®. Use the Unity Integration tool to import and export FBX files directly to and from Unity without specifying filenames, selecting objects, or setting FBX importer or exporter settings.

To customize the **FBX Importer** or **Exporter** settings in Autodesk® Maya® or Autodesk® Maya LT™, use the `unityFbxImportSettings.mel` and `unityFbxExportSettings.mel` files. Both files are in the `Integrations/Autodesk/maya/scripts` folder.

To install Unity Integration for Autodesk® Maya®, Autodesk® Maya LT™, or Autodesk® 3Ds Max®, open Fbx Export Settings (**https://docs.unity3d.com/Packages/com.unity.formats.fbx@2.0/manual/options.html**), Menu: **Edit** | **Project Settings** | **Fbx Export** in Unity:

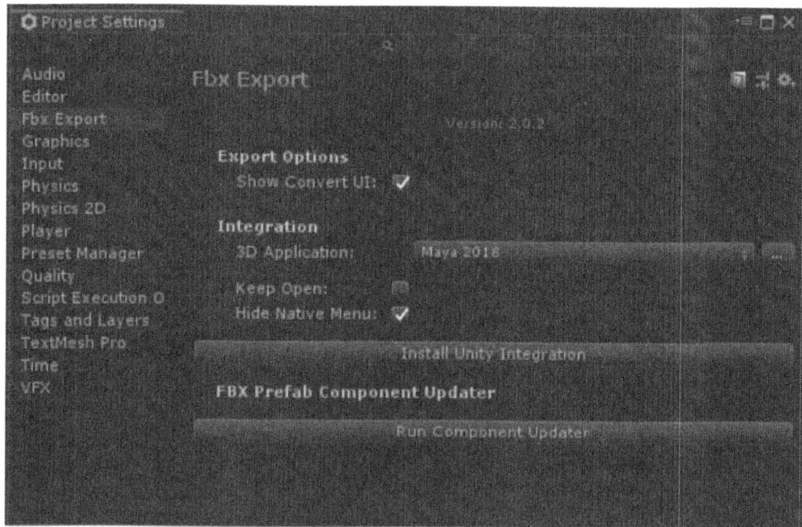

***Figure 11.1**: Illustration of Unity workspace project setting window*

Use the 3D Application property to choose the 3D modeling software and version where you want to install the Unity Integration. To select a version of Autodesk® Maya®, Autodesk® Maya LT™, or Autodesk® 3Ds Max® installed outside the default location, click the **Browse** button.

Refer to the following figure:

***Figure 11.2**: Illustration of Unity workspace Maya LT Integration*

Before installing Unity Integration, close all instances of the selected 3D modeling software that matches the specified version. Click **Install Unity Integration** to install the Unity Integration for the selected 3D modeling software.

If you have unpacked a previous integration in the selected folder, Unity prompts you to use the existing integration or overwrite it with the newer version.

Unity Integration comes packaged in several zip files (one zip file per supported application). When prompted, select a target folder where you want to extract the Unity Integration. The target folder can be outside of your current Project. Autodesk® Maya® and Autodesk® Maya LT™ both use the same zip folder.

The application starts, configures the plug-in, and automatically exits. Unity reports whether the installation was a success.

If an error occurs during startup, Autodesk® Maya® or Autodesk® Maya LT™ may not close. If this happens, check the Autodesk® Maya® or Autodesk® Maya LT™ console to see if you can resolve the issue, and then manually close Autodesk® Maya® or Autodesk® Maya LT™.

If you enabled the Keep Open option in the Fbx Export Settings window (**https://docs.unity3d.com/Packages/com.unity.formats.fbx@2.0/manual/options.html**), then Autodesk® Maya® or Autodesk® Maya LT™ stays open after installation completes.

Unity workflow

Creating a VR application in Unity involves several steps, from setting up a new project to importing assets and configuring the scene. Here is a comprehensive overview of the Unity workflow for creating a VR application:

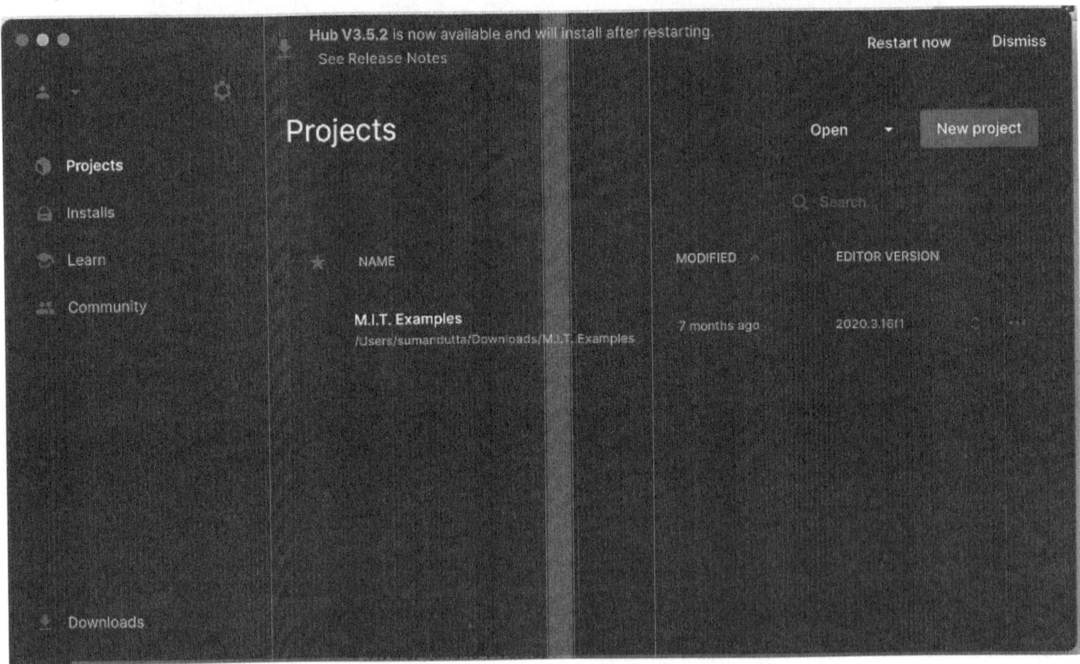

Figure 11.3: *Illustration of Unity workspace*

Creating a VR application in Unity involves a series of steps encompassing project setup, asset importation, and scene configuration. To begin, developers typically start by creating a new Unity project tailored for VR. Unity offers specific project templates for various VR platforms, such as Oculus Rift, HTC Vive, or PlayStation VR. Selecting the appropriate template helps set up the project with the necessary configurations for the chosen VR hardware.

Once the project is established, the next step is importing assets. VR applications often require 3D models, textures, audio files, and other resources. Unity's Asset Store provides a vast repository of pre-made assets that can be utilized in VR projects. Additionally, developers can import custom assets created in external software tools, ensuring the VR environment is visually and auditorily immersive.

Configuring the scene is a critical aspect of VR development. Unity's scene editor allows developers to arrange and manipulate 3D objects within the virtual space. In a VR context, considerations such as player height, scale, and the placement of VR cameras are crucial for a realistic and comfortable experience. Unity provides specific components and settings for VR cameras to ensure proper stereoscopic rendering and head tracking, allowing users to explore the virtual environment seamlessly.

Interaction design is another essential component of VR application development. Unity offers a variety of input methods for VR, including motion controllers, hand tracking, and gaze-based interactions. Developers need to implement these input methods to enable users to interact with the virtual world intuitively. This involves scripting interactions, defining triggers, and handling user inputs to create a responsive and immersive experience.

Optimization is a key concern in VR development to ensure smooth performance and avoid motion sickness. Unity provides tools to profile and optimize the application, including techniques such as **level-of-detail (LOD)** for 3D models, occlusion culling, and efficient rendering. Testing the VR application on the target hardware is essential to identify and address performance issues.

Finally, deploying the VR application involves building it for the specific VR platform. Unity supports various VR platforms, and developers must configure build settings accordingly. Once the application is built, it can be deployed to the target VR device for testing and distribution.

In summary, creating a VR application in Unity involves setting up a new project, importing assets, configuring the scene for VR, designing interactions, optimizing performance, and deploying the application to the target hardware. Each step requires careful consideration to ensure a seamless and immersive VR experience for users.

Tools and features to edit game objects

Unity offers robust tools and features for creating and editing game objects. Here is an overview of some key tools and features that Unity provides:

- **GameObject system**: Unity revolves around the concept of GameObjects, the basic entities in a Unity scene. GameObjects can represent characters, props, lights, cameras, and more. They can hold various components that define their behavior, appearance, and functionality.

- **Inspector**: The Inspector window allows developers to view and edit the properties and components of selected GameObjects. It provides a user-friendly interface for tweaking object attributes, adding components, and configuring scripts.
- **Transform component**: The Transform component defines an object's position, rotation, and scale in 3D space. Developers can manipulate objects in the scene view by adjusting their transforms directly or using gizmos and handles.
- **Components**: Unity's components are scripts and modules that define specific behavior for GameObjects. For example:
    - **Mesh Renderer**: Renders 3D meshes.
    - **Collider**: Defines the shape for collision detection.
    - **Rigidbody**: Enables physics interactions.
    - **Animator**: Controls animations.
    - **Audio Source**: Plays audio.
    - **Script Components**: Custom scripts for specific functionalities.
- **Prefab system**: Prefabs are templates of GameObjects that allow developers to reuse GameObject configurations. Prefabs streamline creating and managing multiple similar objects, ensuring consistency and simplifying updates across scenes.
- **Particle system**: Unity's built-in Particle System allows developers to create various visual effects like fire, smoke, rain, and explosions. It provides a range of parameters for controlling particle behavior and appearance.
- **Lighting and shading**: Unity offers multiple lights, such as directional, point, and spotlights. Real-time lighting and baked lighting techniques are supported. Unity also provides various shaders for achieving different visual styles, including Standard, Unlit, and Custom shaders.
- **Physics system**: Unity's physics engine allows for realistic simulations. Developers can use Rigidbody components and colliders to create interactive and dynamic environments. Unity supports 2D and 3D physics.
- **Animation system**: Unity's Animation System allows developers to create complex animations for characters and objects. It supports skeletal animation, blend trees, and state machines, enabling the creation of lifelike movements and behaviors.
- **Navigation system**: Unity provides a built-in navigation system that allows developers to create AI-driven characters that can move intelligently through the game world. NavMesh components define walkable areas, and the navigation system calculates paths for characters to follow.

- **Terrain system**: Unity's Terrain System enables the creation of vast, detailed outdoor environments. It supports painting textures, trees, and grass onto the terrain, providing tools for realistic landscape design.
- **Asset store integration**: Unity's Asset Store offers a vast library of 3D models, textures, scripts, and plugins that developers can use to enhance their projects. It is an excellent resource for finding ready-made assets and tools to accelerate development.

These tools and features, combined with Unity's intuitive interface and extensive documentation, empower developers to create diverse and interactive game objects and environments. Unity's flexibility and scalability make it a popular choice for indie developers and large studios working on various games and interactive applications.

VR development in Unity

Building VR applications in Unity involves understanding and integrating various components that create immersive virtual reality experiences. Here is a detailed overview of the key components and input methods commonly used in VR development:

- **VR headsets**: VR headsets are the primary interface between the user and the virtual environment. Popular VR headsets include Oculus Rift, HTC Vive, PlayStation VR, and Valve Index. Unity provides built-in support for these headsets and their respective SDKs, allowing developers to create VR experiences tailored to specific platforms.
- **Controllers**: VR controllers are handheld devices that allow users to interact with the virtual world. They can feature buttons, triggers, thumbsticks, and sensors to detect motion and gestures. Unity supports various controller types, enabling developers to design intuitive user interactions. For example:
    - **Oculus Touch**: Oculus Rift controllers with hand tracking and buttons.
    - **HTC Vive Wand**: HTC Vive controllers with touch-sensitive pads and triggers.
    - **PlayStation Move**: PlayStation VR controllers with buttons and motion tracking.
- **Tracking systems**: Tracking systems monitor the position and movement of VR headsets and controllers in real-time. They accurately represent the user's actions within the virtual environment. Common tracking systems include:
    - **Inside-out tracking**: Cameras and sensors on the headset track the surroundings.
    - **Outside-in tracking**: External sensors (lighthouse base stations for HTC Vive) track headset and controller positions.

- **Room-scale tracking**: Allows users to move freely within a designated physical space.

- **Input methods:** Unity supports various input methods for VR applications, allowing developers to create diverse and engaging interactions. Some common input methods include:
  - **Hand tracking:** Utilizes sensors to track hand movements and gestures without needing controllers. This method provides a natural and immersive experience.
  - **Voice recognition:** Integrates speech recognition software to enable users to control the VR environment using voice commands. This method enhances accessibility and hands-free interaction.
  - **Gaze-based interactions:** Tracks the user's gaze direction. Users can interact with objects or UI elements by looking at them, making it suitable for simple selection and navigation tasks.
  - **Gesture recognition:** Utilizes machine learning or predefined patterns to recognize hand gestures made by users. This method enables users to act by making specific gestures in the air.
  - **Physical controllers:** Allows users to interact with the virtual environment using handheld controllers, triggering actions through buttons, triggers, and thumbsticks.
  - **Haptic feedback:** Provides tactile feedback to users, simulating sensations like touch, impact, or vibration. Unity supports haptic feedback for controllers, enhancing the sense of presence in VR experiences.

Developers can choose and combine these input methods based on the VR platform, user experience goals, and the complexity of interactions they want to achieve.

In Unity, the integration of these components is typically handled through the Unity XR API, which provides a unified interface for different VR platforms. Unity's XR Interaction Toolkit offers tools for creating interactive VR experiences, including handling input events, object manipulation, and locomotion systems, streamlining the development process for VR applications. Developers can create compelling and immersive VR experiences in Unity by understanding and leveraging these components and input methods.

Creating scenes and environments

Creating scenes and environments in Unity involves several essential steps and techniques, from designing 3D models to optimizing the scene for performance and quality. Here is a comprehensive guide to help you understand the process:

- **Planning your scene**:
  - **Conceptualize**: Start by brainstorming and sketching your ideas. The purpose of the scene and its theme.
  - **Layout**: Plan the layout of your scene. Consider the placement of objects, characters, and camera angles.
  - **References**: Gather references for the environment, objects, and textures you plan to create. This helps maintain consistency and realism.
- **Creating 3D models**:
  - **Modeling software**: Use 3D modeling software like Blender, Maya, or 3ds Max to create your 3D models.
  - **Polygon count**: Optimize your models by keeping the polygon count as low as possible without compromising quality. Use **Level of detail** (**LoD**) models for distant objects.
  - **UV mapping**: Properly unwrap UVs for your models to apply textures accurately.
- **Creating textures**:
  - **Texture maps**: Create texture maps like diffuse (color), normal maps (surface details), specular maps (shininess), and emission maps (self-illumination).
  - **PBR workflow**: Use the **physically based rendering** (**PBR**) workflow for realistic materials. PBR shaders in Unity work based on textures like albedo, metallic, roughness, and normal maps.
  - **Texture compression**: Compress textures to reduce memory usage. Unity supports various texture compression formats.
- **Lighting**:
  - **Light sources**: Place light sources strategically. Unity supports point lights, directional lights, spotlights, and area lights.
  - **Global illumination**: Use baked or real-time global illumination for realistic lighting effects.
  - **Light probes**: Use light probes to capture lighting information for dynamic objects.
- **Optimizing for performance**:
  - **Occlusion culling**: Implement occlusion culling to avoid rendering objects invisible to the camera.

  - **LOD groups**: Use LOD groups for models to switch to lower-detail versions as the camera moves away.
  - **Batching**: Combine objects that share the same material to reduce draw calls. Static objects can be batched during the baking process.
  - **Shader optimization**: Write efficient shaders or use Unity's built-in optimized shaders.

- **Testing and iteration**:
  - **Playtesting**: Regularly playtest your scene to identify performance bottlenecks and visual issues.
  - **Profiling**: Use Unity Profiler to analyze the performance of your scene. Identify CPU and GPU usage and optimize accordingly.
  - **Feedback**: Gather feedback from peers or players. Iterate on your scene design based on feedback.

- **Version control**:
  - **Version control system**: Use a version control system like Git to track changes in your project. This ensures collaboration and allows you to revert to previous versions if needed.

- **Documentation and collaboration:**
  - **Documentation**: Document your scene layout, used assets, and special configurations. This helps other team members understand your work.
  - **Collaboration**: Communicate effectively with team members, especially if multiple people work on different aspects of the scene.

Remember, creating compelling scenes and environments requires combining creativity and technical proficiency. Continuously improve your skills, stay updated with Unity's latest features, and do not hesitate to seek feedback from the community to enhance your creations.

Best practices for scene optimization

Here are some very important aspects of optimizing scenes for performance and quality.

Occlusion culling

Occlusion culling is a rendering optimization technique employed in computer graphics and game development to enhance performance by selectively excluding non-visible objects from the rendering process. The fundamental objective is to avoid expending computational resources on rendering objects obstructed by other elements or lying outside the camera's field of view. The system identifies which objects are currently visible through dynamic and static occlusion culling algorithms and actively updates this determination during runtime. By excluding occluded or distant objects from the rendering pipeline, occlusion culling significantly reduces the workload on the graphics processing unit, resulting in improved frame rates and overall rendering efficiency, especially in complex and dynamic 3D scenes.

For instance, in a virtual environment, if a player is inside a building, occlusion culling would identify and omit rendering objects outside the building that are not visible from the player's viewpoint, such as structures or characters behind walls. This ensures that only the objects within the player's line of sight are rendered, leading to improved frame rates and more efficient use of graphical resources.

Level of detail system

LOD is a system used in computer graphics to optimize rendering performance by adjusting the detail of 3D models based on their distance from the viewer. The idea is to use simpler, lower-polygon versions of models when they are farther away and switch to more detailed versions as they get closer. This helps balance visual quality with computational efficiency.

Consider a scenario where you have a detailed 3D model of a tree in a game. As the player moves away from the tree, it becomes smaller on the screen, and the intricate details become less noticeable. Using LOD, you can create multiple versions of the tree model with varying levels of detail. For example:

- **High detail LOD (LOD0)**: This version includes all the fine details of the tree, suitable for close-up views.
- **Medium detail LOD (LOD1)**: A simplified version with fewer polygons and less intricate textures, suitable for medium distances.
- **Low detail LOD (LOD2)**: An even more simplified version, often a basic representation like a billboard or a simple shape, is used for distant views.

As the player moves through the game world, the LOD system dynamically switches between these versions based on the distance between the camera and the object. When the tree is far away, the engine renders the low-detail version, significantly reducing the number of polygons and textures processed by the GPU. As the player approaches, the system switches to higher LODs, ensuring a balance between visual fidelity and performance.

This LOD system is a crucial parameter for scene optimization because it minimizes the computational load during rendering. By rendering simpler versions of objects when they are distant and progressively adding detail as needed, LOD helps maintain a visually appealing scene while preventing unnecessary strain on the hardware. This is particularly important for large and open game environments where numerous objects may be visible simultaneously. LOD systems contribute to smoother performance, allowing games and applications to run efficiently without sacrificing visual quality.

Batching

Batching is a technique in computer graphics and game development that involves combining multiple objects or elements into a single batch for more efficient rendering. This process helps optimize performance by reducing the number of draw calls, which are commands sent to the GPU to render individual objects. Batching is particularly useful for scenes with many objects, as it minimizes the overhead of processing and transmitting data to the GPU.

Here is a simple example of how batching works and its benefits: consider a scene with multiple trees, each represented by a separate 3D model. Without batching, each tree would require its draw call, leading to many draw calls for the entire scene. However, batching can combine these trees into a single batch, resulting in a much smaller number of draw calls.

- **Without batching**
    - o 10 trees in the scene would result in 10 draw calls (one for each tree).
    - o This can increase CPU overhead and potentially impact performance, especially in scenes with numerous objects.
- **With batching:**
    - o The 10 trees are combined into a single batch.
    - o Only one draw call is needed to render the entire batch of trees.

Shader optimization

Shader optimization is crucial in scene optimization in computer graphics and game development. Shaders are programs that run on the GPU to determine the appearance of objects in a scene. Optimizing shaders involves improving their efficiency to enhance overall rendering performance. Here is a simple example illustrating how shader optimization can be a helpful parameter for scene optimization. Consider a scene with multiple objects using a complex shader that calculates advanced lighting, reflections, and other visual effects. Without shader optimization, these shaders might be computationally expensive, significantly impacting frame rates.

By optimizing shaders, developers can balance visual fidelity and performance. This is particularly important for real-time applications, such as games or simulations, where maintaining a high frame rate is essential for a smooth and immersive user experience. Unity and other game engines provide tools and guidelines for shader optimization to help developers achieve optimal performance in their scenes.

Texture atlasing

Texture atlasing is used in computer graphics and game development to optimize rendering performance by combining multiple textures into a single texture atlas. This approach helps reduce the number of draw calls and memory overhead associated with managing individual textures, improving efficiency in rendering large scenes. Here is a simple example to illustrate how texture atlasing can be a helpful parameter for scene optimization. Consider a game environment with several objects, each requiring its unique texture. Without texture atlasing, each object would have a separate texture, leading to more draw calls and increased memory usage.

Many game engines, including Unity, provide tools and workflows to facilitate texture atlasing. Unity's Sprite Packer, for example, allows developers to automatically pack multiple textures into a single atlas, optimizing 2D game assets. This approach also applies to 3D environments, where objects can share a texture atlas for efficient rendering. Overall, texture atlasing is a valuable technique for scene optimization, particularly in scenarios where there are numerous objects with individual textures.

Physics optimization

Physics optimization is a critical aspect of scene optimization in game development, ensuring the physics simulations run efficiently without sacrificing realism. Physics simulations can be computationally expensive, especially in complex scenes with numerous interacting objects. Optimizing physics involves adjusting and reducing computational load while maintaining a realistic and responsive environment. Here is a simple example of how physics optimization is a helpful parameter for scene optimization. Consider a game with many rigid bodies representing objects in the environment, such as crates, barrels, and other physics-enabled entities. Without physics optimization, the simulation may become a bottleneck, impacting overall performance.

By implementing these physics optimization techniques, developers can maintain a realistic and interactive game environment while ensuring that physics simulations are efficiently managed. This is particularly crucial in scenes with a high density of interacting objects, dynamic physics-based gameplay, or simulations involving complex physics interactions.

Audio optimization

Audio optimization is a crucial aspect of scene optimization in game development, ensuring that sound processing is efficient and doesn't adversely impact overall performance. Optimizing audio involves managing the playback of sounds and music to minimize computational resources while providing an immersive and realistic auditory experience. Here is a simple example to illustrate how audio optimization is a helpful parameter for scene optimization, consider a game environment with various audio sources, including ambient sounds, footsteps, and dynamic music. Without audio optimization, processing numerous simultaneous audio elements may strain system resources.

Key strategies for audio optimization include:

- **Audio occlusion and attenuation**: Implement occlusion and attenuation techniques to simulate the realistic behavior of sound in the game world. Sounds occluded (behind obstacles) or distant from the player can have reduced processing requirements, contributing to performance optimization.
- **Prioritization of sounds**: Prioritize sounds based on their relevance to the player's experience. Focus on processing critical sounds that contribute significantly to the player's immersion while minimizing the impact of less crucial ambient noises.
- **Audio pooling**: Use audio pooling to recycle and manage audio instances efficiently. Instead of creating and destroying audio objects dynamically, maintain a pool of pre-allocated audio instances that can be reused. This reduces the overhead associated with audio instantiation during gameplay.
- **Dynamic loading and unloading**: Dynamically load audio assets based on the player's location in the game world. This helps manage memory usage and prevents unnecessary audio resource processing that is not immediately relevant.
- **Compression and format selection**: Compress audio files appropriately and choose audio formats that balance quality with file size. Compressed audio files require less bandwidth and storage space, resulting in faster loading times and reduced memory usage.

By implementing these audio optimization techniques, developers can achieve a balance between realistic soundscapes and efficient resource utilization. This is particularly important in scenes with numerous audio sources, and optimizing audio processing contributes to a smoother and more responsive gaming experience.

Scripting in Unity

Scripting plays a fundamental role in Unity game development, allowing developers to create interactive gameplay, implement game mechanics, and control various aspects of the game. Unity primarily supports two programming languages for scripting: C# and JavaScript (`UnityScript`). Let us explore the role of scripting in Unity:

- **Role of scripting in Unity:**
  - **Game logic**: Scripts define the behavior of game objects, including player characters, enemies, NPCs, and interactive elements. Game logic, such as movement, combat, and AI, is implemented through scripts.

- **User interaction**: Scripts handle user input, such as keyboard, mouse, and touch events, enabling players to interact with the game world.
- **Animations**: Scripts control animations, allowing developers to create dynamic and responsive character animations and visual effects.
- **Physics**: Scripts can apply forces, detect collisions, and control physics behaviors, influencing the movement and interactions of objects in the game.
- **UI and menus**: Scripts manage UIs, menus, and HUD elements, providing a seamless user experience.
- **Networking**: Scripts enable multiplayer functionality, allowing players to interact and collaborate in real-time over the network.

Programming languages in Unity

Let us now discuss the pros and cons of the programming languages in Unity.

C#

The following are the pros and cons of C#:

- **Pros:**
  - **Strongly typed**: C# is a statically typed language, providing robust error checking and improved code quality.
  - **Performance**: C# offers excellent performance and memory management, making it suitable for complex games.
  - **Unity's primary language**: C# is the officially recommended language by Unity and has extensive support and documentation.
  - **Ecosystem**: C# has a large, active developer community providing resources and support.
- **Cons:**
  - **Learning curve**: For beginners, C# might have a steeper learning curve than JavaScript.

Refer to the following figure:

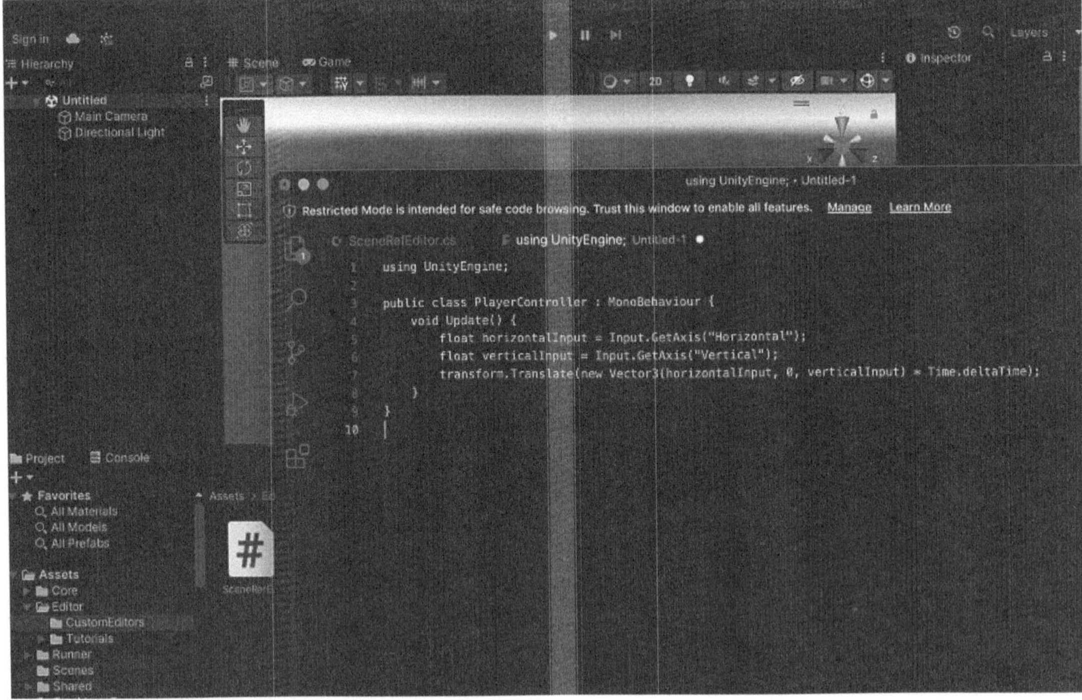

Figure 11.4: Illustration of Unity workspace coded in C#

JavaScript (UnityScript)

UnityScript was a scripting language used in Unity game development. It was a JavaScript-like language specifically designed for scripting in the Unity game engine. UnityScript shared similarities with JavaScript, making it accessible to developers familiar with JavaScript syntax.

Developers are strongly encouraged to use C# for new Unity projects and when following modern Unity tutorials and documentation. C# has become the standard scripting language for Unity game development due to its performance, readability, and extensive support within the Unity ecosystem.

Unity announced that UnityScript (JavaScript) is deprecated and will be removed in future versions. It is not recommended for new projects.

UI Design in VR

Designing UIs for VR applications presents unique challenges due to the immersive and three-dimensional nature of the VR environment. Here are some techniques and best practices to create intuitive and immersive UIs for VR applications:

- **Understand the VR environment:**
  - **Spatial awareness:** VR interfaces exist in 3D space, so understanding spatial relationships is crucial. Design UI elements that fit naturally within the VR environment.
  - **Comfort:** Avoid elements that may cause discomfort or motion sickness. Keep user experience smooth and pleasant.
- **Use 3D UI elements:**
  - **Depth and layers:** Utilize depth and layers to create a sense of hierarchy and importance among UI elements. Important elements can be closer to the user, while secondary elements can be farther away.
  - **3D widgets:** Use 3D objects like buttons, sliders, and panels that users can interact with using VR controllers.
- **Interactivity and feedback:**
  - **Physicality:** Mimic real-world interactions. For example, users can grab and manipulate objects directly using motion controllers.
  - **Haptic feedback:** Provide haptic feedback through controllers to simulate the sense of touch and enhance the feeling of interaction.
- **Optimize text and legibility:**
  - **Font size and type:** Use legible fonts and ensure the text size is large enough to be readable in the VR environment.
  - **Contrast:** Ensure a proper contrast between text and background to enhance readability.
- **Gaze-based interaction:**
  - **Gaze input:** Use the user's gaze as a form of input. Menus or buttons can activate based on where the user is looking.
  - **Gaze feedback:** Provide visual cues, such as highlighting, when the user's gaze intersects with interactive elements.
- **Gesture-based controls:**
  - **Hand gestures:** Implement hand gestures recognized by VR controllers for intuitive navigation and interaction.
  - **Pinching and grabbing:** Use gestures like pinching and grabbing to interact with objects and UI elements.

- **UI placement and anchoring:**
  - **Fixed versus world-space UI**: Decide whether UI elements are fixed in the user's view or anchored to specific objects in the VR environment.
  - **Comfortable viewing**: Place important UI elements within the user's comfortable viewing range without forcing them to strain their neck or eyes.
- **Audio feedback:**
  - **Spatial audio**: Use spatial audio cues to guide users' attention to specific UI elements or interactions.
  - **Audio feedback**: Provide audio feedback when users interact with UI elements to reinforce the interaction feeling.
- **User testing and iteration:**
  - **Playtesting**: Regularly test your VR application with real users to gather feedback on the UI/UX. VR experiences can be highly subjective, so user testing is invaluable.
  - **Iterate**: Based on user feedback, iterate on the design to improve usability and user satisfaction.
- **Performance optimization:**
  - **Optimized assets**: Keep 3D models and textures optimized for performance to ensure a smooth experience, especially in resource-intensive VR environments.

Designing UIs for VR applications requires a deep understanding of VR technology and human-computer interaction principles. You can create compelling and user-friendly VR interfaces by focusing on intuitive interactions, user comfort, and immersive experiences.

Conclusion

In this chapter, we embarked on a comprehensive journey through the intricate world of Unity. This powerful game development engine has revolutionized how we create interactive and immersive experiences. We began with an insightful exploration of Unity's fundamentals, delving into its architecture and workflow, laying the foundation for our understanding of this dynamic platform.

Most of our exploration was dedicated to scripting, where we learned the art of bringing our creations to life through programming. Whether manipulating game logic, designing interactive elements, or controlling animations, we harnessed the power of scripting languages like C# and JavaScript to craft dynamic and responsive experiences.

Furthermore, we dived into the intriguing realm of UI design in VR. Understanding the nuances of spatial awareness, interactivity, and user feedback, we deciphered the complexities of designing intuitive and immersive interfaces in three-dimensional space.

As we conclude this chapter, we stand equipped with a wealth of knowledge. From the foundational concepts of Unity to the intricacies of VR development, from scene creation to scripting intricacies and UI design, we have traversed a diverse and fascinating terrain.

In the next chapter, we will provide practical advice for building successful VR and AR applications, including tips for marketing and monetizing these products.

Points to remember

- **Introduction to Unity:**
    - Unity is a powerful and versatile game development engine that creates games, simulations, and interactive experiences across various platforms.
    - It provides a user-friendly interface and supports both 2D and 3D game development.
- **Unity architecture:**
    - Unity follows an entity-component system architecture, allowing flexibility and modularity in-game object design.
    - Understanding components, GameObjects, and the hierarchy system is crucial for effective Unity development.
- **Unity workflow:**
    - Unity's workflow includes asset import, scene creation, scripting, and deployment to target platforms.
    - Familiarity with the Unity Editor, including the Scene view, Game view, and Inspector, is essential for efficient development.
- **VR development in Unity:**
    - VR development in Unity involves creating immersive experiences for virtual reality headsets, such as Oculus Rift, HTC Vive, or PlayStation VR.
    - Unity provides specialized tools and components for VR development, enabling developers to create interactive and realistic VR environments.
- **Creating scenes and environments:**
    - Designing scenes involves creating 3D models, textures, and lighting and optimizing for performance.

  - Techniques such as LOD, occlusion culling, and light baking are essential for creating visually appealing and performant environments.

- **Scripting in Unity:**
  - Unity supports scripting in C# and JavaScript (UnityScript), with C# being the recommended and widely used language.
  - Scripts control game logic, animations, and interactions, making them the backbone of Unity development.

- **UI design in VR:**
  - VR UI design requires a deep understanding of spatial awareness, interactivity, and user comfort.
  - Techniques such as gaze-based interaction, gesture controls, and spatial audio feedback enhance user experience in VR environments.

- Remember, Unity development is both an art and a science. Mastering these concepts and techniques will empower you to create immersive, engaging, and performant experiences in the exciting world of Unity game development and virtual reality.

Chapter 12
Building and Monetizing Successful VR and AR Applications

Introduction

In this chapter, we will provide practical advice for building successful VR and AR applications, including tips for marketing and monetizing these products. We will discuss the key factors contributing to the success of VR and AR applications, including user experience, design, and performance. We will also explore the various strategies that can be used to market and monetize VR and AR applications, such as advertising, sponsorships, and in-app purchases.

Structure

In this chapter, we will discuss the following topics:

- Understanding your audience
- Engaging user experience for retention
- Optimal application boosts retention
- Monetizing your app
- Marketing your app
- Leveraging analytics
- Engaging with your community

Objectives

At the end of this chapter, you will understand how **Virtual Reality (VR)** and **Augmented Reality (AR)** technologies have ushered in a new era of immersive experiences. To harness the full potential of VR and AR applications, developers need to understand their audience, design user-friendly interfaces, optimize performance, effectively monetize their apps, implement strategic marketing, analyze user data, and engage with their community. This chapter explores essential strategies in these areas, guiding developers toward building and monetizing successful VR and AR applications.

Understanding your audience

Understanding your audience is the cornerstone of a successful VR or AR application. In the dynamic realm of virtual and augmented reality, knowing your users intimately can be the difference between an app that soars and one that fizzles out. Here are key considerations for understanding the audience:

- **Demographic profiling:** Begin by defining the demographic characteristics of your target audience. Age, gender, location, interests, and occupation are pivotal in shaping user preferences. For instance, an educational AR app might target students and educators, whereas a VR gaming app could cater to a younger, tech-savvy demographic.

- **Psychographic insights:** Go beyond demographics and delve into psychographics, the study of attitudes, aspirations, and values of your audience. Understanding the psychographic profile helps in crafting experiences that resonate emotionally. For instance, an AR meditation app might cater to users seeking stress relief and mindfulness, shaping the content and design accordingly.

- **Behavioral analysis:** Study user behavior patterns. Knowing what users are doing within your app, popular features, and their engagement. Behavioral analysis offers real-time insights into user interactions. Tracking user journeys helps identify pain points and preferences, guiding iterative app development.

- **Technological proficiency:** Assess the technological proficiency of your audience. Whether they are early adopters comfortable with cutting-edge tech or beginners needing intuitive interfaces, this insight guides the complexity of your application. A tech-savvy audience might appreciate intricate VR environments, while beginners might favor simplicity and ease of use in AR interfaces.

- **Feedback loops:** Engage your audience actively through surveys, feedback forms, and social media channels. User feedback is a goldmine of information. Pay attention to user reviews, both positive and negative. Positive reviews highlight what users love, while negative feedback points to areas for improvement. Addressing user concerns fosters trust and loyalty.

- **Accessibility and inclusivity:** Design your app, keeping accessibility in mind. Ensure compatibility with assistive technologies for users with disabilities. VR and AR have immense potential in education and therapy for people with disabilities. By creating inclusive experiences, you tap into an often-underserved market.
- **Competitor analysis:** Study successful VR and AR applications in your niche. Analyze their user base and user reviews. Specific features that the users are praising and the areas where the competitors are falling short. Identifying gaps in existing offerings helps you position your app uniquely, catering to unmet needs and preferences.

Understanding your audience is not a one-time task but an ongoing process. As technology evolves and user preferences shift, staying attuned to your audience ensures your VR or AR application remains relevant and continues captivating users. By empathizing with your users, tailoring experiences to their needs, and actively incorporating their feedback, you pave the way for a loyal user base and sustainable monetization strategies.

Engaging user experience for retention

Designing for user experience in VR and AR applications is a multifaceted challenge. Unlike traditional interfaces, VR and AR offer immersive, interactive environments that demand careful consideration of user interactions, spatial design, and sensory engagement.

Here are some of the key points that you can create for a user experience that captivates and retains users:

- **Intuitive interfaces**: Simplicity is key. Design intuitive menus and controls that users can grasp naturally. Consider hand gestures and motion-based interactions in VR for a more immersive feel. In AR, utilize gestures and taps that align with real-world movements. Intuitive interfaces reduce the learning curve, ensuring users can engage with your application effortlessly.
- **Spatial design**: In VR, users inhabit a 3D space. Thoughtful spatial design is essential for guiding user movement and interactions. Create clear paths, interactive zones, and focal points within the virtual environment. Spatial audio cues can enhance the sense of presence, guiding users toward points of interest. In AR, consider the physical environment design overlays that blend seamlessly with the real world, enhancing immersion.
- **Feedback and responsiveness:** Provide immediate feedback for user actions. Visual cues, haptic feedback, and audio responses confirm user interactions, reinforcing a sense of control. Responsive interfaces enhance user confidence, making the experience more engaging and enjoyable. Feedback also includes loading times to optimize your application's performance to minimize waiting, ensuring a seamless experience.

- **Comfort and motion sickness**: Motion sickness is a concern in VR. Implement comfort features like teleportation, snap turning, and adjustable movement speeds. Minimize sudden movements and disorienting camera shifts. Consider the user's physical comfort design interactions in AR that do not require prolonged device holding up. Prioritize user comfort to enhance the overall experience.
- **Realism and immersion**: Strive for realism without compromising performance. High-quality textures, realistic lighting, and lifelike animations enhance immersion. In VR, consider hand presence; accurately mirroring hand movements and gestures creates a powerful connection between the user and the virtual world. In AR, realistic object placement and lighting effects deepen the sense of presence in the real environment.
- **Consistent branding**: Maintain consistent branding elements throughout the application. From logos to color schemes, cohesive branding creates a memorable user experience. Consistency instills trust and brand recognition, vital for user retention and monetization efforts.
- **User testing and iteration:** User testing is invaluable. Gather feedback from diverse users, including novices and experienced VR/AR enthusiasts. Identify pain points and areas of confusion. Use this feedback for iterative design improvements. A user-centric approach ensures your application aligns with user expectations and preferences.
- **Accessibility**: Consider diverse user needs. Implement subtitles, adjustable text sizes, and color contrasts for visually impaired users. Ensure compatibility with assistive technologies. Designing for accessibility not only broadens your user base but also reflects ethical design practices.

Optimal application performance boosts retention

Creating immersive VR and AR experiences exceeds stunning visuals; it hinges on meticulous performance optimization. First and foremost, developers must optimize assets, meticulously balancing visual fidelity with resource efficiency. This involves compressing textures, utilizing LOD models, and implementing asynchronous loading techniques.

Clean, streamlined code is paramount, eliminating redundancies and employing occlusion culling to render only what users see, preventing unnecessary processing. Consistent frame rates, ideally 90 FPS or higher, ensure smooth interactions, necessitating rendering techniques and dynamic resolution scaling optimizations.

Memory management is key, requiring developers to employ strategies like object pooling and texture atlases while ensuring proper garbage collection. Network optimizations, such as client-side prediction and lag compensation, are vital for real-time interactions, especially in multiplayer scenarios. Tailoring applications to specific devices and continuous testing on diverse platforms ensure optimal performance across different hardware configurations.

Lastly, user experience testing provides invaluable feedback, helping developers identify and address performance-related frustrations and ensuring a seamless and immersive user experience.

So, we can say that building high-performance VR and AR applications demands a multifaceted approach encompassing asset optimization, streamlined coding, consistent frame rates, memory efficiency, network optimizations, device-specific tailoring, and rigorous user experience testing. By meticulously addressing each aspect, developers can create applications that captivate users and serve as the foundation for successful monetization. These optimizations are not merely technical necessities but the building blocks for user satisfaction, positive reviews, and prolonged user engagement. In the dynamic landscape of VR and AR, a high-performing application catalyzes user retention, positive word-of-mouth, and sustainable revenue streams, marking the pathway toward building and monetizing successful VR and AR applications.

Monetizing your app

Monetizing VR and AR applications involves carefully considering diverse strategies with advantages and challenges. Here, we explore various approaches to monetization, along with their respective pros and cons.

Paid apps

The pros and cons of paid apps are as follows:

- **Pros**: Paid apps generate direct revenue, ensuring developers get paid upfront for their efforts. This model often implies a higher level of user commitment, potentially resulting in more engaged users due to the initial investment.
- **Cons**: The barrier to entry is higher for users, leading to a potentially smaller user base. Users might hesitate to purchase apps without first experiencing them, limiting the number of downloads and potential earnings.

Tip: Provide a compelling app description and high-quality screenshots or videos on app stores to showcase the app's value and features.

In-app purchases and virtual goods

The pros and cons of **In-App Purchases (IAPs)** are as follows:

- **Pros**: IAPs and virtual goods allow developers to offer free apps while monetizing through microtransactions. Users can access basic features for free, with the option to purchase additional content or virtual items, enhancing user engagement.
- **Cons**: Balancing the fine line between enticing purchases and not alienating free users is crucial. Overemphasis on IAPs may lead to user frustration and negative reviews if perceived as pay-to-win or excessively monetized.

Tip: Offer enticing, limited-time offers or discounts on virtual items to encourage purchases.

Freemium models

The pros and cons of freemium models are as follows:

- **Pros**: Freemium models combine free access with premium features or content available through purchases. This approach attracts a broad user base while incentivizing users to upgrade for enhanced experiences.
- **Cons**: Careful balancing is necessary to avoid creating a significant disparity between free and premium content. Striking the right balance ensures users find value in the premium features without feeling pressured to spend excessively.

Tip: Offer a generous amount of free content or features to hook users, and then introduce premium features gradually to maintain their interest.

Subscriptions

The pros and cons of subscriptions are as follows:

- **Pros**: Subscriptions provide a steady revenue stream, fostering a long-term relationship with users. Regular updates and exclusive content for subscribers enhance user retention.
- **Cons**: Users may hesitate to commit to ongoing payments, expecting substantial value in return. Maintaining consistent, high-quality content is essential to justify the subscription model.

Tip: Regularly update and expand subscription-exclusive content to keep subscribers engaged and justify the recurring payment.

Ads and sponsorships

The pros and cons of ads and sponsorship are as follows:

- **Pros**: Ad-supported models offer free access to users while generating revenue from advertisers. Brand sponsorships align the app with specific products or services, creating mutually beneficial partnerships.
- **Cons**: Excessive ads can disrupt the user experience, leading to user dissatisfaction and potential uninstallation. Balancing ad frequency and relevance is crucial. Sponsorship deals need careful negotiation and may restrict the app's creative freedom.

Tip: Implement non-intrusive ad formats, such as rewarded ads, which users can opt into for in-app rewards, ensuring a positive user experience.

Location-based services and partnerships

The pros and cons of location-based services and partnerships are as follows:

- **Pros**: Utilizing location-based services for augmented reality experiences can create unique monetization opportunities, such as sponsored location-based events or offers. Partnerships with businesses for AR advertising or special promotions can enhance revenue.
- **Cons**: The success of location-based services relies heavily on the app's user base and geographic reach. Initial efforts in building partnerships and securing sponsored events can be time-consuming.

Tip: Foster relationships with local businesses for mutually beneficial partnerships, creating immersive AR experiences tied to real-world locations.

Data monetization

The pros and cons of data monetization are as follows:

- **Pros**: Data-driven insights from user behavior can be monetized by selling anonymized, aggregated data to third parties. This approach leverages analytics to create additional revenue streams without impacting the user experience directly.
- **Cons**: Data privacy concerns are paramount. Striking a balance between monetization and user privacy is challenging. Transparent policies and ensuring user consent are essential.

Tip: Communicate your data usage policies to users and ensure their data is anonymized and secure. Transparency builds trust and user confidence.

In conclusion, the monetization strategy for VR and AR applications depends on the app's nature, target audience, and developer goals. Choosing the right approach involves understanding user preferences and market trends while carefully weighing the pros and cons of each method. Ultimately, successful monetization aligns user value with revenue generation, creating a sustainable and profitable ecosystem for developers in the dynamic landscape of VR and AR applications.

Marketing your app

Effective marketing ensures your app stands out and reaches its intended audience in the competitive landscape of VR and AR applications. A well-thought-out marketing strategy drives initial downloads, sustains user engagement, and fosters a loyal user base. Here, we delve into the importance of marketing and explore diverse channels and tactics to effectively promote your VR and AR applications.

Here are some of the examples from the industry where effective and multi-facet marketing helped product outreach and increase market capitalization:

- IKEA Place is an AR app that allows users to place and visualize IKEA furniture in their homes virtually before making a purchase.

  Effective marketing strategies:

  - **Educational content**: IKEA used the app to create educational content using AR features, making it user-friendly.
  - **Social media integration**: Customers were encouraged to share their AR-designed spaces on social media, creating user-generated content.
  - **Incentivized purchases**: The app indirectly increased sales by allowing customers to confidently visualize products in their homes before buying.

- Pokémon GO by Niantic Labs is an AR mobile game that allows players to catch virtual Pokémon in the real world using their smartphones.

  Effective marketing strategies:

  - **Social media engagement**: Niantic used social media extensively to tease the game's release, creating excitement and anticipation.
  - **Word of mouth and community building**: The game leveraged the nostalgia associated with Pokémon and encouraged social interactions among players.
  - **In-app purchases**: The app monetized through in-app purchases for items like Poke Balls and other virtual goods.

- Oculus VR by Oculus, a subsidiary of Meta (formerly Facebook) is a leading VR platform offering a range of VR experiences and games.

Effective marketing strategies:

- **Influencer partnerships**: Oculus collaborated with influencers in the gaming and tech industry to promote its VR devices and experiences.
- **Content exclusivity**: Oculus secured exclusive VR content, making its platform more appealing to users.
- **In-store demos**: Oculus set up in-store VR demo stations to allow potential customers to experience the technology firsthand.
- **Regular software updates**: Frequent updates introduced new features and improved the user experience, encouraging user retention.

Importance of effective marketing

Let us discuss the importance of effective marketing:

- **Visibility and awareness**: Effective marketing enhances the visibility of your VR or AR application, ensuring it reaches a broader audience. Increased awareness among potential users is the first step towards building a dedicated user base.
- **User engagement and retention**: Marketing campaigns keep users interested and invested in your application. Regular updates, sneak peeks, and interactive content maintain user interest, encouraging them to explore new features and functionalities, thereby enhancing retention rates.
- **Building credibility and trust**: A well-executed marketing strategy establishes your VR or AR app as a credible and trustworthy choice among users. Positive user testimonials, expert endorsements, and professional branding contribute to building trust, which is vital for sustained success.
- **Competition and market differentiation**: In a market flooded with options, effective marketing helps your application stand out. Highlighting unique features and benefits through marketing channels differentiates your app, making it appealing to potential users.

Exploring various channels and tactics

Let us explore various channels and tactics in this section:

- **Social media platforms**: Utilize platforms like Facebook, Instagram, Twitter, and LinkedIn to create engaging content, including videos, teasers, and interactive posts. Social media offers a direct channel to connect with potential users, fostering a community around your app.
- **Influencer partnerships**: Collaborate with influencers and content creators within the VR and AR community. Their endorsement and firsthand experience

can significantly impact their followers' perception of your application, driving downloads and user engagement.

- **App Store Optimization (ASO)**: Optimize your app store presence with relevant keywords, appealing visuals, and compelling descriptions. A well-optimized app store page increases the likelihood of your app being discovered by users searching for VR and AR experiences.
- **Email marketing and newsletters**: Build an email list of interested users and send regular newsletters showcasing updates, new features, and exclusive offers. Personalized communication keeps users engaged and informed, increasing the chances of app re-engagement.
- **Content marketing**: Create blog posts, tutorials, and how-to guides related to VR and AR technology. Share valuable insights, tips, and industry news. Quality content establishes your authority in the field, attracting users interested in your expertise.
- **Partnerships and collaborations**: Collaborate with VR/AR hardware manufacturers, event organizers, or relevant industry stakeholders. Partnerships can lead to cross-promotion opportunities, increasing your app's reach and credibility.

In conclusion, effective marketing is not just a one-time effort but an ongoing process that nurtures user relationships, sustains interest, and promotes user loyalty. By leveraging diverse marketing channels and tactics, VR and AR developers can create a compelling narrative around their applications, ensuring that they not only reach their target audience but also create a lasting impact in the competitive landscape of immersive technologies.

App store optimization

Having a stellar VR or AR application is only half the battle in the vast ocean of app marketplaces. To ensure your app gets the attention it deserves, mastering the art of ASO is essential. ASO involves optimizing various elements of your app store listing to improve its discoverability and visibility. Here is how a strategic approach to ASO can significantly impact the success of your VR and AR applications:

- **Keyword research**: Conduct in-depth research to identify relevant keywords related to your VR or AR application. Think from the user's perspective, the terms they are likely to search for when looking for an app like yours, and incorporate these keywords naturally into your app title, description, and backend keywords to enhance search relevance.
- **Compelling app title and description**: Craft an engaging and informative title that conveys your app's purpose. Utilize the description space to highlight key features and benefits. Use concise language, emphasizing what sets your VR or AR

application apart. A compelling description captures user interest, encouraging them to explore further.

- **Eye-catching visuals**: Visual elements, including app icons, screenshots, and promotional videos, are crucial for grabbing user attention. Design an eye-catching app icon that represents your app's essence. Use high-quality, captivating screenshots that showcase different app features and experiences. Include a compelling promotional video that provides a glimpse into the immersive world of your VR or AR application.
- **Positive ratings and reviews**: Encourage satisfied users to leave positive reviews and ratings. Positive feedback enhances your app's reputation and credibility, influencing potential users. Address negative reviews promptly and professionally, demonstrating your commitment to user satisfaction. High ratings and positive testimonials increase user trust and app appeal.
- **Regular updates and user engagement**: App stores favor actively maintained apps that engage users regularly. Regularly update your VR or AR application, introducing new features, content, or bug fixes. Engage with your user base through in-app notifications, emails, or social media, keeping them informed and involved in your app's evolution.
- **Localization and internationalization**: Localize your app store listing, including the app title, description, and keywords, for different languages and regions. Tailoring your content to specific languages and cultures increases your app's visibility in international markets, attracting a diverse user base.
- **A/B testing and iterative optimization**: Utilize A/B testing to experiment with different elements of your app store listing, such as titles, descriptions, and visuals. Analyze the performance of different variations to identify what resonates best with users. Continuously iterate and optimize your listing based on user behavior and feedback.

In conclusion, ASO is a dynamic and ongoing process that significantly impacts your VR or AR application's discoverability and visibility in app marketplaces. By meticulously optimizing keywords, crafting compelling titles and descriptions, designing eye-catching visuals, encouraging positive reviews, engaging with users, localizing content, and employing data-driven iterative approaches, developers can maximize their app's potential, ensuring it reaches the right audience and thrive in the competitive landscape of app marketplaces.

Leveraging analytics

Understanding user behavior and app performance is pivotal for building and monetizing successful VR and AR applications. Developers gain valuable insights that drive informed decisions by tracking key metrics and employing effective analytics tools. Here, we explore essential metrics and offer tips on how to utilize analytics tools effectively to maximize your app's potential:

- **User engagement**: User engagement metrics, such as session duration, feature interactions, and user feedback, reveal how users interact with your VR or AR application. Regularly monitor these metrics to identify popular features and user preferences. Engage users through surveys or in-app messages to gather qualitative data, providing deeper insights into their experiences.
- **Retention rate**: The retention rate measures the percentage of users who return to your app after the initial download. High retention indicates satisfied users and a compelling app experience. Analyze user journeys to pinpoint drop-off points. Enhance onboarding processes, introduce new content, or send personalized notifications to boost retention rates over time.
- **Monetization metrics**: Key monetization metrics include **Average Revenue Per User (ARPU)**, **Customer Lifetime Value (CLV)**, and conversion rates for in-app purchases. Track these metrics to assess revenue generation. Experiment with pricing strategies, offer limited-time promotions or introduce exclusive content for paying users to enhance monetization opportunities.
- **User acquisition and sources**: Understand where your users come from. Track acquisition channels and referral sources to identify the most effective marketing efforts. Allocate resources to channels that yield high-quality users. Analyze user behavior based on acquisition sources to tailor marketing strategies for specific user segments, optimizing conversion rates.
- **Performance and technical metrics**: Technical metrics, such as app crashes, loading times, and hardware compatibility issues, directly impact user experience. Regularly monitor these metrics to ensure a seamless app performance. Address technical issues promptly to prevent user frustration, negative reviews, and uninstallations.

Tips for using analytics tools effectively

Let us discuss how we can effectively use analytics tools:

- **Choose the right analytics tool**: Select analytics tools tailored for VR and AR applications. Look for platforms offering features like heatmap analysis, 3D interaction tracking, and real-time user feedback collection, catering specifically to immersive experiences.
- **Set clear goals and KPIs**: Establish **Key Performance Indicators (KPIs)** aligned with your app's objectives. Define specific goals, such as increasing user engagement or improving retention rates. Analytics tools are most effective when used to measure progress toward these objectives.

- **Implement event tracking**: Implement event tracking within your app to monitor user interactions. Define and track events like level completion, feature usage, or in-app purchases. Granular event tracking provides detailed insights into user behavior, guiding app enhancements.
- **Utilize A/B testing**: A/B testing allows you to experiment with different app variations. Test UI, features, or pricing structure changes and analyze user responses. A/B testing provides data-driven insights, helping you make informed decisions for optimal user engagement and revenue generation.
- **Combine quantitative and qualitative data**: Combine quantitative data (metrics and numbers) with qualitative data (user feedback, reviews) to gain a holistic understanding of user experiences. Quantitative data provides patterns, while qualitative data offers context, enriching your analytical insights.

Incorporating a data-driven approach into your VR or AR application development process empowers you to make informed decisions, iterate on user feedback, and enhance the overall user experience. By understanding and utilizing metrics effectively, developers can create immersive, engaging, and monetizable experiences that captivate users and thrive in the competitive landscape of virtual and augmented reality applications.

Engaging with your community

In the ever-evolving realm of VR and AR applications, the symbiotic relationship between developers and their user community is the cornerstone of success. Engaging with users and fans is a practice and an ethos that shapes exceptional applications. By establishing vibrant online spaces, social media channels, and interactive forums, developers create platforms where users can share their experiences and contribute meaningfully to the app's evolution. Transparent communication, whether through regular updates or behind-the-scenes glimpses, builds trust, fostering a sense of belonging among users. Actively seeking feedback through surveys, in-app questionnaires, and beta testing programs provides invaluable insights into user preferences and pain points. Hosting live Q&A sessions, interactive webinars, and community events creates a personal connection, enabling direct conversations with users. Implementing feedback loops, where user suggestions directly influence the app's features, demonstrates a profound commitment to user satisfaction. By acknowledging and acting upon user feedback, developers refine their applications and cultivate a loyal, enthusiastic user base, setting the stage for successful monetization and enduring user engagement.

In conclusion, engaging with your community of users and fans is not merely a strategy but a fundamental ethos of successful VR and AR application development. By fostering a sense of community, maintaining transparent communication, actively soliciting feedback through various channels, and demonstrating responsiveness to user input, developers can create a loyal user base invested in the application's success. This symbiotic relationship between developers and users forms the foundation for building a user-centric, immersive experience that not only meets user expectations but exceeds them, ensuring long-term success and sustainable monetization strategies.

Conclusion

In this chapter, we embarked on a comprehensive journey through the intricate landscape of developing and monetizing cutting-edge VR and AR applications. We unveiled the crucial elements that form the foundation of prosperous VR and AR ventures.

Understanding your audience became the compass guiding our development, enabling us to tailor experiences that resonate deeply with users. Designing for user experience emerged as an art, blending innovation with usability, ensuring every interaction feels intuitive and immersive. Building for performance transformed our visions into reality, demanding meticulous optimization to deliver seamless, high-quality experiences.

Monetization strategies were explored, from paid apps to in-app purchases, subscriptions, ads, and strategic partnerships, each avenue revealing unique opportunities for revenue generation. Marketing initiatives unfolded across social media platforms, influencer engagements, app store optimizations, and data-driven campaigns, fostering visibility and user acquisition.

Our journey into analytics shed light on the invaluable insights garnered from user behavior, guiding strategic decisions and iterative improvements. Lastly, engaging with our community of users and fans became the heart of our approach, fostering not just a user base but a passionate, devoted following. Their feedback, ideas, and enthusiasm catalyzed our applications toward greatness.

As we conclude this chapter, we emphasize the interconnectedness of these topics. Successful VR and AR applications are not just about sophisticated technology; they are about human experiences. Understanding the audience's desires, crafting seamless interactions, optimizing performance, and fostering genuine connections lay the groundwork for financial success and enduring user satisfaction. By integrating these facets into our development journey, we empower ourselves to build exceptional applications and shape the future of immersive technology, where innovation meets user delight, and every interaction becomes a memorable experience.

Points to remember

- Tailor your VR/AR experiences to match the preferences and needs of your target audience. An in-depth understanding of user demographics and behaviors lays the foundation for engaging and relevant applications.
- Prioritize user-centric design, ensuring every interaction is intuitive, immersive, and delightful. Seamless and enjoyable experiences enhance user engagement and retention.

- Explore diverse monetization strategies, from paid apps to in-app purchases, subscriptions, ads, and collaborations. Choose a model aligned with your audience and app features to maximize revenue potential.
- Develop a comprehensive marketing strategy that utilizes social media, app store optimization, influencer partnerships, and targeted campaigns. Effective marketing builds visibility, attracts users, and creates a loyal customer base.
- Utilize analytics tools to gather actionable insights about user behavior, preferences, and engagement patterns. Data-driven decisions empower you to refine features, optimize marketing efforts, and enhance user satisfaction.
- Cultivate a vibrant user community by fostering transparent communication, active engagement, and responsive feedback mechanisms. A dedicated user base becomes your advocate, contributing to the app's growth and success.
- By combining technical excellence with user empathy, strategic monetization, effective marketing, data-driven insights, and genuine community engagement, you pave the way for your applications to thrive in immersive technologies' competitive and ever-evolving landscape.

Index

Symbols

3D model animation 144
  blend shapes and morph targets 144
  challenges 145
  Inverse Kinematics (IK) 144
  keyframe animation 144
  motion capture 145
  physics-based animation 145
  rigging and skinning 145
3D modeling 138, 139
  key concepts 139

A

Absorption-Realism-Attention (ARA) model 16
AccuVein 92
Adobe XD 150
ads and sponsorship 183
AI, in VR/AR
  adaptive learning 63
  computer vision 62
  content generation 63
  graphic rendering 62
  intelligent avatars 63
  Natural language processing (NLP) 62
  personalized experiences 63
  predictive analytics 63
  realistic simulations 62
analytics tools
  leveraging 187, 188
  monetization metrics 188
  performance and technical metrics 188
  retention rate 188
  usage tips 188, 189
  user acquisition and sources 188
  user engagement 188
animation and rigging modeling technique 142

Apple 73
application of presence 22
architectural design 25
examples 24, 25
importance 23
medical training 24
mental health therapy 25
military training 24
occupational safety training 24
sports training 24
therapy 23, 24
tourism and cultural heritage 25
training 23
applications of game engines
architectural visualization 147
entertainment and media 147
simulators 147
video games 147
VR and AR 147
app marketing 184, 185
app store optimization 186, 187
channels and tactics, exploring 185, 186
effective marketing 185
app monetizing 181
ads and sponsorship 183
data monetization 183, 184
freemium models 182
In-App Purchases (IAPs) 182
location-based services and partnerships 183
paid apps 181
subscriptions 182
app store optimization 186, 187
artificial intelligence (AI) 61
in AR, VR and XR 61, 62
AR, VR, and XR in education 107, 108
benefits 110, 111
current state 108, 109
evolution 109, 110
simulations 112, 113
AR, VR, and XR in healthcare 90
case studies 103
current state 91
diagnosis and treatment 93, 94
doctors and nurses practice 94, 95
evolution 91, 92
key trends 92, 93
major players 92
medical realities 104
mental health treatment 96
pain management 96
surgical training 95, 96
AR, VR, and XR in rehabilitation and physical therapy 97
balance and proprioception training 97
enhanced engagement and adherence 97
feedback and progress tracking 98
gamified rehabilitation 98
home-based rehabilitation 98
pain management 98
personalized therapy programs 97
realistic simulations 97
attentional tunneling model 16
audience 178
audio optimization 169
strategies 170
Augmented Reality (AR) 1-3, 28
milestones 5
Autodesk® Maya® 150, 158
Average Revenue Per User (ARPU) 188

B

batching 168
behavioral analysis 178

behavioral measures 20
interaction logs 20
task performance metrics 20
Blender 150
business of VR/XR 72
business landscape and key trends 73-75
current state and evolution 72, 73

C

C#
advantages 171
disadvantages 171, 172
California Consumer Privacy Act (CCPA) 128
channels and tactics
App Store Optimization (ASO) 186
content marketing 186
email marketing and newsletters 186
influencer partnerships 185
partnerships and collaborations 186
social media platforms 185
Cinema 4D 150
cognitive rehabilitation 133
collaboration 166
collaborative learning 115
benefits 116
VR/XR for team building and project learning 117
competitor analysis 179
consumer VR 48
technology advancement 48, 49
co-presence theory 15
Customer Lifetime Value (CLV) 188

D

data monetization 183
demographic profiling 178
Depth of Presence (DoP) model 15
documentation 166

E

effective marketing 185
electroactive polymers (EAPs) 55
emotional immersion
designing 34
powerful emotions, with immersive experience 34, 35
role of design 35, 36
empathy building 134
ethics, in immersive technologies 124
ethical challenges 124, 125
ethical consideration 126
experience sampling 20
exposure therapy 133
Extended Reality (XR) 1, 3, 4

F

factors, for development of immersive experience
attentional guidance 18
compelling storytelling 18
emotional feedback 19
emotion, evoking through visuals and audio 18, 19
haptic feedback 18
interactive elements 18
meaningful interactions 18
spatial audio 18
visual realism 18
factors, influencing presence
cognitive processes 17
emotional responses 17
sensory inputs 17
feedback loops 178
Figma 150
freemium models 182

funding and investment 75
  challenges, for VR/XR industry 75, 76
  funding options and investment-securing strategies 76-78

G

game engines 146
  applications 147
  functionalities 146, 147
GameObject system 161
General Data Protection Regulation (GDPR) 127
Google 73
graphic rendering 63
  AI, for improving realism and details 63, 64
  complex scenes and environments, rendering 65
Graphics Processing Units (GPUs) 49
Gravity Sketch 150
group problem-solving 117

H

haptic feedback 33, 34
  evolution 54, 55
  force feedback 55
  Haptic text and Braille 56
  role, on VR hardware 54
  tactile pressure 56
  temperature feedback 56
  texture feedback 55
  types 55
  vibration 55
haptic force 55
haptic technology
  benefits 56, 57
  limitations 57
Head-Mounted Display (HMD) system 44
HTC Vive 73
HTC Vive Wand 163

I

immersion 28
  importance 28, 29
immersive content creation
  democratization 147
immersive design 28
immersive experience principles 32
  haptic feedback 33, 34
  sound design 32, 33
  spatial design 32
immersive experiences 27
  architectural and design visualization 29
  emotional impact 28
  enhanced engagement 28
  entertainment and media 29
  learning and training 28
  psychology and impact 29, 30
immersive learning environments 111, 112, 117
Immersive Realm 12
immersive technologies 1, 2
  Augmented Reality (AR) 2, 3
  current state 6, 7
  Extended Reality (XR) 3, 4
  limitations 9
  overview 4, 5
  potential 8
  statistical data 7
  Virtual Reality (VR) 3
immersive user experiences
  challenges 150
  considerations 150
Immersive Virtual Environment (IVE) model 17

In-App Purchases (IAPs) 182
inclusivity and accessibility 117
Inertial Measurement Units (IMUs) 49
input methods 164
gaze-based interactions 164
gesture recognition 164
hand tracking 164
haptic feedback 164
physical controllers 164
voice recognition 164
Internet of Things (IoT) 74
Interpupillary Distance (IPD) 130
Inverse Kinematics (IK) animation 144

K

keyframe animation 144
Key Performance Indicators (KPIs) 188

L

Level of Detail (LoD) 145
optimization 65
Level of Detail (LoD) system 167
high detail LOD (LOD0) 167
low detail LOD (LOD2) 167
medium detail LOD (LOD1) 167
linear resonant actors (LRAs) 55
location-based services and partnerships 183

M

machine learning-based anti-aliasing 65
Magic Leap 74
Magic Leap case study 86, 87
market capitalization examples
IKEA Place 184
Oculus VR 184
Pokémon GO 184
medical education and training 99, 100
immersive technologies, using 101, 102
VR/XR, using 100, 101
medical realities 104
design principles 104, 105
meditation and mindfulness exercises 134
MedyMatch 92
Meta (Oculus) 73
methods, to measure presence
advantages 21
behavioral measures 20
experience sampling 20
hybrid approaches 20
limitations 21, 22
physiological measures 19
self-report measures 19
Microsoft 73
MindMaze 92
Minecraft Earth 4
Mixed Reality (MR) 90
modeling technique 140
animation and rigging modeling technique 142
artistic and technical balance 144
optimization technique 144
parametric modeling 142
photogrammetry 142
polygonal modeling 140
procedural modeling 142
rigging 142
sculpting 141
subdivision surface modeling 141
texturing and material modeling technique 143
models of presence
Absorption-Realism-Attention (ARA) model 16
attentional tunneling model 16
cognitive models 16

Depth of Presence (DoP) model 15
overview 15
Perceptual Illusion of Non-Embodiment (PINE) model 15
monetization models
advertising 81
in-app purchases 80
paid content/software 80
pros and cons 79-82
sponsorships and brand partnerships 81, 82
subscription models 80, 81
monetization strategies, in VR/XR industry 78
challenges 78, 79
motion capture 145

N

narrative immersion
compelling narrative and user engagement, crafting 38, 39
designing 37
importance of storytelling 37, 38
National Center for Biotechnology Information (NCBI) 99
natural language processing (NLP) 66
contribution in natural and intuitive interaction 66
popularity 66
Non-uniform rational B-spline (NURBS) 138

O

occlusion culling 65, 166, 167
Oculus case study 85, 86
Oculus Touch 163
optimal application performance boosts retention 180, 181
optimization technique 144
Osso VR 92, 104
design principles 104

P

paid apps 181
parametric modeling 142
patient education and engagement 102
immersive technologies, using 102, 103
Perceptual Illusion of Non-Embodiment (PINE) model 15
personalized learning 113
customized and personalized learning experience 113, 114
photogrammetry 142
physics-based animation 145
physics optimization 169
physiological measures 19
Electrocardiography (ECG/EKG) 20
Electroencephalography (EEG) 20
Galvanic Skin Response (GSR) 20
PIPEDA 128
PlayStation Move 163
Pokemon Go 4
Pokémon GO case study 134, 135
polygonal modeling 140
Post-Traumatic Stress Disorder (PTSD) 25
predictive analytics 68
for better user experience 68, 69
presence 11, 12
definition 12
explanation 12
factors contributing 17
models 15
theories 14
presence, for immersion and user experience
emotional engagement 13

enhanced learning and skill development 14
increased focus and attention 13
realism and believability 13
sense of agency and control 13
social interaction and collaboration 14
presence, in immersive technologies.
audio immersion 12
body sensations 12
interaction and input 12
narrative and context 13
social presence 13
visual realism 12
presence, measuring 19
methods, using 19
privacy and data protection 126, 127
best practices 128, 129
ethical frameworks 128
legal frameworks 127, 128
privacy of personal data and safeguard 127
Procedural modeling 142
programming languages, Unity
C# 171
JavaScript (UnityScript) 172
Project-Based Learning (PBL) 117
ProtoPie 150
psychographic insights 178
psychological and emotional impact 131, 132
potential risks 132, 133
well-being and mental health, promoting 133, 134
psychological presence theory 15

R

real-time 3D graphics 146
real-time ray tracing 65
rigging 142
room-scale tracking 164

S

safety and physical health
considerations 129
measures, for ensuring user safety 130, 131
physical effects on users 129, 130
scene optimization
audio optimization 169, 170
batching 168
best practices 166
level of detail system 167
occlusion culling 166, 167
physics optimization 169
shader optimization 168
texture atlasing 169
scene reconstruction and depth estimation 65
scripting in Unity
animations 171
game logic 170
networking 171
physics 171
UI and menus 171
user interaction 171
sculpting 141
self-report measures 19
Presence Questionnaire (PQ) 19
Slater-Usoh-Steed Presence Questionnaire (SUS-PQ) 19
subjective mental effort questionnaire 19
sensory immersion
designing 30
immersive experience, with engaging user senses 31, 32
shader optimization 168

simulations, for educational purposes
  distance learning 112
  hazardous environments 112
  historical and cultural exploration 112
  language learning 112
  science and exploration 113
  skill-based training 112
  soft skills development 112
  special education 112
  team collaboration 112
Simultaneous Localization And Mapping (SLAM) techniques 65
situated presence theory 15
Sketch 150
social interaction 133
social presence theory 14
Sony PlayStation VR 73
sound design 32, 33
spatial design 32
spatial presence theory 14
Spinal Cord Injuries (SCI) 98
stress reduction 133
subdivision surface modeling 141
subscriptions 182
Surgical theater 92

T

tactile feedback 33, 54
teacher training and professional development 117
team building 117
technological advancements, in VR industry
  display technology 48
  graphics processing power 49
  input devices and controllers 49
  tracking and positional sensors 49
  wireless and standalone VR 49
technological proficiency 178
texture atlasing 169
texturing and material modeling technique 143
theories, of presence
  co-presence theory 15
  experience 16, 17
  overview 14
  psychological presence theory 15
  situated presence theory 15
  social presence theory 14
  spatial presence theory 14
  transportation theory 14
therapeutic applications, presence
  distraction and pain management 24
  empathy and rapport 24
  enhanced immersion 23
  exposure and desensitization 23
therapeutic creativity 134
tools, for immersive interfaces
  3D modeling and animation 150
  game engines 150
  spatial design 150
  UI/UX design 150
tracking systems 163
  inside-out tracking 163
  outside-in tracking 163
training scenarios
  emotional engagement 23
  memory retention 23
  skill acquisition 23
transportation theory 14
Traumatic Brain Injury (TBI) 98

U

UI Design, in VR 172

3D UI elements, using 173
audio feedback 174
gaze-based interaction 173
gesture-based controls 173
interactivity and feedback 173
performance optimization 174
text and legibility, optimizing 173
UI placement and anchoring 174
user testing and iteration 174
VR environment 173
UIs, in 3D environment
considerations 151
design principles 151
implementation 151
implementation workflow 151, 152
tools and technologies 152
Unity 150, 156
animation system 162
architecture 157
Asset Store 163
components 162
environments, creating 164
hands-on exploration and practical insights 157
Inspector 162
integrating, with 3D modeling and animation 157-160
lighting and shading 162
navigation system 162
Particle system 162
Physics system 162
Prefab system 162
programming languages 171
scenes, creating 164
scripting 170
Terrain system 163
tools and features 161-163
Transform component 162
VR development 163, 164
VR landscape 156
workflow 160, 161
UnityScript 172
Unreal Engine 150
user adoption and effective marketing 82
Marketing strategies, of companies for VR/XR 83, 84
VR/XR's adoption challenges 82, 83
user community 189
engaging with 189, 190
user experience, for retention 179, 180
user interaction 67
with gesture recognition and eye tracking 67
user interface and experience design
audio design for immersion 41
best practices 40
contextual and dynamic user interfaces 41
interactive feedback and responsiveness: 41
intuitive and responsive controls 40
iterative design and user testing 41
seamless navigation and information architecture 40
user-centric interface design 40
visual aesthetics and atmospheric design 41
user interface design principles 148
consistency and familiarity 148
contextual information presentation 148
feedback and animation 148
hierarchy and depth 148
minimalism and simplicity 148
natural gestures and interactions 148

- spatial awareness and context 148
- spatial sound and audio cues 149
- user-centric adaptation 148
- user testing and iteration 149

user interface design software and workflow 149
- 3D animation 149
- 3D modeling 149
- conceptualization 149
- integration 150
- interaction design 149
- optimization 150
- prototyping 149
- user feedback loop 150
- user testing 149
- visual design 149

V

Venture Capital (VC) funding 76

version control system 166

VictoryXR case study 118
- design principles 118-120

Virtual Reality (VR) 1, 3, 28
- education 3
- milestones 6
- therapy 3
- tourism 3

Virtual Reality (VR) hardware 43, 44
- case studies 57-59
- design challenges 50, 51
- emerging technologies 51, 52
- emerging technologies, impact on industries 52, 53
- evolution 44
- first head-mounted displays 47
- future 51

VR controllers 163

VR development in Unity 163

VR hardware, case studies 57-59

VR hardware evolution
- early systems (1960s-1990s) 44, 45
- modern era (2010s onward) 45, 46
- recent advancements 46, 47

VR headsets 163

VR/XR
- for adaptive learning 114
- for embodied learning 115
- for gamification techniques 114
- for inclusivity and accessibility 115
- for personalized assessments 114
- for stroke rehabilitation 98
- for traumatic brain injury 99
- in spinal cord injuries 99
- learning analytics 115

VR/XR industry
- case studies 85
- monetization strategies 78
- technology challenges 84, 85

VR/XR industry case studies
- Magic Leap case study 86, 87
- Oculus case study 85, 86

X

XR applications
- architecture and design 4
- gaming and entertainment 4
- retail and marketing 4
- training 4